KATHARINA FRITSCH

KATHARINA FRITSCH

San Francisco Museum of Modern Art

Museum für Gegenwartskunst Basel

San Francisco Museum of Modern Art

31 October 1996 – 11 March 1997

Museum für Gegenwartskunst

Öffentliche Kunstsammlung Basel

26. April – 31. August 1997

Cover/Umschlag: Mann und Maus (Man and Mouse) 1991-1992

CONTENTS

INHALT

FOREWORD

We are pleased and honored to be the two museums to present the first overview of the work of Katharina Fritsch. She is an artist only now reaching mid-career, but one who over the past fifteen years has established herself as one of the preeminent artists of her generation on both sides of the Atlantic. While steeped in the traditions and history of German and European culture, her work is also acutely attuned to the issues of contemporary art in the West today, and particularly reveals the influence of the Minimal and Pop art movements of the 1960s. The problematic relationships of culture with consumer society and mass media also resonate here, exposing and enfolding in her work their pull on the contemporary imagination. Complementing these elements is the careful attention Fritsch pays to formal issues – balance and structure, weight and material, color and texture – so that an appreciation of its craft and a delight in the visual pleasures it provides are immediately and keenly felt. The resulting synthesis yields an art that is thoroughly of its time but weighted with a ballast that we believe will give it continuing vitality during the years ahead.

It has been a pleasure for each of our institutions to cooperate on this project, particularly in the production of a mid-career catalogue raisonné, which provides a comprehensive and lasting documentation of Fritsch's work to date. While some sculptures will be presented at both museums, the exhibitions are distinct and separate, offering visitors a different experience of the artist's work in each presentation. Since these works will be shown only at our two museums for this project, the exhibitions will be on view for a longer period of time than is customary, with the hope that as many members of the public as possible may have the opportunity to see either one or both shows.

Finally, we are deeply grateful for the initiative and hard work of the curators of these two exhibitions, Gary Garrels, Elise S. Haas chief curator and curator of painting and sculpture at SFMOMA, and Theodora Vischer, curator of contemporary art at the Museum für Gegenwartskunst Basel.

John R. Lane, Director
San Francisco Museum of Modern Art

Katharina Schmidt, Director
Öffentliche Kunstsammlung Basel

Es ist uns eine grosse Freude, in unseren beiden Museen zum ersten Mal einen Überblick über das Gesamt-
werk von Katharina Fritsch geben zu können. Sie ist mit ihrem bisherigen Schaffen im Laufe von fünfzehn
Jahren zu einer der herausragenden Künstlerinnen ihrer Generation auf beiden Seiten des Atlantiks geworden. Ihr Werk ist eingebettet in die Geschichte und Tradition deutscher und europäischer Kultur, zugleich
reagiert es präzise auf die zeitgenössische Kunst des Westens, besonders auf die Minimal und Pop Art der
sechziger Jahre. In den Werken klingen die problematischen Beziehungen zwischen Kultur einerseits, Kon-
sumgesellschaft und Massenmedien andererseits an, deren Einfluss auf die zeitgenössische Vorstellungswelt
ist in ihnen enthalten und vorgeführt. Von entscheidender Bedeutung ist Katharina Fritschs sorgfältiger Umgang mit formalen Elementen wie Gleichgewicht und Struktur, Gewicht und Material, Farbe und Oberflächen-
beschaffenheit, der die handwerkliche Perfektion und die Schönheit der Werke unmittelbar spürbar werden
lässt. Wir haben es mit einer Kunst zu tun, die ganz gegenwärtig ist und die gleichzeitig ein inhaltliches
Potential enthält, das es in Zukunft noch zu entdecken gilt.

Die Zusammenarbeit unserer beiden Institutionen an dem Projekt, besonders an der Herstellung des Katalo-
ges, der eine umfassende Dokumentation über das Schaffen von Katharina Fritsch enthält, war ein Vergnügen.
Einige Skulpturen werden in beiden Museen zu sehen sein; im ganzen unterscheiden sich die Ausstellungen
jedoch deutlich voneinander und ermöglichen den Besuchern und Besucherinnen eine unterschiedliche Erfahrung des Werkes von Katharina Fritsch. Da die Arbeiten nur bei dieser einen Gelegenheit in San Francisco
und in Basel zu sehen sein werden, ist die Ausstellungsdauer grosszügig angesetzt. Wir hoffen, dass auf diese
Weise möglichst viele Menschen eine oder beide Ausstellungen besichtigen können.

    Wir danken den beiden Konservatoren, Gary Garrels, Elise S. Haas chief curator and curator of painting
and sculpture at SFMOMA, und Theodora Vischer, Konservatorin am Museum für Gegenwartskunst, für ihr
grosses Engagement.

John R. Lane, Direktor
San Francisco Museum of Modern Art

Katharina Schmidt, Direktorin
Öffentliche Kunstsammlung Basel

Although works by Katharina Fritsch have been publicly exhibited for more than fifteen years in both Europe and the United States, the full scope of her oeuvre, its development, and the connections among her diverse pieces have not been readily apparent to a public audience. From her first exhibition of sculptures in 1980 at the Art Academy in Düsseldorf until now, Fritsch has concentrated almost exclusively on the specific situation of each public exhibition. Often an individual work or body of works has been isolated in its presentation, sometimes existing only for an exhibition or shown but once. Although the catalogue raisonné published here includes 112 entries, even the most seasoned art professional has found it difficult to see more than a few of them. Given their diversity, ranging from potentially endlessly produced multiples to monumental sculptures, from recordings of sound to ephemeral events, her works have resisted an easy coherence.

With this project, which includes two overview exhibitions and a book – a catalogue raisonné – for the first time Fritsch has given us the opportunity to see in one space works from throughout her career, to begin to knit together the issues and themes that remain as preoccupations, and to recognize the diversity and development of her work over seventeen years. The exhibitions at the San Francisco Museum of Modern Art and the Museum für Gegenwartskunst Basel are each distinct, bringing together different pieces selected in response to the unique settings of each museum and reflecting the relative familiarity that the American or European audience may have with some more than others. Because of the scale, spatial requirements, and physical complexities of handling and presenting the sculptures, only a small number of them can be exhibited at each museum; consequently this book, which completely documents Fritsch's output to date, is an important complement to the exhibitions themselves.

We are extremely grateful to Katharina Fritsch, who accepted our invitation to pursue this project and has worked closely with us on the conception and realization of all phases of the exhibitions and book. Our admiration for her work has only been enhanced by our direct personal contact; our appreciation for her patience and persistence, professionalism and commitment to this project is genuinely felt.

The work of Valeria Liebermann, assistant to Katharina Fritsch, and author of the catalogue raisonné, has been of critical importance. We thank Matthias Winzen who undertook a lengthy interview with the artist, portions of which are included here. Alexej Koschkarow and Heiner Frohn provided special assistance to the artist with the installation of her works in San Francisco.

8

Obwohl die Arbeiten von Katharina Fritsch seit mehr als fünfzehn Jahren sowohl in Europa als auch in den Vereinigten Staaten öffentlich gezeigt werden, ist ihr Schaffen, seine Entwicklung und die Beziehungen der einzelnen Werke untereinander in der Öffentlichkeit bisher noch nicht in vollem Umfang sichtbar geworden. Seit der ersten Präsentation ihrer Arbeiten 1980 in der Düsseldorfer Kunstakademie konzentriert sich Katharina Fritsch immer auf die jeweilige Situation einer Ausstellung. Oft wurde ein einzelnes Werk oder eine Gruppe von Werken isoliert gezeigt, manchmal existierten sie nur für die Dauer dieser einen Ausstellung. Auch wenn das hier veröffentlichte Werkverzeichnis 112 Katalognummern umfasst, haben selbst die erfahrensten Ausstellungsbesucher selten mehr als einige wenige Werke gesehen. Mit ihrer Vielfalt, die von unendlich reproduzierbaren Multiples bis zu monumentalen Skulpturen reicht, von Tonaufnahmen bis zu ephemeren Ereignissen, entziehen sich die Arbeiten einem sofort einsehbaren Zusammenhang.

Mit diesem Projekt, das zwei Ausstellungen und eine Publikation mit einem Werkverzeichnis der Arbeiten bis heute umfasst, gibt Fritsch uns zum ersten Mal Gelegenheit, Werke aus ihrem gesamten Schaffen in einem Zusammenhang zu sehen. So können wir allmählich das Geflecht jener Elemente und Themen knüpfen, die sich als Hauptanliegen herauskristallisiert haben, und gleichzeitig die Vielfalt und Entwicklung ihrer Arbeit über siebzehn Jahre hinweg verfolgen. Die Ausstellungen im San Francisco Museum of Modern Art und im Museum für Gegenwartskunst Basel sind jeweils verschieden und präsentieren eine Zusammenstellung von Arbeiten, die auf die jeweilige Museumssituation sowie auf den unterschiedlichen Bekanntheitsgrad der Werke in Europa beziehungsweise in Amerika abgestimmt ist. Aufgrund der Grösse und der räumlichen Bedingungen, der komplexen Handhabung und Präsentation der Skulpturen zeigt jedes Museum nur eine kleine Auswahl von Arbeiten. Das Buch, welches das Werk der Künstlerin bis heute dokumentiert, ist daher eine wichtige Ergänzung zu den Ausstellungen.

Unser erster grosser Dank richtet sich an Katharina Fritsch. Sie hat unsere Einladung zu diesem Projekt angenommen und sowohl bei der Konzeption als auch bei der Realisierung der Ausstellungen und des Buches eng mit uns zusammengearbeitet. Ihre Geduld und Beharrlichkeit, ihre Professionalität und Engagiertheit waren bewundernswert und wertvoll.

Einen entscheidenden Beitrag zum Gelingen des Projekts leistete Valeria Liebermann, Assistentin von Katharina Fritsch und Autorin des Werkverzeichnisses. Unser Dank gilt Matthias Winzen, der für dieses Buch ein Interview mit der Künstlerin führte. Alexej Koschkarow und Heiner Frohn haben der Künstlerin bei der Installation der Werke in San Francisco assistiert.

The works in the exhibitions are fragile and often demanding in their requirements for handling and installation. We are deeply indebted and grateful to the lenders who have entrusted their works to the care of our museums for these two exhibitions.

A project of this scale and complexity could not be undertaken without substantial financial support. Major funding for the San Francisco presentation and the book has been provided by the Lannan Foundation; The Andy Warhol Foundation for the Visual Arts; the National Endowment for the Arts, a Federal agency; Coutts International Private Banking & Coutts Contemporary Art Foundation; and the Institut für Auslandsbeziehungen, Stuttgart. Additional generous support has been provided by Mimi and Peter Haas, Frances and John Bowes, Doris and Donald G. Fisher, Elaine McKeon, Helen and Charles Schwab, Phyllis C. Wattis, and Pat and Bill Wilson. Exhibition expenses have been supported by generous in-kind donations from the San Francisco Marriott and from Lufthansa German Airlines.

Major funding for the Basel presentation and the book has been provided by the Fonds für künstlerische Aktivitäten im Museum für Gegenwartskunst der Emanuel Hoffmann-Stiftung und der Christoph Merian Stiftung and Coutts International Private Banking & Coutts Contemporary Art Foundation.

Colleagues and friends have contributed their assistance and insights in myriad ways. We wish especially to thank Jean-Christophe Ammann, Rolf Lauter, and Mario Kramer, Museum für Moderne Kunst, Frankfurt; Gerhard Storck and Julian Heynen, Kaiser Wilhelm Museum, Krefeld; Anne d'Harnoncourt and Ann Temkin, Philadelphia Museum of Art; Matthew Marks, Matthew Marks Gallery, New York; Maja Oeri, Emanuel Hoffmann-Stiftung, Basel; Kathy Halbreich, Walker Art Center, Minneapolis; Kaspar König, Städelschule and Portikus, Frankfurt; and Charles Wright, Seattle.

Staff members at both museums have worked with diligence and care and brought goodwill to this project. We would like to thank these colleagues, who are listed individually on the last page of this publication for their assistance and support.

Gary Garrels
Elise S. Haas Chief Curator and Curator of Painting and Sculpture
San Francisco Museum of Modern Art

Theodora Vischer
Curator of Contemporary Art, Museum für Gegenwartskunst Basel

Zu grossem Dank verpflichtet sind wir den Leihgebern. Sie haben die Werke von Katharina Fritsch, die sehr fragil und in ihrer Handhabung oft extrem schwierig sind, in grosszügiger Weise der Fürsorge unserer Museen anvertraut.

Ein Projekt von solcher Grösse und Schwierigkeit wäre ohne massgebliche finanzielle Unterstützung nicht zu realisieren. Einen wesentlichen Beitrag zur Ausstellung in San Francisco und zum Buch leisteten die folgenden Institutionen: The Lannan Foundation, The Andy Warhol Foundation for the Visual Arts, The National Endowment for the Arts, a Federal Agency, Coutts International Private Banking & Coutts Contemporary Art Foundation, und das Institut für Auslandsbeziehungen, Stuttgart; bedeutende Unterstützung kam auch von den folgenden Personen: Mimi und Peter Haas, Frances und John Bowes, Doris und Donald G.Fisher, Elaine McKeon, Helen und Charles Schwab, Phyllis C.Wattis und Pat und Bill Wilson. Das San Francisco Marriott Hotel und die Lufthansa haben während der Ausstellungsvorbereitungen grosses Entgegenkommen gezeigt.
    Einen grosszügigen Beitrag zur Ausstellung in Basel und zur Publikation leistete der Fonds für künstlerische Aktivitäten im Museum für Gegenwartskunst der Emanuel Hoffmann-Stiftung und der Christoph Merian Stiftung und Coutts International Private Banking & Coutts Contemporary Art Foundation.

Kollegen und Freunde haben auf vielfältige Weise ihre Hilfe und ihr Wissen zur Verfügung gestellt. Unser besonderer Dank gilt hier Jean-Christophe Ammann, Rolf Lauter und Mario Kramer vom Museum für Moderne Kunst, Frankfurt, Gerhard Storck und Julian Heynen vom Kaiser Wilhelm Museum in Krefeld, Anne d'Harnoncourt und Ann Temkin vom Philadelphia Museum of Art, Matthew Marks von der Matthew Marks Gallery, New York, Maja Oeri von der Emanuel Hoffmann-Stiftung in Basel, Kathy Halbreich vom Walker Art Center, Minneapolis, Kasper König, Städelschule und Portikus, Frankfurt sowie Charles Wright, Seattle.

Die Mitarbeiter beider Museen haben viel Einsatz und Sorgfalt gezeigt und dem Projekt ihren guten Willen entgegengebracht. Am San Francisco Museum of Modern Art und am Museum für Gegenwartskunst Basel danken wir unseren Kollegen für ihre Hilfe und Unterstützung.

Gary Garrels,
Elise S.Haas Chief Curator and Curator of Painting and Sculpture,
San Francisco Museum of Modern Art

Theodora Vischer,
Konservatorin am Museum für Gegenwartskunst Basel

Gary Garrels

Katharina Fritsch:
An Introduction

Katharina Fritsch:
Eine Einführung

THE WORK OF KATHARINA FRITSCH HAS LEFT AN INDELIBLE mark in the realm of contemporary art. Her first work to gain widespread international attention was *Elefant* (Elephant, 1987; pl. 12, cat. 64), shown in 1987 at the Kaiser Wilhelm Museum in Krefeld, Germany. This work stirred the interest of the general press and inspired numerous visitors to journey to Krefeld to see it, while also arousing discussion throughout the pages of European and American art journals. The *Madonnenfigur* (Madonna Figure, 1987; pl. 13, cat. 67), made for the 1987 *Skulptur Projekte*, a large summer exhibition of public artworks in Münster, Germany, followed and was quickly one of the most controversial and discussed works of an exhibition that in general received broad attention. The next year Fritsch made her *Tischgesellschaft* (Company at Table, 1988; pl. 17, cat. 75) for an exhibition in Basel, Switzerland, a work that subsequently has been on long-term exhibition at the Museum of Modern Art in Frankfurt, Germany, where it has become the public emblem of the museum. In the United States, her *Rattenkönig* (Rat-King, 1991-1993; pl. 20, cat. 97), which was presented at the Dia Center for the Arts in New York City for a year during 1993-1994, elicited the same controversy and acclaim as had her sculpture in Europe, including a rare two-page photograph of the work in *Newsweek* magazine. Most recently, *Museum, Modell 1:10* (Museum, Model 1:10, 1995; pl. 21, cat. 100), the work by which she represented Germany at the Venice Biennale in the summer of 1995, ignited heated discussions in the German press and graced the cover of the *Artforum* issue that focused on the oldest and grandest international art exhibition at its one hundredth anniversary.

One of the remarkable features of Fritsch's work has been its ability both to capture the popular imagination by its immediate appeal and to be a focal point for the specialized discussions of the contemporary art world. This all too infrequent meeting point is at the center of her work, as it addresses the ambiguous and difficult relationships between artists and the public and between art and its display – that is, the role of art and exhibitions and of the museum in the late twentieth century.

Fritsch's work, however, is not concerned primarily with theoretical issues but rather with the nature of human perception and experience. Each of her works is intended to be distinct, to respond to a particular environment, and to take a form contingent upon the artist's purpose. Some works are small and intimate, others grand and monumental; some works are rational and geometric, others are psychological and expressive. She has made

DAS WERK VON KATHARINA FRITSCH HAT IM BEREICH DER zeitgenössischen Kunst ein unauslöschliches Zeichen gesetzt. Internationales Aufsehen erregte sie erstmals mit «Elefant» (Taf. 12, Kat. 64), der 1987 im Krefelder Kaiser Wilhelm Museum gezeigt wurde. Er weckte das Interesse der Tageszeitungen und lockte zahlreiche Besucher nach Krefeld, während er zugleich Diskussionen in den europäischen und amerikanischen Kunstzeitschriften auslöste. Im selben Jahr war bei «Skulptur Projekte» in Münster, einer grossen Sommerausstellung von Kunst im öffentlichen Raum, die eigens dafür geschaffene «Madonnenfigur» (Taf. 13, Kat. 67) zu sehen und erwies sich schnell als eine der meist diskutierten und kontroversesten Arbeiten in einer Ausstellung, die insgesamt auf breites Interesse stiess. Im darauffolgenden Jahr schuf Fritsch ihre «Tischgesellschaft» (1988, Taf. 17, Kat. 75) für eine Ausstellung in der Kunsthalle Basel. Anschliessend wurde sie im Frankfurter Museum für Moderne Kunst permanent ausgestellt, wo sie zum Markenzeichen des Museums wurde. In den Vereinigten Staaten zeigte das New Yorker Dia Center for the Arts 1993-1994 ein Jahr lang ihren «Rattenkönig» (1991-1993, Taf. 20, Kat. 97) und löste dort ein ebenso kontroverses Echo aus wie ihr Werk zuvor in Europa; sogar das «Newsweek»-Magazin widmete der Arbeit eine Photo-Doppelseite. Hitzige Diskussionen entzündeten sich in jüngster Zeit in der deutschen Presse über «Museum, Modell 1:10» (Taf. 21, Kat. 100). Die Arbeit, mit der die Künstlerin im Sommer 1995 Deutschland an der Biennale in Venedig vertrat, zierte ausserdem die Titelseite derjenigen «Artforum»-Ausgabe, die dem hundertsten Geburtstag der ältesten und bedeutendsten internationalen Kunstausstellung gewidmet war.

Eine der bemerkenswerten Qualitäten des Werks von Katharina Fritsch ist die Fähigkeit, mit seiner unmittelbaren Anziehungskraft die Phantasien des breiten Publikums zu bannen und zugleich ein Brennpunkt für die spezialisierte Diskussion der zeitgenössischen Kunstwelt zu sein. Diese allzu seltene Verknüpfung liegt unmittelbar im Kern ihrer Arbeit, denn sie handelt von den vieldeutigen und schwierigen Beziehungen zwischen Künstlern und Publikum, zwischen Kunst und deren Präsentation – das heisst, es geht um die Rolle von Kunst und Ausstellungen sowie des Museums im späten 20. Jahrhundert.

Doch Katharina Fritschs Werk bemüht sich nicht um primär theoretische Fragen, sondern um solche der menschlichen Wahrnehmung und Erfahrung. Jedes einzelne Stück ist für sich eine Besonderheit, eine spezifische Reaktion auf die Umgebung und entspricht in seiner Form der Absicht der Künstlerin. Einige Arbei-

ten sind klein und intim, andere mächtig und monumental; einige Stücke sind rational und geometrisch, andere psychologisch und expressiv. Sie hat Objekte und Skulpturen gemacht, aber auch mit Klang gearbeitet und ephemere Ereignisse inszeniert. Man hat nicht viele ihrer Arbeiten gleichzeitig sehen können, weil ihre Präsentation jeweils ganz bestimmte Anforderungen stellt. Dabei wollte Fritsch nicht schwer zu fassen sein, sondern einfach mit jedem einzelnen Stück ein ganz präzises Ziel verfolgen – Vervollkommnung und Ganzheit eines Bildes, das eine unauslöschliche Spur im Kopf des Besuchers hinterlässt, auf dass Erfahrung und Erinnerung untrennbar miteinander verschmelzen.

Katharina Fritsch wurde 1956 in der deutschen Stadt Essen geboren; von dort, aus dem Herzen des Ruhrgebiets, stammen auch ihre Grosseltern väterlicherseits. Die ersten Lebensjahre verbrachte sie zusammen mit der Familie bei den Grosseltern mütterlicherseits in Langenberg, ebenfalls einer kleinen Stadt im Ruhrgebiet, bevor ihre Eltern nach Münster umzogen, in eine Stadt nördlich der Ruhr, die das Zentrum einer blühenden Landwirtschaftsregion bildet. Zwar blieb Münster ihr Wohnort, bis sie Ende der siebziger Jahre nach Düsseldorf zog, doch fühlten weder sie noch ihre Eltern sich in dieser Stadt verwurzelt. Oft besuchte sie als Kind ihre Grosseltern an der Ruhr. Die Sommer und die Feiertage verbrachte sie im süddeutschen Franken, von wo die Familie ihrer Mutter stammte; der Grossvater war aus Nürnberg, die Grossmutter aus einer ländlichen Gegend in der Nähe von Bamberg.

Katharina Fritsch erinnert sich an den Eindruck, den ihr als Kind die mittelalterlichen und barocken Kirchen und Paläste in Franken machten. Ihr Vater war Architekt und diskutierte manchmal mit ihr die Architektur und Kunst, auf die sie trafen. Ihre Familie war katholisch und nahm sie gelegentlich zu Gottesdiensten mit; sie war fasziniert von den kirchlichen Traditionen und Riten – was durch die Tatsache, dass sie in der sehr katholischen Stadt Münster lebte, sicherlich gefördert wurde. Ihre vom Land stammende Grossmutter war dem Aberglauben und den Bräuchen der alten Naturreligionen noch sehr verbunden, die teilweise mit dem Christentum verschmolzen. Als Kind interessierte sich Fritsch sowohl für germanische als auch für griechische Mythen. Diese «Bildwelt» habe sie immer lebendig vor Augen gehabt, sagt sie.

Ab dem fünften Lebensjahr, so erinnert sie sich, wollte sie Künstlerin werden. Ihr Grossvater war Vertreter für Faber-Castell-Stifte gewesen, die in seiner Heimatstadt Nürnberg hergestellt wurden; er gab ihr Stifte und Feder, unterrichtete sie im Zeichnen.

13

objects and sculptures but she has also worked with sound and staged ephemeral events. It has been difficult to see many of her works because the requirements of presentation are extremely specific. Yet Fritsch's intention has not been to remain elusive but simply to achieve with each work a precise goal – the perfection and completeness of an image, indelibly left in the mind of the visitor, so that experience and memory are indissolubly fused.

Katharina Fritsch was born in 1956 in the German town of Essen, the home of her paternal grandparents, in the heart of the industrial Ruhr district. Her first years were spent living with her family in the apartment of her maternal grandparents in Langenberg, a small town also in the Ruhr district, before her parents moved to Münster, north of the Ruhr and center of a prosperous farming region. Although Münster remained her home until she moved to Düsseldorf in the late 1970s, neither she nor her parents ever felt completely rooted in that city, and during her childhood she frequently visited her grandparents in the Ruhr. Summers and holidays were spent in the Franken region in southern Germany where her mother's family had its roots, her grandfather having come from Nuremberg and her grandmother from the countryside near Bamberg.

Fritsch recounts her wonder as a child visiting the medieval and Baroque churches and palaces in the Franken region. Her father was an architect, and he sometimes discussed with her the architecture and the works of art they encountered. Her family was Catholic, and she occasionally attended services and recalls being fascinated by the traditions and rituals of the church – an interest no doubt reinforced by living in Münster, which remains a very Catholic city. Her grandmother, who had come from the countryside, carried links to the superstitions and customs held over from the ancient nature religions, often fused partially with Christianity. As a child Fritsch was also interested in both Germanic and Greek myths. She has said that during her youth this "image world" was always near and vivid in her mind.

From the age of five, she recalls, she wanted to be an artist. Her grandfather had been a salesman of Faber-Castell pencils, which were made in his hometown of Nuremberg, and he would give her pencils and pens, as well as instruct her in drawing. In addition to being an architect, her father enjoyed drawing and taught her also. Artistic aspirations may have been inspired by Fritsch's mother, too, who had studied dancing and acting and had wanted to become an actress.

After secondary school (*Gymnasium*), Fritsch attended the university in Münster to study history and art history. At the same time, she studied studio art in the evenings at the Münster *Volkshochschule* with Hermann Josef Kuhna, drawing, as she has said, anything from bags to naked women and "everything you can put on a table."

The year 1978 marked a turning point for Fritsch. She increasingly felt the need for more freedom and autonomy. That year she went to Düsseldorf to attend the now famous performance given at the Art Academy by Joseph Beuys and Nam June Paik in memory of the Fluxus artist George Maciunas. Fritsch encountered many artists at the concert; outside on the streets her attention was captured by the spectacle of the city's punks, and she discovered an active music scene with many connections around the Art Academy. At that point Fritsch decided she must study at the Academy and move to Düsseldorf, because, as she put it, "Da spielt die Musik," literally "There plays the music," – i.e., "That's where it's happening."

With modest financial support from her parents, who had initially resisted her plan, Fritsch moved in 1979 to Düsseldorf, finding an apartment to share with another young woman. By then she had gained admittance to the Art Academy and was accepted into the class of Fritz Schwegler. Her curriculum there included courses that would prepare her for a teaching career, as her parents believed that if she wanted to study art, she should plan to be a teacher. At first she primarily painted, though not from the modernist position of an interest in abstraction but rather with an interest in depicting objects. She aspired to achieve the atmosphere of the American painter Edward Hopper (fig. 1), the feeling of his painting echoing her own sentiments at the time of a melancholy loneliness. This mood did not simply reflect the struggles of finding a new life as a student in Düsseldorf, however; she believes it also was a response to the character of the Ruhr district, which she experiences as her *Heimat*, or homeland – an industrial landscape, rooted in the nineteenth century, with a history that is threatened and vanishing in the late twentieth century.

While Fritsch was still in Münster she had been introduced to the work of artists active around the Düsseldorf Academy by Johannes Brus, a teacher who had studied at the Academy and was friends with artists there. Through Brus, she saw the paintings of Sigmar Polke and Gerhard Richter, whose works she found shocking and unsettling. In them Fritsch sensed an ambivalence toward or even negation of the act of painting which

Ihr Vater war nicht nur Architekt, er zeichnete auch gern und lehrte sie zeichnen. Künstlerische Ambitionen mögen zudem auch von der Mutter ausgegangen sein, die Tanz und Schauspiel studiert und Schauspielerin hatte werden wollen.

Nach dem Gymnasium studierte Fritsch Geschichte und Kunstgeschichte an der Universität in Münster. Gleichzeitig nahm sie abends Zeichenkurse an der Volkshochschule bei Hermann Josef Kuhna. Sie zeichnete – so sagt sie – alles, vom Sack bis zum Akt und «alles, was man auf einen Tisch legen kann».

Das Jahr 1978 markiert einen Wendepunkt für Katharina Fritsch. Sie sehnte sich zunehmend nach mehr Freiheit und Eigenständigkeit. In diesem Jahr besuchte sie in der Düsseldorfer Kunstakademie die berühmte Performance von Joseph Beuys und Nam June Paik zu Ehren des Fluxus-Künstlers George Maciunas. Bei diesem Konzert begegnete Fritsch vielen Künstlern. Auf den Strassen erregten die Punks ihre Aufmerksamkeit, und sie entdeckte eine aktive Musikszene rund um die Kunstakademie. An diesem Punkt entschied sie sich, nach Düsseldorf zu gehen, um dort an der Akademie zu studieren, denn «da spielte die Musik», wie sie sich ausdrückte.

Mit einer bescheidenen finanziellen Unterstützung durch die Eltern, die anfänglich gegen ihren Plan waren, zog Fritsch 1979 nach Düsseldorf und teilte sich dort eine Wohnung mit einer anderen jungen Frau. Sie wurde zum Studium an der Kunstakademie zugelassen und in die Klasse von Fritz Schwegler aufgenommen. Sie belegte zusätzlich auch Fächer, die sie auf eine Lehrerlaufbahn vorbereiteten, da ihre Eltern wünschten, dass sie ihr Kunststudium auf den Lehrberuf ausrichtete. Zunächst malte sie hauptsächlich, allerdings nicht aus einem modernistischen Interesse an der Abstraktion heraus, sondern mit dem Ziel, Gegenstände abzubilden. Sie strebte eine Atmosphäre wie beim amerikanischen Maler Edward Hopper an (Abb. 1), in dessen Malerei sie damals ihre eigene melancholische Einsamkeit wiederfand. Doch diese Stimmung erwuchs nicht nur aus den Kämpfen ihres neuen Lebens als Studentin in Düsseldorf; vielmehr sieht Fritsch darin auch eine Reaktion auf den Charakter des Ruhrgebiets, das sie als ihre Heimat begreift – eine Industrielandschaft, die ihre Wurzeln im 19. Jahrhundert hat, deren Geschichte am Ende des 20. Jahrhunderts aber zu verschwinden droht.

Noch während ihrer Zeit in Münster hatte Johannes Brus, ein Lehrer, der an der Akademie studiert hatte und mit Künstlern dort befreundet war, Fritsch mit der Arbeit von Künstlern rund um die Düsseldorfer Akademie vertraut gemacht. Durch ihn sah sie zum ersten Mal Bilder von Sigmar Polke und Gerhard Richter, deren Arbeiten sie schockierten und beunruhigten. Fritsch spürte in ihnen eine Ambivalenz gegenüber dem Akt des Malens oder gar

verged on nihilism, but which compelled her to want to understand the issues of modern painting as completely as possible. In response she went to a library and read everything she could find on modern art. She also saw the sculptures of Reiner Ruthenbeck during this period and particularly remembers his sculpture of a table with a tablecloth (fig. 2), which she perceived as extremely simple but powerful and unlike anything she had seen before. In his work she sensed not irony as much as a directness and seriousness, which seemed to open up new possibilities for making art. In art magazines she discovered reproductions of the work of the American sculptor Richard Artschwager (fig. 3), whose work fascinated her, although she did not understand it.

Although Fritsch had made some sculptures in Münster, it was during 1979, her first year at the Art Academy studying with Schwegler, that her attention shifted from painting to sculpture. Her first works were small, handmade models: *Schornstein* (Chimney, 1979; cat. 4), and *Dunkelgrüner Tunnel* (Dark Green Tunnel, 1979; cat. 3). For her these objects specifically evoked the Ruhr district and expressed a compression of experience, a distillation of memory. The chimney, while easily recalling the chimneys in the paintings of de Chirico (fig. 4), was taken, in fact, from the memory of a specific chimney in Langenberg; the tunnel was recalled from experiences of driving through the countryside as a child. Render-

ing these objects as clear, sharp images released Fritsch from the more atmospheric effects of her early paintings. This shift expanded the possibilities of meaning for her work, she felt, so that she could now deal with proportion, material, and color – the form of things – but also maintain the potential of stories and history.

During her first year at the Academy, Fritsch made most of her small sculptures by hand in her apartment. She recalls the atmosphere at the Academy as highly competitive, and she experienced the burden of its history and tradition as both intimidating and potentially paralyzing. In making these early objects, she felt exposed and uncertain, working intuitively and trying to create a language for her own work, though she feared it might be perceived as not serious or as unprofessional. In February 1980 for the first time she publicly showed a group of these early objects at the Academy, displayed together on a table, where fellow students and professors could appraise her work from the preceding year (fig. 8).

The tradition of teaching at the Art Academy in Düsseldorf (typical of other academies in Germany) is that a student aligns himself or herself primarily with one professor, and a cohort of students becomes a kind of "class" associated with that professor. A distinct set of attitudes, principles, and ways of working develops around each professor and class. At the Düsseldorf

16

dessen Negation, die an Nihilismus grenzten und in ihr den dringenden Wunsch auslösten, das Wesen der modernen Malerei so umfassend wie möglich zu verstehen. Daraufhin ging sie in eine Bibliothek und las alles, was sie über moderne Kunst finden konnte. In dieser Zeit sah sie auch die Skulpturen von Reiner Ruthenbeck, wobei sie sich vor allem an eine aus einem Tisch mit Tischtuch bestehende Skulptur (Abb. 2) erinnert, die sie als extrem einfach, aber kraftvoll empfand, anders als alles, was sie bis dahin gekannt hatte. In seinem Werk spürte sie nicht so sehr Ironie, sondern eine Direktheit und Ernsthaftigkeit, die neue Möglichkeiten für die künstlerische Arbeit zu eröffnen schienen. In Kunstzeitschriften entdeckte sie zudem Abbildungen von Arbeiten des amerikanischen Bildhauers Richard Artschwager (Abb. 3), von denen sie fasziniert war, ohne sie zu verstehen.

Zwar hatte Fritsch schon in Münster einige Skulpturen gemacht, doch erst 1979, in ihrem ersten Jahr an der Kunstakademie bei Fritz Schwegler, verlagerte sich ihr Interesse von der Malerei zur Skulptur. Ihre ersten Arbeiten bestanden aus kleinen, handgefertigten Modellen: «Schornstein» (1979, Kat. 4), «Dunkelgrüner Tunnel» (1979, Kat. 3). Für sie evozierten diese Objekte vor allem das Ruhrgebiet, waren Ausdruck verdichteter Erfahrung, ein Destillat der Erinnerung. Der Kamin mag einerseits die Kamine in den Gemälden von de Chirico (Abb. 4) ins Gedächtnis rufen, entspringt aber tatsächlich der Erinnerung an einen ganz bestimmten Kamin in Langenberg. Der Tunnel geht zurück auf die ländlichen Ausfahrten ihrer Kindheit. Indem Fritsch aus diesen Gegenständen klare, scharfe Bilder machte, befreite sie sich von den atmosphärischen Effekten ihrer frühen Malerei. Durch diese Veränderung ergaben sich für sie neue Bedeutungsmöglichkeiten in ihrer Arbeit, so dass sie sich nun mit Fragen von Proportion, Material und Farbe – der Form der Dinge – beschäftigen und zugleich das Potential von Geschichten und Geschichte beibehalten konnte.

Während des ersten Jahres an der Akademie formte Fritsch die meisten ihrer kleinen Skulpturen von Hand, zu Hause in ihrer Wohnung. Von der Atmosphäre an der Akademie sagt sie, dass sie sehr von Konkurrenzdenken geprägt gewesen sei. Die Last von Geschichte und Tradition des Hauses war einschüchternd, potentiell lähmend. Als sie in dieser Situation ihre frühen Objekte schuf, fühlte sie sich exponiert und unsicher. Während sie intuitiv arbeitete und eine eigene Sprache für ihre Arbeit zu entwickeln versuchte, fürchtete sie zugleich, für unprofessionell gehalten und nicht ernst genommen zu werden. Im Februar 1980 zeigte sie in der Akademie zum ersten Mal öffentlich eine Gruppe dieser

17

Fig./Abb. 3
Richard Artschwager
Untitled, 1966
Museum of Contemporary Art,
San Diego

Fig./Abb. 4
Giorgio de Chirico
L' énigme de la fatalité, 1914
Emanuel Hoffmann-Stiftung,
Depositum im Kunstmuseum
Basel

Academy at this time were several strong artist-teachers, including Gerhard Richter, Klaus Rinke, Gerhard Hoehme, Bernd Becher, and Schwegler, among others; Joseph Beuys, although no longer formally teaching at the Academy, was still a strong presence there, living and working in Düsseldorf. In Fritsch's case, Schwegler was an important influence in encouraging her own intuitive approach. He was less interested in discussing art history or theory than were most other professors and instead emphasized individual exploration and discussions about general issues of life and being an artist. She has described his credo as one of pushing the work to a point of no longer being able precisely to explain it, of finding a place where it becomes something unknown. Although this approach appealed to Fritsch, she remembers feeling a sense of danger and deep insecurity both artistically and personally in pushing herself to the artistic and existential edge that Schwegler's attitude sanctioned. She was also intimidated as a female student in an environment dominated by men, in which being an independent and assertive woman could cause derision, and in which there were no female role models.[1]

In 1981 Schwegler approved Fritsch to advance to the *Meisterschüler*, equivalent in the American system to an advanced degree status.[2] In a situation similar to that of many other young artists, Fritsch retained her affiliation with the Academy in order to continue having access to a workshop there, as well as the health insurance the Academy continued to provide. Not until 1984 did she separate completely from the school.

Through 1981 she continued to make sculptures, but now sometimes rather than making models she created works closer to the actual scale of their worldly counterparts, such as the *Käse* (Cheese, 1981; cat. 21) which she later incorporated into *Acht Tische mit acht Gegenständen* (Eight Tables with Eight Objects, 1984; pl. 3, cat. 48). She also occasionally began to work with objects that could be readily purchased rather than having to be fabricated. For example, the *Töpfe* (Cooking Pots, 1981; cat. 22), slightly larger in scale than usual pots and later included also in *Acht Tische mit acht Gegenständen*, were first purchased to become one of her works. At this time she also began to develop ideas for making objects as multiples.[3] Invited to participate in a newspaper started by New Wave musicians and called *Deutscher Realitätsdienst* (Germany Reality Service), she conceived of the *Werbeblatt I* (Advertising Leaflet I, 1981; pl. 1, cat. 24), as a newspaper insert from which people could order the objects she was making, priced cheaply and with no limit to the number

of copies that could be made. The newspaper was never published, but Fritsch did go ahead and publish the small leaflet offering her objects for sale, of which some were sold.

Typically, Fritsch develops many ideas simultaneously, and her work takes many forms. In addition to making the sculptures for which she is best known, very early in her career she began to think about projects on a large, architectural scale. In the formative years of 1980 and 1981, Fritsch along with another young artist, Peter Josef Abels, first conceived of an alternative place in which art might be presented, a kind of motel where visitors could stay overnight and which would have a garden around it. The project was never developed and remained only an idea the two artists would discuss occasionally. At this time Fritsch was living in the southern part of Düsseldorf, and she would go for walks in the *Südfriedhof*, the cemetery just outside the city. She also began to develop ideas for her own gardens and cemeteries, and during 1982 she made the first of the drawings of these plans. That same year she also began to work with sound by making a recording of croaking toads, although not until 1988 did she turn the recording into a record *Unken* (Toads, 1982/88, cat. 32), one of four multiples with sound she has made to date. In later years she also used sound as an essential component for creating rooms as sculptural environments.

Of primary importance to Fritsch in all of her works is finding or creating a borderline of perception between the physicality or materiality of an object and its existence as an image in the mind, that is, as something essential and pictorial. For each work, locating a point of tension in form and proportion that corresponds to a personal and intuitive sense of rightness is critical. She has described this search as finding a standard, a specificity of scale and material, so that an object is transformed and removed from its ordinary function or association, existing apart from its normal circumstances.

She is also interested in the social dimension of the objects as they give expression to beliefs about the role of art in society, especially in relation to structures of economic exchange. Fritsch has studied the traditions of the Arts and Crafts movement in nineteenth–century England and the German *Werkbund* and later *Bauhaus* movements of the early twentieth century, all of which shared a desire to create standard, good forms for the objects of daily use, which could be produced readily for a large, mass market and at moderate cost. The utopian ideals of these

frühen Objekte, auf einem Tisch arrangiert, so dass Studenten und Professoren ihre Arbeit des vergangenen Jahres begutachten konnten (Abb. 8).

An der Düsseldorfer Kunstakademie ist es (wie auch an den meisten anderen Akademien in Deutschland) üblich, dass die Studenten sich einem bestimmten Professor anschliessen, zu dessen Klasse sie dann gehören. Um jeden Professor bilden sich in dessen Klasse bestimmte Haltungen, Prinzipien und Arbeitsweisen heraus. Damals unterrichteten an der Düsseldorfer Kunstakademie einige starke Künstlerpersönlichkeiten, darunter Gerhard Richter, Klaus Rinke, Gerhard Hoehme, Bernd Becher und Fritz Schwegler. Joseph Beuys lehrte zwar formal nicht mehr an der Akademie, war aber dennoch sehr präsent; er lebte und arbeitete in Düsseldorf. Für Fritsch war Schwegler ein wichtiger Einfluss, weil er sie in ihrem eigenen, intuitiven Zugriff ermutigte. Im Vergleich zu den anderen Professoren interessierte er sich weniger für kunstgeschichtliche und theoretische Diskussionen und legte stattdessen Wert auf die individuelle Erforschung und Diskussion allgemeiner Fragen des Lebens und des Künstlerseins. Sein Credo bestand nach ihrer Beschreibung darin, die Arbeit bis zu einem Punkt voranzutreiben, an dem man sie nicht mehr genau erklären kann, einen Ort zu finden, wo sie zu etwas Unbekanntem wird. Auch wenn Fritsch dieser Ansatz entsprach, erinnert sie sich, dass sie es sowohl in persönlicher als auch in künstlerischer Hinsicht als eine Gefahr und tiefe Verunsicherung empfand, sich an jene künstlerische und existentielle Schwelle vorzuwagen, die Schwegler propagierte. Darüberhinaus fühlte sie sich als Studentin eingeschüchtert in einer von Männern dominierten Umgebung, in der man als unabhängige und selbstbewusste Frau nicht selten Spott erntete; es fehlten auch weibliche Rollenvorbilder.[1]

1981 wurde Katharina Fritsch Meisterschülerin bei Fritz Schwegler.[2] Wie viele andere junge Künstler schrieb sie sich weiterhin an der Akademie ein, um dort Zugang zu einer Werkstatt zu haben und die studentische Krankenversicherung in Anspruch nehmen zu können. Erst 1984 verliess sie die Akademie endgültig.

1981 schuf sie weitere Skulpturen, die nun manchmal nicht mehr Modellcharakter besassen, sondern sich dem Format ihrer weltlichen Gegenstücke annäherten, so beispielsweise der «Käse» (1981, Kat. 21), der später in «Acht Tische mit acht Gegenständen» (1984, Taf. 3, Kat. 48) wieder auftauchte. Zudem begann sie gelegentlich mit Objekten zu arbeiten, die sie nicht selbst herstellen musste, sondern fertig kaufen konnte. Die «Töpfe» (1981,

Kat. 22) zum Beispiel, nur wenig grösser als gewöhnliche Töpfe und später in «Acht Tische mit acht Gegenständen» verwendet, hatte sie in der Absicht gekauft, daraus eine Arbeit zu machen. Zu diesem Zeitpunkt entwickelte sie auch Ideen für Objekte als Multiples.[3] Eingeladen, sich an einer von New Wave-Musikern gegründeten Zeitung mit dem Titel «Deutscher Realitätsdienst» zu beteiligen, entwarf sie das «Werbeblatt I» (1981, Taf. 1, Kat. 24) als Zeitungsbeilage, nach der man ihre Objekte bestellen konnte; sie waren billig und die Anzahl der möglichen Kopien unbegrenzt. Die Zeitung erschien zwar nie, aber Fritsch veröffentlichte das Blatt auf eigene Faust und offerierte so ihre Objekte, von denen auch einige verkauft wurden.

Typisch für Katharina Fritsch ist, dass sie viele Ideen gleichzeitig entwickelt und ihre Arbeit in vielen Formen daherkommt. Zusätzlich zu ihren Skulpturen, mit denen sie am meisten bekannt wurde, begann sie schon sehr früh über Projekte im grossen, architekturalen Massstab nachzudenken. In den prägenden Jahren 1980 und 1981 fasste sie zusammen mit Peter-Josef Abels, einem anderen jungen Künstler, zum ersten Mal die Idee für einen alternativen Ort der Kunstpräsentation, eine Art Motel mit Garten, wo die Besucher über Nacht bleiben können. Das Projekt wurde nicht weiterverfolgt, sondern blieb eine Idee, die die beiden Künstler von Zeit zu Zeit diskutierten. Damals wohnte Fritsch im Süden Düsseldorfs und ging oft auf dem dort gelegenen Südfriedhof spazieren. So entwickelte sie Ideen für ihre eigenen Gärten und Friedhöfe, bis 1982 die ersten Zeichnungen dazu entstanden. Im selben Jahr begann sie auch mit Tönen zu arbeiten. Sie nahm das Geräusch rufender Unken auf, woraus 1988 die Platte «Unken» (1982/88, Kat. 32) wurde, eines von vier Ton-Multiples, die bis heute entstanden sind. Später verwendete sie Ton auch als wichtige Komponente bei der Gestaltung von Räumen als skulpturale Environments.

In allen ihren Werken geht es Fritsch hauptsächlich darum, zwischen dem physischen bzw. materiellen Charakter eines Objekts einerseits und dessen Existenz als Bild im Geiste, das heisst als etwas wesenhaft Bildliches andererseits eine Wahrnehmungsgrenze zu ziehen oder aufzuspüren. In jedem einzelnen Stück muss ein Ort der Spannung in Form und Proportion gefunden werden, der einem persönlich-intuitiven Gefühl der Richtigkeit entspricht. Sie hat dies als die Suche nach einem Standard beschrieben, nach einer bestimmten Eigenart in Grösse und Material, die den Gegenstand verwandelt, aus seiner gewöhnlichen

19

movements aspired to find a language of form which could fuse art and utility and which would be easily and universally understood and accepted. Fritsch believes such idealism is now impossible, subverted by contemporary mass media, commercialism, and popular culture. The appeal and strength of these new forces are their ability to create powerful images, whether the advertising of products on television or the projection of a lifestyle on MTV. Although potent, these images are in her view largely superficial, fleeting, and insubstantial.

Fritsch identifies the situation of the artist as one that cannot be disengaged either from the search to find a truth for oneself or from commerce. She has said, "You have to sell something you can't sell. I wanted to deal with that situation. I wanted to do that without losing a kind of honesty." Her conundrum has been to find some way out from the dead ends of both utopian modernism and contemporary commercialism: to create a language of form that is accessible without claiming universality and to create images that are broadly appealing but do not relinquish their subjectivity.

Especially as she experimented with and developed the sculptures that often became multiples, she has most specifically addressed these issues. In some cases she has made an object by hand and it remains unique. But her intention was always that pieces could be industrially produced, though the expense of doing so was frequently prohibitive. Sometimes relatively simple molds were fabricated, which allowed multiple copies to be made. The *Madonnenfigur* (Madonna Figure, 1982; cat. 31), for example, was a simple recreation of a small, plaster Madonna sold in tourist shops in Lourdes, which Fritsch painted a bright, shocking yellow. Copies were produced in a small workshop by hand from a mold. The final forms for *Katze* (Cat, 1981/89; cat. 25) and *Gehirn* (Brain, 1987/89; cat. 72), by contrast, were made working with the product development section of the huge German corporation Bayer, where prototypes could be developed. *Vase mit Schiff* (Vase with Ship, 1987/88; cat. 68) was made with an industrial form, produced in a factory using cast polyester.

Fritsch often traces her choice of objects to memories, frequently from childhood – to moments when an object is secured as an image by the mind. For example, *Katze* was based on a cat-shaped object made for putting out cigarettes which had been used by her mother. Other works may be based on visions, what she calls "moments in between reality." Sometimes she may work her way through to the final form of an object by making sketches and then models, first in cardboard, sometimes in plas-

ter, to determine scale, proportion, and degree of detail. The final sculpture often is highly abstracted and formalized, as well as changed in size, material, and color from the object that was the direct source.

In 1983 Fritsch was asked by Rüdiger Schöttle to present work at his gallery in Munich. She already had begun to realize that making clear decisions about the presentation of the objects was as important as the decisions about the making of the objects themselves. This gallery invitation crystallized her need to find the right solution for showing many of the objects made up to that date. The result was *Warengestell* (Display Stand, 1979-1984; pl. 2, cat. 40), a stand with five glass shelves for presenting small objects, in which the form of presentation became fully and precisely developed. The sculpture intentionally alludes to a counter for presenting objects for sale that might be found in a small shop, or to a knickknack stand that could be found in someone's home. But in her positioning of the objects and through their associations, Fritsch elicits a much more psychological reading. The top shelf is left empty, and on the shelf below is placed a green emerald, a crystal, which might be associated with the head. At the center of the middle shelf she placed a Madonna, evoking religion and the soul. Under it are objects pronounced by the simple beauty of their material, such as a ring of beads arranged like a bracelet. Finally, under all the other objects she placed jars of anthurium, alluding to sex as the unconscious level. The stand thus becomes a kind of anthropomorphic cosmos, the objects transformed into contemporary charms and fetishes, becoming surrogates for subliminal yearnings and dreams.

In the midst of creating *Warengestell*, Fritsch was invited by the curator Kasper König to present work in an enormous survey of contemporary German art titled *von hier aus* (from here onwards), which he was organizing for presentation in Düsseldorf in the fall of 1984 at the city trade fair halls. She responded by creating a large sculpture for display of larger objects she had made, *Acht Tische mit acht Gegenständen* (Eight Tables with Eight Objects, 1984; pl. 3, cat. 48). The piece is like a concession stall in the middle of which someone could conceivably stand and sell goods or food. Characteristically, Fritsch considers each sculpture for a particular situation, what she describes as "the right thing for the right place." At any time she has many ideas for potential works, but the context draws out and determines the final realization of an idea. In many cases, such as the *Acht*

Funktion bzw. Assoziation herauslöst und ausserhalb seiner normalen Umgebung existieren lässt.

Auch die gesellschaftliche Dimension der Objekte interessiert Fritsch, schlägt sich in ihnen doch die Vorstellung einer Gesellschaft von der Rolle der Kunst nieder, vor allem was die Strukturen des ökonomischen Austauschs betrifft. Fritsch hat das Bemühen der englischen Arts and Crafts-Bewegung des 19. Jahrhunderts, des Deutschen Werkbundes und des Bauhauses studiert. Diese teilten das Streben nach guten Standardformen für die Gegenstände des täglichen Gebrauchs, die mit geringen Kosten für den Massenabsatz geschaffen werden sollten. Ihr utopisches Ideal war eine Formensprache, die Kunst und Nützlichkeit miteinander verbindet; dabei sollte sie leicht und weltweit verstanden und akzeptiert werden. Fritsch hält solchen Idealismus heutzutage nicht mehr für möglich, er sei den zeitgenössischen Massenmedien, Kommerzialismus und Popkultur zum Opfer gefallen. Anziehung und Stärke dieser neuen Kräfte liegen in deren Fähigkeit, machtvolle Bilder zu schaffen, sei es bei der Produktwerbung im Fernsehen oder im Entwurf eines Lebensstils auf MTV. Doch bei aller Macht, die diesen Bildern innewohnt, hält Fritsch sie weitgehend für oberflächlich, unbeständig und substanzlos.

Fritsch hat erkannt, dass ein Künstler sich weder von der Suche nach einer eigenen Wahrheit noch vom Kommerz losmachen kann. «Man muss etwas verkaufen, das man gar nicht verkaufen kann», sagt sie. «Auf diese Situation wollte ich eingehen. Ich wollte das tun, ohne eine gewisse Aufrichtigkeit einzubüssen.» Die Aufgabe war, einen Ausweg sowohl aus der Sackgasse des utopischen Modernismus als auch des zeitgenössischen Kommerzialismus zu finden: eine Formensprache zu schaffen, die verfügbar ist, ohne einen Anspruch auf Universalität zu erheben, und Bilder zu schaffen, die ein breites Publikum ansprechen, ohne ihre Subjektivität preiszugeben.

Vor allem beim Experimentieren mit und Entwickeln von jenen Skulpturen, aus denen oft Multiples wurden, hat sie sich auf diese Problematik konzentriert. In einigen Fällen machte sie ein Objekt von Hand und es blieb ein Unikat. Die Stücke sollten aber grundsätzlich industriell herstellbar sein, auch wenn die Kosten dafür es oft verboten. Manchmal fertigte sie einfache Hohlformen an, die ein mehrfaches Ausgiessen erlaubten. Die «Madonnenfigur» (1982, Kat. 31) beispielsweise ist eine schlichte Nachbildung einer kleinen Gipsmadonna von Lourdes, wie sie in Touristenläden verkauft wird; die Figur hat Fritsch schliesslich mit leuchtend gelber Schockfarbe bemalt. Die Kopien wurden in einer kleinen Werk-

statt von Hand mit einer Hohlform gefertigt. Dagegen entstanden die endgültigen Formen für «Katze» (1981/89, Kat. 25) und «Gehirn» (1987/89, Kat. 72) in Zusammenarbeit mit der Abteilung für Produktentwicklung des grossen deutschen Konzerns Bayer, wo die Prototypen entwickelt werden konnten. Die «Vase mit Schiff» (1987/88, Kat. 68) schliesslich wurde in einer Fabrik nach einer Industrieform in Kunststoff gegossen.

Oft kann Fritsch die Auswahl ihrer Objekte auf Erinnerungen zurückführen, aus der Kindheit zumal – auf jene Augenblicke, in denen der Geist einen Gegenstand als Bild festhält. Die «Katze» zum Beispiel basiert auf einem Glutlöscher in Katzenform, den ihre Mutter für Zigaretten benutzte. Anderen Arbeiten liegen vielleicht eher Visionen zugrunde, was sie «Momente zwischen der Realität» nennt. Manchmal durchläuft die Entwicklung bis zur endgültigen Form eines Objekts auch Zeichnungen und Modelle, zunächst aus Pappe, gelegentlich aus Gips, mit denen sie Grösse, Proportionen und Detailliertheit festlegt. Im Vergleich zu dem Gegenstand, der als unmittelbare Quelle diente, ist die endgültige Skulptur oft stark abstrahiert und formalisiert sowie in Grösse, Material und Form verändert.

1983 schlug Rüdiger Schöttle der Künstlerin eine Ausstellung in seiner Münchener Galerie vor. Damals hatte sie bereits erkannt, dass klare Entscheidungen über die Präsentation der Objekte ebenso wichtig sind wie Beschlüsse im Herstellungsprozess der Objekte selbst. Diese Galerieeinladung nun konkretisierte ihren Wunsch, für die bis dahin entstandenen Objekte die richtige Präsentationsform zu finden. Das Ergebnis war das «Warengestell» (1979-1984, Taf. 2, Kat. 40), ein Gestell mit fünf Glasflächen für die Präsentation kleiner Objekte, bei dem die Form der Präsentation ebenso systematisch wie präzise entwickelt war. Die Skulptur spielt gezielt auf ein Regal an, wie es beispielsweise in einem kleinen Laden als Warenauslage dienen könnte, oder auf ein Nippesregal in irgendeiner Wohnung. Doch durch die Plazierung der Objekte und deren Assoziationen entlockt Fritsch ihnen eine weitaus psychologischere Lesart. Die obere Glasplatte ist leer, und auf der Etage darunter liegt ein grüner Smaragd, ein Kristall, den man dem Kopf zuordnen könnte. Im Zentrum der mittleren Glasplatte steht eine Madonnenfigur, die die Vorstellung von Religion und Seele weckt. Darunter befinden sich Objekte, die sich durch die schlichte Schönheit ihres Materials auszeichnen, zum Beispiel ein Ring aus Perlen, der wie ein Armband arrangiert wurde. Und schliesslich hat sie unter all den anderen Objekten noch Vasen mit

Tische mit acht Gegenständen, the sculpture may be presented later in other situations, but the initial creation occurred in response to a specific context.

Simultaneous with these two sculptures, in 1984 Fritsch made her first work in which no physical object was present but the environment itself became the work. Called *Parfüm im Hausflur* (Perfume in the Hallway, 1984; pl. 5, cat. 41), this work simply involved scenting the air of a stairwell with perfume. She describes the piece as a kind of negative of a person who has passed through the stairwell: the smell of the perfume is something that is left, physical but imperceptible as material – the effect of an apparition, but to the nose rather than to the eyes. This work, Fritsch says, derived from memories of the house in which she lived with her grandparents when she was four years old. She always knew when another woman living in the house had been present by the lingering smell of her perfume. Sometime after making this work, Fritsch asked her mother if she knew which perfume the woman had used, and her mother told her it was called *Je reviens* (I will come again), the name echoing precisely Fritsch's conflation of experience and memory.

Throughout the mid-1980s Fritsch made a number of sculptures, always in response to an invitation to show work in a particular place. This phase of her work culminated in exhibitions in 1987 in Krefeld and Münster, from which her work first gained widespread international attention. In Krefeld, Fritsch was invited to make a new work to be presented in the Kaiser Wilhelm Museum and to participate in a group exhibition organized by the museum at the nearby Haus Lange. The Kaiser Wilhelm Museum, built at the turn of the century in the center of the city, is a grand Beaux-Arts structure whose monumental galleries have arching skylights. For one of these galleries Fritsch made the *Elefant* (Elephant, 1987; pl. 12, cat. 64). Cast in polyester from a stuffed elephant in the Natural History Museum in Bonn, the sculpture resembled its naturalistic counterpart, except that it was tinted a peculiar green. Echoing the vaulted curve of the overhead skylight, a high elliptical pedestal elevated the sculpture, which appeared like a supernatural apparition: enormous, displaced, dematerialized by its color and shimmering surface, yet perfectly poised and balanced, alone in the stark white salon. In contrast, Fritsch responded to the setting of Haus Lange, a modernist villa built by Mies van der Rohe in Krefeld in the mid-1920s, by creating an intimate domestic tableau. A small, light gray table with latticed sides, *Beistelltisch mit Engel und Flasche* (Side Table with Angel and Bottle, 1985; cat.

57), was set in a small room, on three sides of which Fritsch had stenciled a green and red pattern – *Tapetenmuster* (Wallpaper Pattern, 1980; cat. 16) – copying a 1950s-style wallpaper that she had seen in a hotel when she was a child. On the table sat a tiny silver angel and a tall, square green bottle. The overall effect was of a private space of great delicacy, beauty, and mystery. In a nearby corridor the space remained empty except for the recorded sound of lightly falling rain, *Regen* (Rain, 1987; cat. 63).

Only weeks after this exhibition, in a plaza in Münster Fritsch unveiled the *Madonnenfigur* (Madonna Figure, 1987; pl. 13, cat. 67), again based on tourist figurines of the Madonna of Lourdes and painted a brilliant, acidic yellow but now shifted to human scale. Positioned in the plaza midway between a Catholic church and a large department store, the *Madonnenfigur* appeared again like a phantom, recalling the otherworldly aspirations of the church as well as the often colorful merchandising of the department store. The piece was almost immediately destroyed at night, only to be replaced and destroyed again, a charged and high-profile target. Evidence makes clear that the destruction was at the hands of hooligans rather than defenders of the faith, and during its brief appearance the *Madonnenfigur* inspired poems and letters to the artist and discussions in schools and throughout the town, as much in praise as in distrust of its appearance, bringing the subject of faith and its material emblems in contemporary society to lively reconsideration.

The next year, 1988, marked a shift in Fritsch's work away from the relative simplicity of the earlier, iconic sculptures. That year she presented in the Basel Kunsthalle the enormous sculpture of thirty-two identical male figures seated at a long refectory-style table, the *Tischgesellschaft* (Company at Table, 1988; pl. 17, cat. 75). By using the human figure, Fritsch introduced an explicit psychological resonance to her work, a brooding existential darkness. This sculpture evoked feelings of isolation and loneliness, of vulnerability and withdrawal, even in the midst of such a multitude of human forms. Characteristic of her sculpture, the piece exploits symmetry and balance to allude to both infinity and containment. She had intended to show two other, related new sculptures for that exhibition, including a two-part sculpture called *Gespenst und Blutlache* (Ghost and Pool of Blood, 1988; pl. 18, cat. 76), consisting of a tall, white, shrouded figure opposite what appeared to be a shallow pool of shimmering, garnet-colored liquid. It was not completed in time for the Basel presentation and was shown late that fall in the Carnegie International exhibition in Pittsburgh. The

Anturien aufgestellt, eine Anspielung auf das Geschlecht als unbewusste Ebene. Auf diese Weise wird das Gestell zu einer Art anthropomorphen Kosmos und die Objekte – verwandelt in zeitgenössische Talismane und Fetische – zu Surrogaten unbewusster Sehnsüchte und Träume.

Noch während Fritsch an ihrem «Warengestell» arbeitete, erhielt sie von Kasper König die Einladung zu einer grossen Übersichtsausstellung für zeitgenössische deutsche Kunst mit dem Titel «von hier aus», die er für den Herbst 1984 in den Düsseldorfer Messehallen organisierte. Darauf antwortete sie mit einer grossen Skulptur für die Präsentation ihrer grösseren Objekte: «Acht Tische mit acht Gegenständen» (1984, Taf. 3, Kat. 48). Das Stück ist wie ein Verkaufsstand, in dessen Mitte jemand stehen und Waren oder Lebensmittel anbieten könnte. Typisch für Fritsch ist, dass sie jede Skulptur auf eine bestimmte Situation hin entwirft; sie selbst nennt das «die richtige Sache für den richtigen Ort.» Zwar hat sie immer viele Ideen für mögliche Arbeiten auf Lager, aber erst der Kontext provoziert und bestimmt die endgültige Realisierung einer Idee. In vielen Fällen, wie beispielsweise bei «Acht Tische mit acht Gegenständen», kann die Skulptur später auch in anderem Zusammenhang gezeigt werden, aber ihre ursprüngliche Entstehung war eine Reaktion auf eine konkrete Situation.

Gleichzeitig mit diesen beiden Skulpturen produzierte Fritsch 1984 ihre erste Arbeit, bei der es kein physisches Objekt gab, sondern die Umgebung selbst zum Werk wurde: «Parfüm im Hausflur» (1984, Taf. 5, Kat. 41). Diese Arbeit bestand einfach darin, dass sie ein Treppenhaus parfümierte. Sie beschreibt das Stück als eine Art Negativabdruck von einer Person, die durch das Treppenhaus gegangen ist; was bleibt, ist der Geruch des Parfüms, physisch zwar, aber als Material nicht wahrnehmbar – wie eine Erscheinung, allerdings nicht für die Augen sondern für die Nase. Fritsch erklärt dazu, dass dieses Stück auf die Erinnerung an jenes Haus zurückgeht, in dem sie als Vierjährige mit ihren Grosseltern wohnte. Wenn eine andere, im selben Haus wohnende Frau anwesend war, wusste sie es immer wegen des Parfüms, dessen Duft dann in der Luft lag. Einige Zeit nach der Entstehung dieser Arbeit fragte Fritsch ihre Mutter, ob sie noch wisse, welches Parfüm die Frau damals benutzt hatte, und sie sagte, es sei «Je reviens» gewesen – ein Name, der Fritschs Verschmelzung von Erfahrung und Erinnerung genau trifft.

Bis Mitte der achtziger Jahre gestaltete Katharina Fritsch verhältnismässig wenige Skulpturen, mit denen sie jeweils auf einen bestimmten Ausstellungsort reagierte. Höhepunkt dieser Werkphase waren 1987 Ausstellungen in Krefeld und Münster, wo ihre Arbeit zum ersten Mal internationale Beachtung fand. In Krefeld hatte man Fritsch eingeladen, für das Kaiser Wilhelm Museum ein neues Werk zu schaffen und an einer vom Museum im nahegelegenen Haus Lange veranstalteten Gruppenausstellung teilzunehmen. Das Kaiser Wilhelm Museum ist ein grosser Gründerzeit-Bau der Jahrhundertwende inmitten der Stadt; die grosszügigen Ausstellungsräume verfügen über gewölbte Oberlichter. Für einen davon schuf Fritsch den «Elefanten» (1987, Taf. 12, Kat. 64). Die Skulptur war nach einem ausgestopften Elefanten im Bonner Naturkundemuseum in Polyester nachgegossen und ihrem naturalistischen Vorbild sehr ähnlich, ausser dass sie mit einem eigenartigen Grün angestrichen war. Ein hohes, ellipsenförmiges Podest, das die Wölbung des Oberlichts aufgriff, erhöhte die Skulptur so, dass sie wie eine übernatürliche Erscheinung wirkte: gigantisch, abgehoben, durch Farbe und schimmernde Oberfläche entmaterialisiert, doch ausgewogen in vollkommener Balance, allein im leeren weissen Saal. Als Kontrast dazu reagierte Fritsch auf die Situation im Haus Lange, einer von Mies van der Rohe Mitte der zwanziger Jahre erbauten modernistischen Villa, mit einem häuslich-intimen Tableau. Ein kleiner, hellgrauer Tisch mit Gittern an den Seiten, «Beistelltisch mit Engel und Flasche» (1985, Kat. 57), stand in einem kleinen Raum, in dem Fritsch drei Wände mittels Schablone mit einem grünroten Muster versah: «Tapetenmuster» (1980, Kat. 16). Es war die Kopie einer Tapete im Stil der fünfziger Jahre, die sie als Kind in einem Hotel gesehen hatte. Auf dem Tisch standen ein kleiner Silberengel und eine hohe, rechteckige, grüne Flasche. Das Ganze wirkte wie ein privater Raum voller Zartheit, Schönheit und Geheimnis. In einem nahegelegenen Durchgang blieb der Raum leer, nur das aufgezeichnete Geräusch von leichtem Regen war zu hören: «Regen» (1987, Kat. 63).

Einige Wochen nach dieser Ausstellung enthüllte Fritsch auf einem Platz in Münster die «Madonnenfigur» (1987, Taf. 13, Kat. 67). Auch dieser Skulptur, in beissendem Gelb bemalt, lag wieder eine Souvenirfigur der Madonna von Lourdes zugrunde; nun allerdings in Menschengrösse. Aufgestellt auf einem Platz zwischen einer katholischen Kirche und einem grossen Kaufhaus, wirkte die «Madonnenfigur» auch hier wie eine Erscheinung, die einerseits an die Jenseitsgerichtetheit der Kirche und andererseits an die bunte Warenwelt des Kaufhauses erinnerte. Das Stück wurde noch am selben Abend zerstört, wieder aufgestellt und wieder zerstört, ein überaus reizvolles Angriffsziel also. Offensichtlich war die Zerstörung das Werk von Randalierern und nicht von

two works are seen together for the first time in the San Francisco exhibition. A third work intended for the Basel exhibition, a large shark in a basin, was never completed.

Shown the next year and contrasting with the starkness and inward mood of the previous year's work was a series of sculptures – including *Warengestell mit Vasen* (Display Stand with Vases, 1987/89; pl. 11, cat. 69) and *Warengestell mit Madonnen* (Display Stand with Madonnas, 1987/89; pl. 10, cat. 70) – that concentrated on the stunning visual effects of repeated patterns and the play of negative and positive spaces. Towers of objects were precariously balanced and stacked, making a wonderfully delicate and rich visual effect, more formal than psychological, more rational than organic. Made soon after the towers and related to them by a cool beauty and the formal effect of repeated shapes was a series of highly colored wall reliefs, *Acht Bilder in acht Farben* (Eight Pictures in Eight Colors, 1990/91; pl. 15, cat. 93) – geometric, appearing like framed pictures but with no image. These works were followed by *Mann und Maus* (Man and Mouse, 1991/92; pl. 19, cat. 96), which brought back the form of the male figure seated at the long table, but now drained of color, isolated, prostrate, and immobile under the great weight of a huge black mouse: truly a nightmare, but also delightfully and absurdly funny. Fritsch increasingly came to see a dialogue in her work between what she refers to as the "dark" pieces and the "light" pieces, a contrast and tension she has continued to develop up to the present.

In the early 1990s Fritsch concentrated on making her largest-scale work to date, a monumental sculpture commissioned by the Dia Center for the Arts in New York, the *Rattenkönig* (Rat-King, 1991/93; pl. 20, cat. 97).[4] Fritsch made her first trip to the United States at the invitation of Dia in 1989 and at the end of three weeks in New York arrived at the initial idea of making this work. The sculpture was in part a response to the gallery space offered for the project, a vast ground-floor room in a building formerly used for manufacturing and as a warehouse on the far west side of Manhattan, near the docks and piers of the Hudson River. It also brought together many aspects of her works from the prior years, especially the fusing of monumental form with repeated elements. The appearance of the rats was highly stylized and abstracted, not cast from an existing object but conceived and developed slowly in the artist's imagination through stages of enlargement and refinement. The knot at the middle, which joined the tails of the rats, became an independent sculpture of its own: *Knoten* (Knot, 1992/93; cat. 98), one of the most compressed and geometric works yet done by Fritsch.

For the exhibitions in San Francisco and Basel, Fritsch has completed a new sculpture, *Kind mit Pudeln* (Child with Poodles, 1995/96; pl. 22, cat. 102), which shares some of the same psychological qualities of *Mann und Maus*: a feeling of entrapment and the standoff between innocence and evil. A prototype for this work was presented in the spring of 1995 for an exhibition at the Zürich Kunsthaus titled *Zeichen und Wunder* (Signs and Wonders), just prior to the opening of the Venice Biennale. In the prototype 32 poodles were stationed in elegant, spacious rings around an infant at the center. In the final sculpture the ranks of the poodles have been closed, with four tight, densely packed rings comprising 224 poodles, heightening and intensifying the sense of menace, shutting off any possibility of escape. Fritsch chose the image of the poodle as a dog that is cute and beguiling but also can be aggressive and mean. Soon after completing the piece, she recalled that a poodle appears in Johann Wolfgang von Goethe's story of Faust: while walking, Faust sees a black poodle which he brings home, unknowingly inviting into his study Mephistopheles, the devil. The child represents humanity, innocent at birth, which cannot escape encountering evil, and which once it begins the journey of life must face the tensions of civilization and the potential for corruption. An intentional ambiguity inhabits the work, however, because the poodles also seem to be on alert watch, guarding over the child. And aside from the ominous atmosphere, a strange sense of humor and an uneasy feeling of delight are elicited by the quirky oddness of both the poodles and the baby. Fritsch is loath to attach a single meaning to any of her sculptures, intending them to be open to a variety of interpretations and responses from individual viewers.

Soon after the Dia commission Fritsch was invited to represent Germany in the 1995 Venice Biennale, and she began work on *Museum, Modell 1:10* (Museum, Model 1:10, 1995; pl. 21, cat. 100), a large-scale sculpture for the German pavilion. In contrast to the *Rattenkönig*, this work evokes a consideration of philosophical ideas and creates a forum for discussion of art and society, bringing together an extremely complex and layered set of references and sources. Specifically, the work addresses the dilemma of liberal humanism in the West at the end of the twentieth century, particularly the meaning of art and of the frame for its presentation – that is, the site where we experience art, namely the institution of the museum, and how that place conditions our experience.

Glaubensverteidigern. Während ihres kurzen Auftritts regte die «Madonnenfigur» zu Gedichten und Briefen an die Künstlerin an und löste Diskussionen in Schulen und in der ganzen Stadt aus, in denen sowohl Lob als auch Misstrauen formuliert wurde. Eine lebhafte Debatte über den Glauben und seine materiellen Sinnbilder in der heutigen Gesellschaft kam in Gang.

Im darauffolgenden Jahr 1988 entfernte sich Fritschs Werk von der relativen Einfachheit ihrer früheren ikonenhaften Skulpturen. In der Basler Kunsthalle präsentierte sie eine riesige Skulptur: «Tischgesellschaft» (1988, Taf. 17, Kat. 75). An einem langen Tisch, der aus einem Refektorium stammen könnte, sitzen zweiunddreissig identische männliche Figuren. Mit der menschlichen Figur bringt Fritsch ein explizit psychologisches Moment in ihre Arbeit, eine latente existentielle Düsternis. Die Skulptur evoziert Gefühle von Isolation und Einsamkeit, von Verwundbarkeit und Rückzug, selbst inmitten so zahlreicher menschlicher Formen. Es ist typisch für die bildhauerische Arbeit dieser Künstlerin, dass auch diese Skulptur wieder Symmetrie und Balance nutzt, um in einem Unendlichkeit und Kontrolle zu suggerieren. Ursprünglich hatte sie zwei weitere Skulpturen bei dieser Ausstellung zeigen wollen, darunter eine zweiteilige Arbeit mit dem Titel «Gespenst und Blutlache» (1988, Taf. 18, Kat. 76). Sie besteht aus einer grossen, mit einem weissen Tuch verhängten Figur und etwas, das wie die Lache einer dünnen, glänzenden, rotgefärbten Flüssigkeit aussieht. Das Stück wurde aber für die Basler Ausstellung nicht rechtzeitig fertig und stattdessen im Herbst desselben Jahres bei der «Carnegie International» in Pittsburgh gezeigt. In San Francisco werden die beiden Arbeiten zum ersten Mal zusammen zu sehen sein. Eine dritte Skulptur für Basel, ein grosser Hai in einem Becken, wurde nie fertiggestellt.

Im darauffolgenden Jahr zeigte Fritsch eine Reihe von Skulpturen, die ganz im Gegensatz zur Strenge und Innerlichkeit der Arbeiten aus dem Vorjahr standen, darunter «Warengestell mit Vasen» (1987/89, Taf. 11, Kat. 69) und «Warengestell mit Madonnen» (1987/89, Taf. 10, Kat. 70). Dabei verblüffen vor allem die optischen Effekte wiederholter Muster und das Spiel mit Negativ- und Positivräumen. Die Türme von Objekten – in labiler Balance gestapelt – wirken wunderbar delikat und eindrücklich, weniger im psychologischen als im formalen Sinne, eher rational denn organisch erscheinend. Wenig später entstand, den Türmen in ihrer kühlen Schönheit und im formalen Effekt wiederholter Formen vergleichbar, eine Serie von stark farbigen Wandreliefs, «Acht Bilder in acht Farben» (1990/91, Taf. 15, Kat. 93) – geometrische Formen, die wie gerahm-

te Gemälde wirken, aber kein Bild zeigen. Darauf folgte «Mann und Maus» (1991/92, Taf. 19, Kat. 96), ein Stück, das die männliche Form aus der Tischgesellschaft wieder aufgreift, jetzt aber der Farbe beraubt, isoliert, reglos hingestreckt unter der schweren Last einer riesigen schwarzen Maus: ein richtiger Alptraum, zugleich aber auch herrlich absurd und komisch. Zunehmend erkannte Fritsch im eigenen Werk einen Dialog zwischen den von ihr so genannten «dunklen» und den «hellen» Stücken. Diese Spannung und Gegensätzlichkeit hat sie bis heute immer weiter entwickelt.

Zu Beginn der neunziger Jahre konzentrierte sich Katharina Fritsch auf die Arbeit an ihrem bis dahin grössten Werk, einer monumentalen Skulptur im Auftrag des Dia Center for the Arts in New York: «Rattenkönig» (1991/93, Taf. 20, Kat. 97).[4] Auf Einladung von Dia unternahm sie 1989 ihre erste Amerika-Reise. Am Ende des dreiwöchigen Aufenthalts in New York kam sie auf die Idee zu diesem Stück. Die Skulptur war auch eine Reaktion auf den für dieses Projekt vorgesehenen Ausstellungsort, ein weitläufiger Raum im Erdgeschoss eines Gebäudes im Westen Manhattans, nahe den Hafenanlagen am Hudson River, das früher einmal als Fabrik und Lagerhaus gedient hatte. Das Stück vereint in sich viele Aspekte von Arbeiten aus früheren Jahren, vor allem die Verbindung einer monumentalen Form mit der Wiederholung von Elementen. Die Ratten präsentieren sich in äusserst stilisiert-abstrahierter Form. Sie ist kein Abguss von einem bereits existierenden Objekt, sondern entwickelte sich nach und nach in der Vorstellung der Künstlerin und durchlief dabei verschiedene Stadien der Vergrösserung und Ausgefeiltheit. Aus dem Knoten in der Mitte, wo die Rattenschwänze zusammenlaufen, wurde eine eigenständige Skulptur mit dem Titel «Knoten» (1992/93, Kat. 98), eine der komprimiertesten und geometrischsten Arbeiten, die Fritsch je schuf.

Für die Ausstellungen in San Francisco und Basel produzierte Katharina Fritsch eine neue Skulptur – «Kind mit Pudeln» (1995/96, Taf. 22, Kat. 102), die einige psychologische Elemente mit «Mann und Maus» gemeinsam hat: das Gefühl einer Falle und die Spannung zwischen Unschuld und Bosheit. Im Frühjahr 1995 gab es kurz vor der Eröffnung der Biennale in Venedig bei der Ausstellung «Zeichen und Wunder» im Kunsthaus Zürich einen Prototypen dieses Stücks zu sehen. Er zeigte 32 Pudel, mit elegantem Schwung in Ringen um ein Kind in ihrer Mitte plaziert. Bei der endgültigen Skulptur sind die Reihen der Pudel geschlossen; vier festgefügte Ringe aus 224 dicht aneinandergedrängten Pudeln verstärken das Gefühl der Bedrohung, indem sie keinen Fluchtweg lassen. Fritsch wählte das Bild des Pudels, weil dieser Hund

The *Museum* is a model made at a one-to-ten scale for a park and building that Fritsch proposes to be built. She describes it as follows:

"The museum is a two-story, octagonal pavilion 24 meters in diameter and 16 meters tall.

The ground floor, designed for the exhibition of sculptures, is glazed on all sides; the outer walls on the second floor, designed for paintings, are gold.

The walls of the stairwell are white on the ground floor and glazed in eight different colors on the second floor – red, blue, green, black, white, yellow, light green, and orange.

Eight doors lead to the inner stairwell, which climbs cone-shaped up to the middle of the first story, where another eight doors lead to an unroofed octagonal inner courtyard. From there the stairs leading up the second floor are funnel-shaped.

The land and lawn around the museum are octagonal. Twenty-five deciduous trees are to be planted on each eighth, forming an exact triangle, the tip of which is aligned with a corner of the building. In winter, a black web of bare branches surrounds the building; in summer it is a leafy green wreath. The trees form a negative star in the grass, with the museum at its center.

The museum has no permanent collection; the exhibitions of contemporary art on view there should be designed specifically for that museum. They remain there for one or two years. Administration and the technical department are housed in adjacent buildings."[5]

Formally *Museum* sets up a series of contrasts. The pedestal is a grand, white, octagonal form, surmounted by a delicate, complex web of black trees, at the center of which is an eight-sided, faceted, colored, jewel-like pavilion. When a visitor walks around the pedestal, the lines of the trees dissolve in and out of focus, a moiré pattern set off against the still, focused center. The brilliance and light of the pavilion, beckoning but unreachable, emerge out of the dark visual barrier of the trees. Tensions between the organic and the geometric, between nature and rationality, between darkness and light are kept in stasis and poised equilibrium.[6]

This work directly harkens back to some of Fritsch's first plans for parks and ideas about the potential of a museum to be a special place of pilgrimage. As precedents, she cites specifically both historical and contemporary sites. One source of inspiration was the Chinese Tea Pavilion (fig. 5) designed by Johann Gottfried Buring for the park of Sanssouci in Potsdam, near Berlin. Built as part of the summer palace complex by Georg Wenzeslaus von Knobelsdorff in the first half of the eighteenth century, it is now, like Versailles, and so many other architectural monu-

26

einerseits niedlich und nett ist und andererseits aggressiv und gemein sein kann. Kurz nachdem sie das Stück fertiggestellt hatte, fiel ihr ein, dass der Pudel auch in Goethes Faust vorkommt: Beim Spaziergang sieht Faust einen schwarzen Pudel, den er mit nach Hause nimmt, ohne zu ahnen, dass er sich auf diese Weise Mephisto, den Teufel, ins Haus holt. Das Kind verkörpert den Menschen schlechthin, der bei der Geburt noch unschuldig ist, aber der Begegnung mit dem Bösen nicht entgehen kann. Sobald er die Reise des Lebens antritt, ist er den Spannungen der Zivilisation und deren korruptem Potential ausgesetzt. Doch das Werk ist mit Absicht doppeldeutig, denn die Pudel scheinen zugleich aufmerksam über das Kind zu wachen. Abgesehen von der ohnehin spannungsgeladenen Atmosphäre entsteht durch die verschrobene Eigentümlichkeit sowohl der Pudel als auch des Kindes etwas Humorvolles und zugleich ein vages Gefühl von Wonne. Weit davon entfernt, ihren Arbeiten jeweils eine einzige Bedeutung zu geben, öffnet Fritsch sie für vielfältige Interpretationen und Reaktionen durch die einzelnen Betrachter.

Schon bald nach dem Dia-Auftrag erhielt Katharina Fritsch die Einladung, Deutschland 1995 bei der Biennale in Venedig zu vertreten. Daraufhin entwickelte sie das «Museum, Modell 1:10» (1995, Taf. 21, Kat. 100), eine grossformatige Skulptur, für den deutschen Pavillon. Im Gegensatz zum «Rattenkönig» legt dieses Stück philosophische Überlegungen nahe und fordert eine Diskussion über Kunst und Gesellschaft heraus, indem es extrem komplexe und vielschichtige Bezüge und Quellen in sich vereint. Im Grunde geht es in dieser Arbeit um das Dilemma des liberalen Humanismus im Westen am Ende des 20. Jahrhunderts, vor allem um die Bedeutung der Kunst und ihres Präsentationsrahmens, das heisst, des Ortes, an dem wir Kunst erfahren, namentlich der Institution Museum, und darum, wie dieser Ort unsere Erfahrung prägt.

Das «Museum» ist ein Modell im Massstab 1:10 für einen Park mit Gebäude. Katharina Fritsch beschreibt es folgendermassen:

«Das Museum ist ein zweistöckiger, achteckiger Pavillon mit einem Durchmesser von 24 Metern und einer Höhe von 16 Metern.

Das untere Stockwerk, zur Ausstellung von Skulpturen gedacht, ist rundum verglast, das obere Stockwerk, der Malerei zugedacht, hat rundum goldene Aussenwände.

Die Wände zum Treppenhaus sind im unteren Stockwerk weiss, im oberen in acht verschiedenen Farben, rot, blau, grün, schwarz, weiss, gelb, hellgrün, orange verglast.

Acht Türen führen ins Treppenhaus im Inneren, das bis zur halben Höhe des ersten Stockwerks kegelförmig ansteigend, sich mit ebenfalls acht Türen zu einem achteckigen Innenhof unter freiem Himmel öffnet. Von dort aus führen die Stufen umgekehrt trichterförmig zum zweiten Stockwerk.

Das Museum liegt auf einem achteckigen Rasengrundstück. Bepflanzt ist jedes Achtel mit 25 Laubbäumen, die ein exaktes, jeweils auf eine Ecke des Museums zulaufendes Dreieck bilden. Im Winter bildet der kahle Wald ein schwarzes Gespinst, im Sommer einen grünen Kranz. Die Form des Waldes bildet negativ im Rasen einen grünen Stern, der seinen Mittelpunkt im Museum hat.

Das Museum soll keine ständige Sammlung beherbergen. Es soll extra auf das Museum zugeschnittene Ausstellungen von zeitgenössischen Künstlern zeigen. Die Ausstellungen sollen ein bis zwei Jahre dort zu sehen sein. Verwaltungs- und technische Dinge sind in umliegenden Gebäuden untergebracht.»[5]

In formaler Hinsicht birgt «Museum» eine Reihe von Gegensätzen. Der Sockel ist ein grosses weisses Achteck, umgeben von einem ebenso zarten wie komplexen Gespinst aus schwarzen Bäumen, in dessen Zentrum sich wie ein Edelstein ein achtseitiger, facettierter farbiger Pavillon befindet. Wenn der Besucher um den Sockel herumgeht, changieren die Baumreihen in seinem Blick zwischen Schärfe und Unschärfe, bilden Moiré-Muster vor dem Fixpunkt im Zentrum. Verlockend aber unerreichbar, leuchtet der Pavillon hinter der dunklen optischen Schranke der Bäume hervor. Die Spannung zwischen Organischem und Geometrischem, zwischen Natur und Rationalität, zwischen Dunkelheit und Licht schwebt in kalkulierter Balance.[6]

Mit dieser Arbeit greift Katharina Fritsch unmittelbar auf ihre ersten Pläne für Parks und ihre Ideen zum Museum als potentiellem Wallfahrtsort zurück. Wie schon andere Künstler vor ihr zitiert sie vor allem sowohl historische als auch zeitgenössische Standorte. So liess sie sich beispielsweise vom chinesischen Teepavillon (Abb. 5) anregen, den Johann Gottfried Buring für den Park von Sanssouci in Potsdam entwarf. Er wurde in der ersten Hälfte des 18. Jahrhunderts als Ergänzung zum Sommerpalast von Georg Wenzeslaus von Knobelsdorff erbaut; heute ist er wie das Schloss von Versailles und viele andere Architekturdenkmäler in Europa eine grosse Touristenattraktion. Generell hat auch die deutsche Barockarchitektur bei dieser Arbeit Pate gestanden. Doch auch das Werk des Architekten Bruno Taut aus dem 20. Jahrhundert hat, nach ihren eigenen Angaben, Fritschs Vorstellung von visionären Strukturen mitgeprägt.

Fig./Abb. 6
Walter De Maria
The Lightning Field,
1977

ments in Europe, a major tourist attraction. In general, German Baroque architecture is an important precedent, but Fritsch also notes the work of the twentieth-century architect Bruno Taut as contributing to her sense of the potential of visionary structures.

Fritsch also cites *The Lightning Field* (fig. 6), a work by contemporary artist Walter De Maria, completed in 1977 in southwestern New Mexico, as offering another alternative model for the experience of art. In this work, as in Fritsch's *Museum*, the sculpture itself is a rigorous geometric configuration set in a landscape, here unspoiled stretches of high desert plateau. Sponsored by the Dia Center for the Arts, *The Lightning Field* is accessible by appointment only to individuals or small groups. Both the journey to reach the field and a requisite overnight stay in a nearby cabin set the experience of this work apart from any other contemporary work of art.

The *Museum* also reaches back to the roots of the cultural traditions of the West, set down through many centuries, built on the classical models of the ancient Mediterranean world. The ninth-century emperor Charlemagne, who established control of what would become France and Germany, aspired to create a center of art and learning like that in Rome in his court at Aachen. One of the structures he built there was a chapel with an eight-sided interior patterned on classical precedents, which survives

today. Having first been exhibited in Italy, *Museum* also recalls the Baptistery in Florence, built in the eleventh and twelfth centuries, which heralded the first stirrings of the Italian Renaissance. With *Museum*, Fritsch attempts to reclaim the humanistic current of spiritual enlightenment at the heart of classicism.

The work contains references as well to the operas of Richard Wagner, one of the great achievements of nineteenth-century German Romanticism. In particular, Fritsch, who deeply admires Wagner, alludes to the opera *Parsifal*. Centering around the struggle for control of the Holy Grail, the story fuses Christian allegory with Germanic myth and is a tale of worldly temptation, fall from grace, redemption, and salvation through faith and discipline. Fritsch's *Museum* evokes metaphors, not unlike those of the Grail, and proposes a state of consciousness and belief in principles to which humanity might aspire. In general, Wagner appeals to Fritsch for his ability to establish emotional, dramatic atmosphere, to evoke the supernatural, and to create a visionary synthesis of music and theater, of form and narrative.

In the presentation of *Museum* at the San Francisco Museum of Modern Art, Fritsch brings about another confrontation. The new SFMOMA building, designed by Swiss architect Mario Botta, also draws strongly on the legacy of Mediterranean classical traditions. Botta fulfilled a program for the new building to be a

Fig./Abb. 7
Mario Botta
San Francisco
Museum of Modern
Art, 1995

Auch «The Lightning Field» (Abb. 6), ein Werk des zeitgenössischen Künstlers Walter de Maria, das dieser 1977 im Südwesten von New Mexico installiert hat, sieht Fritsch als ein alternatives Modell der Kunsterfahrung. Hier, wie auch bei Fritschs Museum, ist die Skulptur selbst ein streng geometrisches Gebilde in der Landschaft, in diesem Fall eines unberührten Wüstenplateaus. «The Lightning Field» ist nur nach Vereinbarung für Einzelpersonen oder kleine Gruppen zugänglich. Sowohl die Anreise als auch die erforderliche Übernachtung in einer nahegelegenen Hütte heben die Erfahrung dieser Arbeit von der anderer zeitgenössischer Kunst ab.

Das «Museum» greift die Wurzeln jener westlichen Kulturtraditionen auf, die sich im Laufe vieler Jahrhunderte herausgebildet haben und auf den klassischen Modellen der antiken mediterranen Welt basieren. Karl der Grosse, der im 9. Jahrhundert das spätere Frankreich und Deutschland beherrschte, wollte an seinem Hof in Aachen ein Zentrum für Kunst und Bildung wie in Rom errichten. Unter anderem baute er eine Kapelle mit achteckigem Innenraum nach klassischem Vorbild, die heute noch erhalten ist. Das «Museum», das ja zum ersten Mal in Italien gezeigt wurde, erinnert zudem an das Florentiner Baptisterium aus dem 11. und 12. Jahrhundert, an dem sich bereits die ersten Regungen der italienischen Renaissance ankündigten. Mit ihrem «Museum» will

Fritsch auch das humanistische Element der geistigen Aufklärung im Kern des Klassizismus zurückgewinnen.

Darüberhinaus enthält das Stück Hinweise auf das Werk Richard Wagners, dessen Meisterwerke der deutschen Romantik. Dabei verweist Fritsch, die Wagner tief bewundert, insbesondere auf dessen Oper «Parzival». Die Geschichte handelt vom Kampf um den Heiligen Gral und verbindet christliche Allegorie mit deutschen Mythen. Es geht um weltliche Versuchung, Sündenfall, Umkehr und Erlösung durch Glaube und Gehorsam. Fritschs «Museum» evoziert Metaphern, die dem Gral nicht unähnlich sind, und handelt von einem Bewusstseinszustand, einem Glauben an Prinzipien, nach denen die Menschheit trachten könnte. Ganz allgemein bewundert Fritsch an Wagner dessen Fähigkeit, eine emotionale dramatische Atmosphäre zu schaffen, Übernatürliches zu beschwören und eine visionäre Synthese aus Musik und Theater, aus Form und Erzählung.

Mit der Präsentation von «Museum» im San Francisco Museum of Modern Art löst Fritsch aber noch eine weitere Konfrontation aus. Auch das neue SFMOMA-Gebäude nach Entwürfen des Tessiner Architekten Mario Botta weist starke Bezüge zum Erbe klassisch-mediterraner Traditionen auf. Botta hatte den Auftrag, mit diesem Gebäude ein weithin sichtbares Wahrzeichen im Stadtzentrum (Abb. 7) und einen weltlichen Tempel zu schaffen. Der Innenhof ist eine Piazza, die Ausstellungs- und Unterrichtsräume

highly visible landmark at the center of the city (fig. 7) and a secular temple – its courtyard a piazza, its galleries and classrooms a conjunction of art and learning for contemporary culture. Thronged by visitors and offering a complex array of collections, temporary exhibitions, and educational and public events, the new SFMOMA is typical of and in many ways a model for the modern urban museum at the end of the twentieth century. Fritsch's *Museum*, however, proposes a radically different model at a further remove from the tempo of daily life: a quiet, relatively unchanging site, where individuals might venture as pilgrims, a place of reflection and philosophical contemplation. The SFMOMA building and Fritsch's "Museum" are not at odds with each other, but rather offer different points along a continuum. Within the exhibition, *Museum* suggests a sanctuary within a sanctuary to further the dialogue about the meaning and place of art for the individual and for society.

Fritsch's work, from its beginnings to the most recent sculpture, is consistent but complex, ranging from modest handmade objects to monumental architectural projects. A development can be traced, but Fritsch is unwilling to foreclose potential for open-ended explorations. Her works are both intimate and idiosyncratic, as well as grand and highly reasoned. Some works are psychological and expressionistic, others are rational, geometric, and abstract.

Julian Heynen, the curator at the Kaiser Wilhelm Museum, analyzed and identified formal characteristics of Fritsch's work early on in her career, and his fundamental points have remained relevant. Fritsch's work is characterized by frontality and symmetry, qualities that "have the ability in a certain way to make pictures out of these sculptures." Color is of central significance, so that the "designated characteristics of a work can also find far-reaching expression." Her work offers a "minimalistic concentration ... an authority of simplicity."[7]

Essential to Fritsch's work is a tension between the apparent and the absolute.[8] The apparent is a conditional state – thus our word *apparition*, with the implication that what is perceived to exist will and must disappear. We continually test the truth of our perceptions by various strategies to determine whether a degree of absoluteness is possible, that is, to know if something will continue to exist despite a change of conditions, or at least to understand the conditions that make the apparent possible.

With Fritsch's work the vividness of the encounter is so at odds with the normal habits of perception that these habits, in which we place such trust, are disarmed. An absoluteness contrary to ordinary experience temporarily suspends the usual understandings by which we orient our sense of perception. When confronted with the inadequacy of the habits that allow us to get by day to day, we recognize how diminished are our perceptual conventions. Immediacy and perfection, a sensate completeness, are evoked and instill feelings of unreality and of an existence apart from the ordinary, which induces a forgotten sense of wonder. We are impelled toward alertness and renewed critical judgment.

This essay is based on numerous encounters with the artist's work and extended discussions with the artist over many years. The author first saw the work of Katharina Fritsch in 1984 in the exhibition *von hier aus* in Düsseldorf, and subsequently in many exhibitions in Germany and the United States. He first met the artist in 1988 and has continued to meet and speak regularly with her since then. In preparation for this book, a formal, lengthy interview was conducted in the artist's studio on May 6, 1996; all direct quotations are taken from that interview.

1. There had been female students earlier at the Academy, including Katharina Sieverding and Isa Genzken, who would go on to establish strong careers as artists, but at this time there were no women faculty.
2. Fritsch had received credit for some of her studies in Münster, which moved her forward to the equivalent of the seventh semester of studies in 1981 at the Academy and qualified her for consideration for the *Meisterschüler*.
3. Multiples are a variety of art object – a continuation of the tradition of printmaking but not limited to works on paper – in which works are made in small, or sometimes very large, editions.
4. For a full discussion of this sculpture, see Lynne Cooke, "Parerga" in: *Katharina Fritsch*, ex.cat., Dia Center for the Arts, New York 1993, pp. 6-11.
5. From the Venice brochure for *Museum*.
6. Fritsch initially had intended that the sculpture would be seen not only from the floor but also from a balcony that surrounds the perimeter of the grand central hall of the pavilion. Due to a shortage of funds, however, the renovation of the pavilion could not be completed, and the balcony remained inaccessible to the public.
7. Julian Heynen, *Katharina Fritsch 1979–1989*, ex.cat., Westfälischer Kunstverein Münster/Portikus, Frankfurt, Köln 1989, pp. 68/69; quoted in Gary Garrels, "Disarming Perception," *Parkett*, no. 25,1990, p. 37.
8. I first developed the argument presented here for the article "Disarming Perception," *Parkett*, no. 25,1990, p. 36.

stellen eine Verbindung zwischen Kunst und Lernen für die zeitgenössische Kultur dar. Mit seinem grossen Besucherandrang und
einem breiten Angebot an Sammlungen, Ausstellungen, Unter-
richt und öffentlichen Veranstaltungen ist das neue SFMOMA typisch und in mancher Hinsicht ein Modell für das moderne urbane
Museum am Ende des 20. Jahrhunderts. Fritschs «Museum» hingegen ist ein radikal anderes Modell, das vom Tempo des Alltags-
lebens abrückt: ein stiller, fast unveränderlicher Ort, den die Leute
als Pilger aufsuchen, ein Ort des Nachdenkens und der philosophi-
schen Betrachtung. Das SFMOMA-Gebäude und Fritschs «Museum» schliessen einander nicht aus, sondern vertreten unterschiedliche Standpunkte in einem zusammenhängenden Ganzen. «Museum» schlägt ein Heiligtum innerhalb eines Heiligtums vor, um den
Dialog über Bedeutung und Ort der Kunst für den Einzelnen und für
die Gesellschaft zu fördern.

Von den Anfängen bis zu den jüngsten Skulpturen ist Fritschs
Werk in sich stringent aber vielschichtig und reicht vom kleinen
handgefertigten Objekt bis zum monumentalen Architekturpro-
jekt. Zwar lässt sich eine Entwicklung ausmachen, doch Fritsch ist
darauf bedacht, den Ausgang ihrer Untersuchungen nie vorweg-
zunehmen. Ihre Arbeiten sind sowohl intim und idiosynkratisch als
auch eindrucksvoll und präzis kalkuliert. Manche Stücke sind psychologisch und expressionistisch, andere sind rational, geometrisch und abstrakt.

Julian Heynen, der Kurator des Kaiser Wilhelm Museums, hat
formale Eigenschaften des Werkes von Katharina Fritsch schon zu
Beginn ihrer Karriere analysiert und beschrieben. Seine Grund-
aussagen sind bis heute gültig. Das Werk zeichnet sich durch eine
Frontalität und Symmetrie aus, die fähig sind, «aus diesen Skulpturen in gewisser Weise Bilder werden zu lassen.» Die Farben sind
von zentraler Bedeutung, damit die «benennbaren Eigenschaften
eines Werkes ... ihren umfassenden Ausdruck finden.» Ihre Arbeit
enthält eine «minimalistische Konzentration ... eine Autorität des
Einfachen.»[7]

Eine wesentliche Rolle in Fritschs Arbeit spielt die Spannung
zwischen dem Augenscheinlichen und dem Absoluten.[8] Das Augenscheinliche ist ein bedingter Zustand – und so impliziert denn
auch das Wort «Erscheinung», dass das, was wir als existent wahrnehmen, wieder verschwinden muss und wird. Immer wieder über-
prüfen wir mit den unterschiedlichsten Strategien die Wahrhaftig-
keit unserer Wahrnehmungen, um auf diese Weise festzustellen, ob
ein bestimmtes Mass an Absolutheit möglich ist. So versuchen wir

herauszufinden, ob etwas auch unter veränderten Bedingungen
weiterexistieren wird, oder doch wenigstens die Bedingungen zu
verstehen, die das Augenscheinliche möglich machen.

Im Werk von Katharina Fritsch steht die Intensität der jeweiligen
Begegnung in so starkem Gegensatz zu den normalen Wahrneh-
mungsgewohnheiten, dass eben diese Gewohnheiten, auf die wir
uns verlassen, ihre Wirksamkeit verlieren. Eine der gewöhnlichen
Erfahrung entgegengesetzte Absolutheit setzt jene gewohnten
Verständnisformen ausser Kraft, an denen sich unsere Wahrnehmung orientiert. Wenn wir mit der Unzulänglichkeit unserer Gewohnheiten, mit deren Hilfe wir tagtäglich über die Runden kommen, konfrontiert werden, erkennen wir, wie eingeschränkt unsere
Wahrnehmungskonventionen sind. Unmittelbarkeit und Perfektion, eine sinnlich wahrnehmbare Vollkommenheit, werden spürbar
und infiltrieren unser Gefühl mit einem Eindruck von Unwirklichkeit,
von einer Existenz jenseits des Gewöhnlichen, die den vergessenen
Sinn für Wunder zu neuem Leben erweckt. Wir werden wachsamer,
auf dass wir unser kritisches Urteil erneuern.

Dieser Aufsatz basiert auf zahlreichen Begegnungen mit dem Werk der Künstlerin
sowie eingehenden Diskussionen mit ihr über viele Jahre hinweg. Zum ersten Mal sah
ich eine Arbeit von Katharina Fritsch 1984 bei der Ausstellung «von hier aus» in Düsseldorf, später bei zahlreichen Ausstellungen in Deutschland und den Vereinigten
Staaten. Die erste Begegnung mit der Künstlerin fand 1988 statt; seither folgten
regelmässige Treffen und Gespräche. Zur Vorbereitung für dieses Buch fand am 6.
Mai 1996 ein ausführliches Interview im Atelier der Künstlerin statt. Alle Zitate sind
diesem Gespräch entnommen.

1. Zwar hatten Frauen an der Akademie schon studiert, unter anderen Katharina
   Sieverding und Isa Genzken, die später Karriere als Künstlerinnen machten, es gab
   jedoch noch keine Professorinnen.
2. Ein Teil ihres Studiums in Münster war Katharina Fritsch angerechnet worden, so
   dass sie 1981 an der Akademie im siebten Semester einsteigen und zur Meisterschülerin ernannt werden konnte.
3. Multiples können viele Arten von Kunstobjekten sein; in ihnen setzt sich die Tradition der Druckkunst fort, ohne auf Papierarbeiten beschränkt zu sein. Die Objekte
   werden in kleinen, manchmal aber auch sehr grossen Auflagen produziert.
4. Eine eingehende Besprechung dieser Skulptur findet sich bei Lynne Cooke, «Parerga», in: Katharina Fritsch, Ausst.kat. Dia Center for the Arts, New York 1993, S.
   6-11.
5. Aus der Broschüre für Venedig zu «Museum, Modell 1:10».
6. Ursprünglich hatte Fritsch geplant, dass die Skulptur nicht nur vom Boden, sondern auch vom Balkon in der grossen Haupthalle des Pavillons aus sichtbar wäre.
   Da aber die Gelder für die Renovierung des Pavillons gekürzt wurden, blieb der
   Balkon für das Publikum gesperrt.
7. Julian Heynen, Katharina Fritsch 1979-1989, Ausst.kat. Westfälischer Kunstverein,
   Münster/Portikus Frankfurt, Köln 1989, S. 62-64.
8. Diese Argumentation habe ich zum ersten Mal vorgestellt in meinem Aufsatz
   «Wahrnehmung entwaffnen», Parkett, Nr. 25, 1990, S. 40.

*In the early 1980s, when we were
students at the Kunstakademie, Prof.
Fritz Schwegler used to refer us to the
following text by Kleist. I think he did this
because it is one of the most beautiful
key texts for the whole of art. (K.Fritsch)*

Heinrich von Kleist
On the
Marionette Theatre

Heinrich von Kleist
Über das
Marionettentheater

*Anfang der achtziger Jahre, während des
Studiums an der Kunstakademie, pflegte
Prof. Fritz Schwegler uns Studenten auf
den folgenden Kleist-Text hinzuweisen.
Ich denke er tat es, weil dies einer der
schönsten Schlüsseltexte zur Kunst überhaupt ist. (K.Fritsch)*

ONE EVENING IN THE WINTER OF 1801 I MET AN OLD friend in a public park. He had recently been appointed principal dancer at the local theatre and was enjoying immense popularity with the audiences. I told him I had been surprised to see him more than once at the marionette theatre which had been put up in the market-place to entertain the public with dramatic burlesques interspersed with song and dance. He assured me that the mute gestures of these puppets gave him much satisfaction and told me bluntly that any dancer who wished to perfect his art could learn a lot from them.

From the way he said this I could see it wasn't something which had just come into his mind, so I sat down to question him more closely about his reasons for this remarkable assertion.

He asked me if I hadn't in fact found some of the dance movements of the puppets (and particularly of the smaller ones) very graceful. This I couldn't deny. A group of four peasants dancing the rondo in quick time couldn't have been painted more delicately by Teniers.

I required about the mechanism of these figures. I wanted to know how it is possible, without having a maze of strings attached to one's fingers, to move the separate limbs and extremities in the rhythm of the dance. His answer was that I must not imagine each limb as being individually positioned and moved by the operator in the various phases of the dance. Each movement, he told me, has its centre of gravity; it is enough to control this within the puppet. The limbs, which are only pendulums, then follow mechanically of their own accord, without further help. He added that this movement is very simple. When the centre of gravitiy is moved in a straight line, the limbs describe curves. Often, shaken in a purely haphazard way, the puppet falls into a kind of rythmic movement which resembles dance.

This observation seemed to me to throw some light at last on the enjoyment he said he got from the marionette theatre, but I was far from guessing the inferences he would draw from it later.

I asked him if he thought the operator who controls these puppets should himself be a dancer or at least have some idea of beauty in the dance. He replied that if a job is technically easy it doesn't follow that it can be done entirely without sensitivity. The line the centre of gravity has to follow is indeed very simple, and in most cases, he believed, straight. When it is curved, the law of its curvature seems to be at the least of

32

ALS ICH DEN WINTER 1801 IN M... ZUBRACHTE, TRAF ICH daselbst eines Abends, in einem öffentlichen Garten, den Herrn C. an, der seit kurzem, in dieser Stadt, als erster Tänzer der Oper, angestellt war, und bei dem Publiko ausserordentliches Glück machte.

Ich sagte ihm, dass ich erstaunt gewesen wäre, ihn schon mehrere Mal in einem Marionettentheater zu finden, das auf dem Markte zusammengezimmert worden war, und den Pöbel, durch kleine dramatische Burlesken, mit Gesang und Tanz durchwebt, belustigte.

Er versicherte mir, dass ihm die Pantomimik dieser Puppen viel Vergnügen machte, und liess nicht undeutlich merken, dass ein Tänzer, der sich ausbilden wolle, mancherlei von ihnen lernen könne.

Da die Äusserung mir, durch die Art, wie er sie vorbrachte, mehr, als eine blosser Einfall schien, so liess ich mich bei ihm nieder, um ihn über die Gründe, auf die er eine so sonderbare Behauptung stützen könne, näher zu vernehmen.

Er fragte mich, ob ich nicht, in der Tat, einige Bewegungen der Puppen, besonders der kleineren, im Tanz sehr graziös gefunden hatte.

Diesen Umstand konnte ich nicht leugnen. Eine Gruppe von vier Bauern, die nach einem raschen Takt die Ronde tanzte, hätte von Teniers nicht hübscher gemalt werden können.

Ich erkundigte mich nach dem Mechanismus dieser Figuren, und wie es möglich wäre, die einzelnen Glieder derselben und ihre Punkte, ohne Myriaden von Fäden an den Fingern zu haben, so zu regieren, als der Rhythmus der Bewegungen, oder der Tanz erfordere?

Er antwortete, dass ich mir nicht vorstellen müsse, als ob jedes Glied einzeln, während der verschiedenen Momente des Tanzes, von dem Maschinisten gestellt und gezogen würde.

Jede Bewegung, sagte er, hätte einen Schwerpunkt; es wäre genug, diesen, in dem Innern der Figur, zu regieren; die Glieder, welche nichts als Pendel wären, folgten, ohne irgend ein Zutun, auf eine mechanische Weise von selbst.

Er setzte hinzu, dass diese Bewegung sehr einfach wäre; dass jedesmal, wenn der Schwerpunkt in einer *graden Linie* bewegt wird, die Glieder schon *Kurven* beschrieben; und dass oft, auf eine bloss zufällige Weise erschüttert, das Ganze schon in eine Art von rhythmische Bewegung käme, die dem Tanz ähnlich wäre.

Diese Bemerkung schien mir zuerst einiges Licht über das Vergnügen zu werfen, das er in dem Theater der Marionetten zu finden vorgegeben hatte. Inzwischen ahndete ich bei weitem die Folgerungen noch nicht, die er späterhin daraus ziehen würde.

Ich fragte ihn, ob er glaubte, dass der Maschinist, der diese Puppen regiere, selbst ein Tänzer sein, oder wenigstens einen Begriff vom Schönen im Tanz haben müsse?

Er erwiderte, dass wenn ein Geschäft, von seiner mechanischen Seite, leicht sei, daraus noch nicht folge, dass es ganz ohne Empfindung betrieben werden könne.

Die Linie, die der Schwerpunkt zu beschreiben hat, wäre zwar sehr einfach, und, wie er glaube, in den meisten Fällen, gerad. In Fällen, wo sie krumm sei, scheine das Gesetz ihrer Krümmung wenigstens von der ersten oder höchstens zweiten Ordnung; und auch in diesem letzten Fall nur elliptisch, welche Form der Bewegung den Spitzen des menschlichen Körpers (wegen der Gelenke) überhaupt die natürliche sei, und also dem Maschinisten keine grosse Kunst koste, zu verzeichnen.

Dagegen würde diese Linie wieder, von einer anderen Seite, etwas sehr Geheimnisvolles. Denn sie wäre nichts anderes, als der *Weg der Seele des Tänzers*; und er zweifle, dass sie anders gefunden werden könne, als dadurch, dass sich der Maschinist in den Schwerpunkt der Marionette versetzt, d.h. mit anderen Worten, *tanzt*.

Ich erwiderte, dass man mir das Geschäft desselben als etwas ziemlich Geistloses vorgestellt hätte: etwa was das Drehen einer Kurbel sei, die eine Leier spielt.

Keineswegs, antwortete er. Vielmehr verhalten sich die Bewegungen seiner Finger zur Bewegung der daran befestigten Puppen ziemlich künstlich, etwa wie Zahlen zu ihren Logarithmen oder die Asymptote zur Hyperbel.

Inzwischen glaube er, dass auch dieser letzte Bruch von Geist, von dem er gesprochen, aus den Marionetten entfernt werden, dass ihr Tanz gänzlich ins Reich mechanischer Kräfte hinübergespielt, und vermittelst einer Kurbel, so wie ich es mir gedacht, hervorgebracht werden könne.

Ich äusserte meine Verwunderung zu sehen, welcher Aufmerksamkeit er diese, für den Haufen erfundene, Spielart einer schönen Kunst würdige. Nicht bloss, dass er sie einer höheren Entwickelung für fähig halte: er scheine sich sogar selbst damit zu beschäftigen.

Er lächelte, und sagte, er getraue sich zu behaupten, dass wenn ihm ein Mechanikus, nach den Forderungen, die er an ihn zu machen dächte, eine Marionette bauen wollte, er vermittelst derselben einen Tanz darstellen würde, den weder er, noch irgend ein anderer geschickter Tänzer seiner Zeit, Vestris selbst nicht ausgenommen, zu erreichen imstande wäre.

Haben Sie, fragte er, da ich den Blick schweigend zur Erde schlug: haben Sie von jenen mechanischen Beinen gehört, welche englische Künstler für Unglückliche verfertigen, die ihre Schenkel verloren haben?

Ich sagte, nein: dergleichen wäre mir nie vor Augen gekommen.

the first and at the most of the second order. Even in the latter case the line is only elliptical, a form of movement natural to the human body because of the joints, so this hardly demands any great skill from the operator. But, seen from another point of view, this line could be something very mysterious. It is nothing other than *the path taken by the soul of the dancer*. He doubted if this could be found unless the operator can transpose himself into the centre of the gravity of the marionette. In other words, the operator *dances*.

I said the operator's part in the business had been represented to me as something which can be done entirely without feeling – rather like turning the handle of a barrel-organ.

'Not at all,' he said. 'In fact, there's a subtle relationship between the movements of his fingers and the movements of the puppets attached to them, something like the relationship between numbers and their logarithms or between asymptote and hyperbola.' Yet he did believe this last trace of human volition could be removed from the marionettes and their dance transferred entirely to the realm of mechanical forces, even produced, as I had suggested, by turning a handle.

I told him I was astonished at the attention he was paying to this vulgar species of an art form. It wasn't just that he thought it capable of loftier development; he seemed to be working to this end himself.

He smiled. He said he was confident, that if he could get a craftsman to construct a marionette to the specifications he had in mind, he could perform a dance with it which neither he nor any other skilled dancer of his time, not even Madame Vestris herself, could equal.

'Have you heard,' he asked, as I looked down in silence, 'of those artificial legs made by English craftsmen for people who have been unfortunate enough to lose their own limbs?'

I said I hadn't. I had never seen anything of this kind.

'I'm sorry to hear that,' he said, 'because when I tell you these people dance with them, I'm almost afraid you won't believe me. What am I saying ... dance? The range of their movements is in fact limited, but those they can perform they execute with a certainty and ease and grace which must astound the thoughtful observer.'

I said with a laugh that of course he had now found his man. The craftsman who could make such remarkable limbs could surely build a complete marionette for him, to his specifications.

'And what,' I asked, as he was looking down in some perplexity, 'are the requirements you think of presenting to the ingenuity of this man?'

'Nothing that isn't to be found in these puppets we see here,' he replied: 'proportion, flexibility, lightness ... but all to a higher degree. And especially a more natural arrangement of the centres of gravity.'

'And what is the advantage your puppets would have over living dancers?'

'The advantage? First of all a negative one, my friend: it would never be guilty of affectation. For affectation is seen, as you know, when the soul, or moving force, appears at some point other than the centre of gravity of the movement. Because the operator controls with his wire or thread only this centre, the attached limbs are just what they should be ... lifeless, pure pendulums, governed only by the law of gravity. This is an excellent quality. You'll look for it in vain in most of our dancers.'

'Just look at that girl who dances Daphne,' he went on. 'Pursued by Apollo, she turns to look at him. At this moment her soul seems to be in the small of her back. As she bends she looks as if she's going to break, like a naiad after the school of Bernini. Or take that young fellow who dances Paris when he's standing among the three goddesses and offering the apple to Venus. His soul is in fact located (and it's a frightful thing to see) in his elbow.'

'Misconceptions like this are unavoidable,' he said, 'now that we've eaten of the tree of knowledge. But Paradise is locked and bolted, and the cherubim stand behind us. We have to go on and make the journey round the world to see if it is perhaps open somewhere at the back.'

This made me laugh. Certainly, I thought, the human spirit can't be in error when it is non-existent. I could see he had more to say, so I begged him to go on.

'In addition,' he said, 'these puppets have the advantage of being for all practical purposes weightless. They are not afflicted with the inertia of matter, the property most resistant to dance. The force which raises them into the air is greater that the one which draws them to the ground. What would our good Miss G. give to be sixty pounds lighter or to have a weight of this size as a counterbalance when she is performing her entrechats and pirouettes? Puppets need the ground only to glance against lightly, like elves, and through this momen-

Es tut mir leid, erwiderte er; denn wenn ich Ihnen sage, dass diese Unglücklichen damit tanzen, so fürchte ich fast, sie werden es mir nicht glauben. – Was sage ich, tanzen? Der Kreis ihrer Bewegungen ist zwar beschränkt; doch diejenigen, die ihnen zu Gebote stehen, vollziehen sich mit einer Ruhe, Leichtigkeit und Anmut, die jedes denkende Gemüt in Erstaunen setzten.

Ich äusserte, scherzend, dass er ja, auf diese Weise, seinen Mann gefunden habe. Denn derjenige Künstler, der einen so merkwürdigen Schenkel zu bauen imstande sei, würde ihm unzweifelhaft auch eine ganze Marionette, seinen Forderungen gemäss, zusammensetzen können.

Wie, fragte ich, da er seinerseits ein wenig betreten zur Erde sah; wie sind denn diese Forderungen, die Sie an die Kunstfertigkeit desselben zu machen gedenken, bestellt?

Nichts, antwortete er, was sich nicht auch schon hier fände; Ebenmass, Beweglichkeit, Leichtigkeit – nur alles in einem höheren Grade; und besonders eine naturgemässere Anordnung der Schwerpunkte.

Und der Vorteil, den diese Puppe vor lebendigen Tänzern voraus haben würde?

Der Vorteil? Zuvörderst ein negativer, mein vortrefflicher Freund, nämlich dieser, dass sie sich niemals *zierte*. – Denn Ziererei erscheint, wie Sie wissen, wenn sich die Seele (vis motrix) in irgend einem anderen Punkte befindet, als in dem Schwerpunkt der Bewegung. Da der Maschinist nun schlechthin, vermittelst des Drahtes oder Fadens, keinen andern Punkt in seiner Gewalt hat, als diesen: so sind alle übrigen Glieder, was sie sein sollen, tot, reine Pendel, und folgen dem blossen Gesetz der Schwere; eine vortreffliche Eigenschaft, die man vergebens bei dem grössesten Teil unsrer Tänzer sucht.

Sehen Sie nur die P... an, fuhr er fort, wenn sie die Daphne spielt, und sich, verfolgt vom Apoll, nach ihm umsieht; die Seele sitzt ihr in den Wirbeln des Kreuzes; sie beugt sich, als ob sie brechen wollte, wie eine Najade aus der Schule Berninis. Sehen Sie den jungen F... an, wenn er, als Paris, unter den drei Göttinnen steht, und der Venus den Apfel überreicht: die Seele sitzt ihm gar (es ist ein Schrecken, es zu sehen) im Ellenbogen.

Solche Missgriffe, setzte er abbrechend hinzu, sind unvermeidlich, seitdem wir von dem Baum der Erkenntnis gegessen haben. Doch das Paradies ist verriegelt und der Cherub hinter uns; wir müssen die Reise um die Welt machen, und sehen, ob es vielleicht von hinten irgendwo wieder offen ist.

Ich lachte. – Allerdings, dachte ich, kann der Geist nicht irren, da, wo keiner vorhanden ist. Doch ich bemerkte, dass er noch mehr auf dem Herzen hatte, und bat ihn, fortzufahren.

Zudem, sprach er, haben diese Puppen den Vorteil, dass sie *antigrav* sind. Von der Trägheit der Materie, dieser dem Tanze entgegenstrebendsten aller Eigenschaften, wissen sie nichts: weil die Kraft, die sie in die Lüfte erhebt, grösser ist, als jene, die sie an der Erde fesselt. Was würde unsere gute G... darum geben, wenn sie sechzig Pfund leichter wäre, oder ein Gewicht von dieser Grösse ihr bei ihren Entrechats und Pirouetten, zu Hülfe käme? Die Puppen brauchen den Boden nur, wie die Elfen, um ihn zu *streifen*, und den Schwung der Glieder, durch die augenblickliche Hemmung neu zu beleben; wir brauchen ihn, um darauf zu *ruhen*, und uns von der Anstrengung des Tanzes zu erholen: ein Moment, der offenbar selber kein Tanz ist, und mit dem sich weiter nichts anfangen lässt, als ihn möglichst verschwinden zu machen.

Ich sagte, dass, so geschickt er auch die Sache seiner Paradoxe führe, er mich doch nimmermehr glauben machen würde, dass in einem mechanischen Gliedermann mehr Anmut enthalten sein könne, als in dem Bau des menschlichen Körpers.

Er versetzte, dass es dem Menschen schlechthin unmöglich wäre, den Gliedermann darin auch nur zu erreichen. Nur ein Gott könne sich, auf diesem Felde, mit der Materie messen; und hier sei der Punkt, wo die beiden Enden der ringförmigen Welt in einander griffen.

Ich erstaunte immer mehr, und wusste nicht, was ich zu so sonderbaren Behauptungen sagen sollte.

Es scheine, versetzte er, indem er eine Prise Tabak nahm, dass ich das dritte Kapitel vom ersten Buch Moses nicht mit Aufmerksamkeit gelesen; und wer diese erste Periode aller menschlichen Bildung nicht kennt, mit dem könne man nicht füglich über die folgenden, um wie viel weniger über die letzte, sprechen.

Ich sagte, dass ich gar wohl wüsste, welche Unordnungen, in der natürlichen Grazie des Menschen, das Bewusstsein anrichtet. Ein junger Mann von meiner Bekanntschaft hätte, durch eine blosse Bemerkung, gleichsam vor meinen Augen, seine Unschuld verloren, und das Paradies derselben, trotz aller ersinnlichen Bemühungen, nachher niemals wieder gefunden. – Doch, welche Folgerungen, setze ich hinzu, können Sie daraus ziehen?

Er fragte mich, welch einen Vorteil ich meine?

Ich badete mich, erzählte ich, vor etwa drei Jahren, mit einem jungen Mann, über dessen Bildung damals eine wunderbare Anmut verbreitet war. Er möchte ohngefähr in seinem sechzehnten Jahre stehn, und nur ganz von fern liessen sich, von der Gunst der Frauen herbeigerufen, die ersten Spuren von Eitelkeit erblicken. Es traf sich, dass wir grade kurz zuvor in Paris den Jüngling gesehen hatten, der sich einen Splitter aus dem Fusse zieht; der Abguss der Statue ist

tary check to renew the swing of their limbs. We humans must have it to rest on, to recover from the effort of the dance. This moment of rest is clearly no part of the dance. The best we can do is make it as inconspicuous as possible.'

My reply was that, no matter how cleverly he might present his paradoxes, he would never make me believe a mechanical puppet can be more graceful than a living human body. He countered this by saying that, where grace is concerned, it is impossible for man to come anywhere near a puppet. Only a god can equal inanimate matter in this respect. This is the point where the two ends of the circular world meet.

I was absolutely astonished. I didn't know what to say to such extraordinary assertions.

It seemed, he said as he took a pinch of snuff, that I hadn't read the third chapter of the book of Genesis with sufficient attention. If a man wasn't familiar with that initial period of all human development, it would be difficult to have a fruitful discussion with him about later developments and even more difficult to talk about the ultimate situation.

I told him I was aware how consciousness can disturb natural grace. A young acquaintance of mine had as it were lost his innocence before my very eyes, and all because of a chance remark. He had never found his way back to that paradise of innocence, in spite of all conceivable efforts. 'But what inferences,' I added, 'can you draw from that?'

He asked me what incident I had in mind.

'About three years ago,' I said, 'I was at the baths with a young man who was then remarkably graceful. He was about fifteen, and only faintly could one see the first traces of vanity, a product of the favours shown him by women. It happened that we had recently seen in Paris the figure of the boy pulling a thorn out of his foot. The cast of the statue is well known; you see it in most German collections. My friend looked into a tall mirror just as he was lifting his foot to a stool to dry it, and he was reminded of the statue. He smiled and told me of his discovery. As a matter of fact, I'd noticed it too, at the same moment, but ... I don't know if it was to test the quality of his apparent grace or to provide a salutary counter to his vanity ... I laughed and said he must be imagining things. He blushed. He lifted his foot a second time, to show me, but the effort was a failure, as anybody could have foreseen. He tried it again a third time, a fourth time, he must have lifted his foot ten times, but it was in vain. He was quite unable to reproduce the same

movement. What am I saying? The movements he made were so comical that I was hard put to it not to laugh.'

'From that day, from that very moment, an extraordinary change came over this boy. He began to spend whole days before the mirror. His attractions slipped away from him, one after the other. An invisible and incomprehensible power seemed to settle like a steel net over the free play of his gestures. A year later nothing remained of the lovely grace which had given pleasure to all who looked at him. I can tell you of a man, still alive, who was a witness to this strange and unfortunate event. He can confirm it word for word, just as I've described it.'

'In this connection,' said my friend warmly, 'I must tell you another story. You'll easily see how it fits in here. When I was on my way to Russia I spent some time on the estate of a Baltic nobleman whose sons had a passion for fencing. The elder in particular, who had just come down from university, thought he was a bit of an expert. One morning, when I was in his room, he offered me a rapier. I accepted his challenge but, as it turned out, I had the better of him. It made him angry, and this increased his confusion. Nearly every thrust I made found its mark. At last his rapier flew into the corner of the room. As he picked it up he said, half in anger and half in jest, that he had met his master but that there is a master for everyone and everything – and now he proposed to lead me to mine. The brothers laughed loudly at this and shouted: "Come on, down to the shed!" They took me by the hand and led me outside to make the acquaintance of a bear which their father was rearing on the farm.

'I was astounded to see the bear standing upright on his hind legs, his back against the post to which he was chained, his right paw raised ready for battle. He looked me straight in the eye. This was his fighting posture. I wasn't sure if I was dreaming, seeing such an opponent. They urged me to attack. "See if you can hit him!" they shouted. As I had now recovered somewhat from my astonishment I fell on him with my rapier. The bear made a slight movement with his paw and parried my thrust. I feinted, to deceive him. The bear did not move. I attacked again, this time with all the skill I could muster. I know I would certainly have thrust my way through to a human breast, but the bear made a slight movement with his paw and parried the thrust. By now I was almost in the same state as the elder brother had been: the

bekannt und befindet sich in den meisten deutschen Sammlungen. Ein Blick, den er in dem Augenblick, da er den Fuss auf den Schemel setzte, um ihn abzutrocknen, in einen grossen Spiegel warf, erinnerte ihn daran; er lächelte und sagte mir, welch eine Entdeckung er gemacht habe. In der Tat hatte ich; in eben diesem Augenblick, dieselbe gemacht; doch sei es, um die Sicherheit der Grazie, die ihm beiwohnte, zu prüfen, sei es, um seiner Eitelkeit ein wenig heilsam zu begegnen: ich lachte und erwiderte – er sähe wohl Geister! Er errötete, und hob den Fuss zum zweitenmal, um es mir zu zeigen; doch der Versuch, wie sich leicht hätte voraussehn lassen, missglückte. Er hob verwirrt den Fuss zum dritten und vierten, er hob ihn wohl noch zehnmal: umsonst! er war ausserstand, dieselbe Bewegung wieder hervorzubringen – was sag ich? die Bewegungen, die er machte, hatten ein so komisches Element, dass ich Mühe hatte, das Gelächter zurückzuhalten: –

Von diesem Tage, gleichsam von diesem Augenblick an, ging eine unbegreifliche Veränderung mit dem jungen Menschen vor. Er fing an, tagelang vor dem Spiegel zu stehen; und immer ein Reiz nach dem anderen verliess ihn. Eine unsichtbare und unbegreifliche Gewalt schien sich, wie ein eisernes Netz um das freie Spiel seiner Gebärden zu legen, und als ein Jahr verflossen war, war keine Spur mehr von der Lieblichkeit in ihm zu entdecken, die die Augen der Menschen sonst, die ihn umringten, ergötzt hatte. Noch jetzt lebt jemand, der ein Zeuge jenes sonderbaren und unglücklichen Vorfalls war, und ihn, Wort für Wort, wie ich ihn erzählt, bestätigen könnte. –

Bei dieser Gelegenheit, sagte Herr C… freundlich, muss ich Ihnen eine andere Geschichte erzählen, von der Sie leicht begreifen werden, wie sie hierher gehört.

Ich befand mich, auf meiner Reise nach Russland, auf einem Landgut des Herrn v. G…, eines livländischen Edelmanns, dessen Söhne sich eben damals stark im Fechten übten. Besonders der ältere, der eben von der Universität zurückgekommen war, machte den Virtuosen, und bot mir, da ich eines Morgens auf seinem Zimmer war, ein Rapier an. Wir fochten; doch es traf sich, dass ich ihm überlegen war; Leidenschaft kam dazu, ihn zu verwirren; fast jeder Stoss, den ich führte, traf, und sein Rapier flog zuletzt in den Winkel. Halb scherzend, halb empfindlich, sagte er, indem er das Rapier aufhob, dass er seinen Meister gefunden habe: doch alles auf der Welt finde den seinen, und fortan wolle er mich zu dem meinigen führen. Die Brüder lachten laut auf, und riefen: Fort! fort! In den Holzstall herab! und damit nahmen sie mich bei der Hand und führten mich zu einem Bären, den Herr v. G…, ihr Vater, auf dem Hofe auferziehen liess.

Der Bär stand, als ich erstaunt vor ihn trat, auf den Hinterfüssen, mit dem Rücken an einen Pfahl gelehnt, an welchem er angeschlossen war, die rechte Tatze schlagfertig erhoben, und sah mir ins Auge: das war seine Fechterpositur. Ich wusste nicht, ob ich träumte, da ich mich einem solchen Gegner gegenüber sah; doch: stossen Sie! stossen Sie! sagte Herr v. G…, und versuchen Sie, ob Sie ihm eins beibringen können! Ich fiel, da ich mich ein wenig von meinem Erstaunen erholt hatte, mit dem Rapier auf ihn aus; der Bär machte eine ganz kurze Bewegung mit der Tatze und parierte den Stoss. Ich versuchte ihn durch Finten zu verführen; der Bär rührte sich nicht. Ich fiel wieder, mit einer augenblicklichen Gewandtheit, auf ihn aus, eines Menschen Brust würde ich ohnfehlbar getroffen haben: der Bär machte eine ganz kurze Bewegung mit der Tatze und parierte den Stoss. Jetzt war ich fast in dem Fall des jungen Herrn v. G… Der Ernst des Bären kam hinzu, mir die Fassung zu rauben, Stösse und Finten wechselten sich, mir triefte der Schweiss: umsonst! Nicht bloss, dass der Bär, wie der erste Fechter der Welt, alle meine Stösse parierte; auf Finten (was ihm kein Fechter der Welt nachmacht) ging er gar nicht einmal ein: Aug in Auge, als ob er meine Seele darin lesen könnte, stand er, die Tatze schlagfertig erhoben, und wenn meine Stösse nicht ernsthaft gemeint waren, so rührte er sich nicht.

Glauben Sie diese Geschichte?

Vollkommen! rief ich, mit freudigem Beifall; jedwedem Fremden, so wahrscheinlich ist sie; um wie viel mehr Ihnen!

Nun, mein vortrefflicher Freund, sagte Herr C…, so sind Sie im Besitz von allem, was nötig ist, um mich zu begreifen. Wir sehen, dass in dem Masse, Grazie darin immer strahlender und herrschender hervortritt. – Doch so, wie sich der Durchschnitt zweier Linien, auf der einen Seite eines Punkts, nach dem Durchgang durch das Unendliche, plötzlich wieder auf der andern Seite einfindet, oder das Bild des Hohlspiegels, nachdem es sich in das Unendliche entfernt hat, plötzlich wieder dicht vor uns tritt: so findet sich auch, wenn die Erkenntnis gleichsam durch ein Unendliches gegangen ist, die Grazie wieder ein; so, dass sie, zu gleicher Zeit, in demjenigen menschlichen Körperbau am reinsten erscheint, der entweder gar keins, oder ein unendliches Bewusstsein hat, d.h. in dem Gliedermann, oder in dem Gott.

Mithin, sagte ich ein wenig zerstreut, müssten wir wieder von dem Baum der Erkenntnis essen, um in den Stand der Unschuld zurückzufallen?

Allerdings, antwortete er; das ist das letzte Kapitel von der Geschichte der Welt.

Geschrieben 1810, hier gedruckt nach: Heinrich von Kleist, Werke in einem Band, hrsg. v. Helmut Sembdner, Carl Hanser Verlag München 1966, S. 802-807.

bear's utter seriousness robbed me of my composure. Thrusts and feints followed thick and fast, the sweat poured off me, but in vain. It wasn't merely that he parried my thrusts like the finest fencer in the world; when I feinted to deceive him he made no move at all. No human fencer could equal his perception in this respect. He stood upright, his paw raised ready for battle, his eye fixed on mine as if he could read my soul there, and when my thrusts were not meant seriously he did not move. Do you believe this story?'

'Absolutely,' I said with joyful approval. 'I'd believe it from a stranger, it's so probable. Why shouldn't I believe you?'

'Now, my excellent friend,' said my companion, 'you are in possession of all you need to know to follow my argument. We see that in the organic world, as thought grows dimmer and weaker, grace emerges more brilliantly and decisively. But just as a section drawn through two lines suddenly reappears on the other side after passing through infinity, or as the image in a concave mirror turns up again right in front of us after dwindling into the distance, so grace itself returns when knowledge has as it were gone through an infinity. Grace appears most purely in that human form which either has no consciousness or an infinite consciousness. That is, in the puppet or in the god.'

'Does that mean,' I said in some bewilderment, 'we must eat again of the tree of knowledge in order to return to the state of innocence?'

'Of course,' he said, 'but that's the final chapter in the history of the world.'

'On the Marionette Theatre' was written in 1810. This translation first appeared in *The Times Literary Supplement*, 20 October 1978, and is included in *Speak Silence: Essays by Idris Parry* published by Carcanet Press, 1988.

Color Plates

Farbtafeln

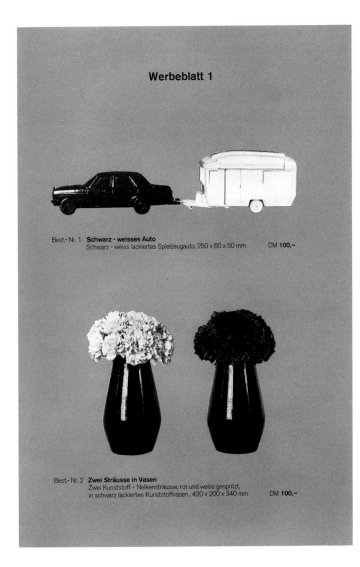

Werbeblatt 1

Best.- Nr. 1 **Schwarz - weisses Auto**
Schwarz - weiss lackiertes Spielzeugauto, 250 x 60 x 50 mm   DM **100,–**

Best.- Nr. 2 **Zwei Sträusse in Vasen**
Zwei Kunststoff - Nelkensträusse, rot und weiss gespritzt,
in schwarz lackierten Kunststoffvasen, 420 x 200 x 340 mm   DM **100,–**

Best.- Nr. 3 **Anturien**
Neun rot - gelb lackierte Kunststoff - Anturien, mit Kupferstielen
in drei weissen Einmachgläsern, 340 x 320 x 360 mm   DM **100,–**

Best.- Nr. 4 **Spiegel**
Zweiseitiger Spiegel, Rand ungeschliffen, 200 x 150 x 4 mm   DM **100,–**

1   Werbeblatt I, 1981 (Kat. 24)
     (Advertising Leaflet I, cat. 24)

Best.- Nr. 5 **Wandvase**
Dunkelgrüne Kunststoffvase, bis zum Rand mit klarem Wasser gefüllt,
wird von einem schwarzen Eisenring gehalten, der an die Wand
angeschraubt wird, 150 x 100 x 280 mm   DM **100,−**

Best.- Nr. 6 **Papageienbild**
Farbfoto in rotem Passepartout, gerahmt, 180 x 240 mm   DM **100,−**

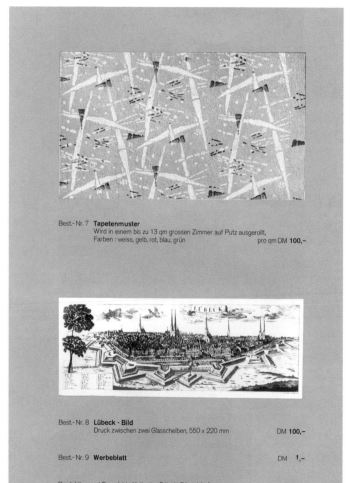

Best.- Nr. 7 **Tapetenmuster**
Wird in einem bis zu 13 qm grossen Zimmer auf Putz ausgerollt,
Farben : weiss, gelb, rot, blau, grün   pro qm DM **100,−**

Best.- Nr. 8 **Lübeck - Bild**
Druck zwischen zwei Glasscheiben, 550 x 220 mm   DM **100,−**

Best.- Nr. 9 **Werbeblatt**   DM **1,−**

Produktion und Copyright : Katharina Fritsch, Düsseldorf
Vertrieb : Ton Bild Wort Vertrieb, DAS BÜRO, Norbert Wehner,
Fürstenwall 64, D - 4000 Düsseldorf, Telefon : (0211) 306855

2   Warengestell, 1979-1984 (Kat. 40)
     (Display Stand, cat. 40)

3   Acht Tische mit acht Gegenständen, 1984 (Kat. 48)
     (Eight Tables with Eight Objects, cat. 48)

4   Spaziergänger mit Hund, 1986 (Kat. 60)   5   Parfüm im Hausflur, 1984 (Kat. 41)
     (Man Out for a Walk with Dog, cat. 60)   (Perfume in the Hallway, cat. 41)

6   Schwarzer Tisch mit eineiigen Zwillingen, 1985 (Kat. 53)
     (Black Table with Identical Twins, cat. 53)

7   Kerzenständer, 1985 (Kat. 54)
     (Candle Stand, cat. 54)

8   Messekoje mit vier Figuren, 1985/86 (Kat. 58)   9   Beistelltisch mit Engel und Flasche, 1985 (Kat.57)
     (Trade Fair Stand with Four Figures, cat. 58)   (Side Table with Angel and Bottle, cat. 57)

10   Warengestell mit Madonnen, 1987/89 (Kat. 70)
      (Display Stand with Madonnas, cat. 70)

11 Warengestell mit Vasen, 1987/89 (Kat. 69)
    (Display Stand with Vases, cat. 69)

12 Elefant, 1987 (Kat. 64)
    (Elephant, cat. 64)

13   Madonnenfigur, 1987 (Kat. 67)   14   Mühle, 1990 (Kat. 78)
     (Madonna Figure, cat. 67)   (Mill, cat. 78)

15   Acht Bilder in acht Farben: Rotes Bild, Blaues
Bild, Grünes Bild, Schwarzes Bild, Weisses
Bild, Gelbes Bild, Hellgrünes Bild, Oranges
Bild, 1990/91 (Kat. 93)

(Eight paintings in Eight Colors: Red Painting,
Blue Painting, Green Painting, Black Painting,
White Painting, Yellow Painting, Light green
Painting, Orange Painting, cat. 93)

16 Roter Raum mit Kamingeräusch, 1991 (Kat. 94)
    (Red Room with Chimney Noise, cat. 94)

17   Tischgesellschaft, 1988 (Kat. 75)
      (Company at Table, cat. 75)

18   Gespenst und Blutlache, 1988 (Kat. 76)
      (Ghost and Pool of Blood, cat. 76)

19 Mann und Maus, 1991/92 (Kat. 96)
    (Man and Mouse, cat. 96)

20 Rattenkönig, 1991-1993 (Kat. 97)
(Rat-King, cat. 97)

21   Museum, Modell 1:10, 1995 (Kat. 100)
(Museum, Model 1:10, cat. 100)

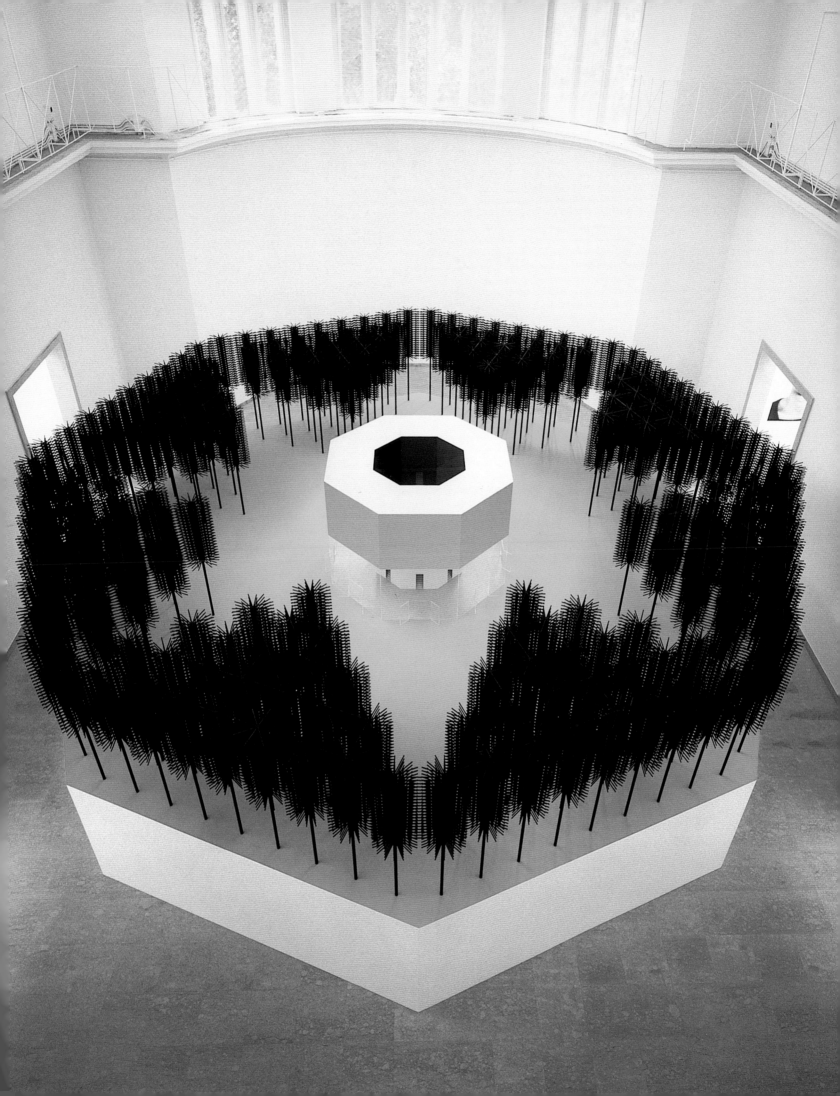

22 Kind mit Pudeln, 1995-1996 (Kat. 102)
    (Child with Poodles, cat. 102)

23　Lexikonzeichnung Schneewittchen, 1996 (Kat. 106)
　　(Lexicon Drawing Snow White, cat. 106)

Matthias Winzen
in Conversation with Katharina Fritsch

Matthias Winzen
im Gespräch mit Katharina Fritsch

Your work Museum, *shown at the 1995 Venice Biennale, seems to me to contain a utopia of cultural policy: the art museum seen not as a leisure activity, but as a crystallization point for public spiritual confrontation. Thinking of real museums, do you see any differences between the U.S.A. and Europe here?*

Yes, my impression is that Americans see museums as public places for showing cultural and spiritual life. Because the U.S.A. is a very young nation they are more actively interested in establishing and updating cultural traditions. I always feel that museums are more popular in the U.S.A.. Of course the influence of individual trustees on American institutions is a double-edged sword, but I do notice that it is a nation for which culture and cultural tradition are very important, and it constantly has to do a great deal to maintain and develop its traditions, because it is so young. Americans would perhaps like to have a national history that goes further back. I thought it was crazy that quite ordinary people were paying outrageous sums for a pair of earrings at the auction of Jackie Kennedy's estate, just to own a piece of American royalty.

How does the difference that you have mentioned between America and Europe show up in the art business?

When I'm preparing an American exhibition, as for the Dia Center for the Arts in 1993, for example, everyone makes me feel as if we're planning something big and exciting. That is more flattering for an artist than what happens with German museum people. But I don't want to say too much against dry German understatement, which does have a great deal going for it. At the moment I'm experiencing the tension between hot and cold in America and Europe. In America presenting yourself in public always involves a bit of Hollywood. There's more of a sense that you're making an entrance in America, being glamorously staged, and that suits my work as well.

Your Tischgesellschaft *(Company at Table), in all its dominant length, has something of a great theatrical entrance about it.*

Yes, I do stage my works, and not just for certain spaces, but for visitors as well. And that all starts with scale. A lot of works like *Rattenkönig* (Rat-King) are larger than life; others are reduced. Or the display stands, which refer to a department store situation,

In deiner Arbeit «Museum», die 1995 bei der Biennale in Venedig zu sehen war, scheint mir eine kulturpolitische Utopie enthalten zu sein: das Kunstmuseum nicht als Freizeitbeschäftigung, sondern als ein Kristallisationspunkt der öffentlichen geistigen Auseinandersetzung. Wenn man an reale Museen denkt, siehst du da Unterschiede zwischen den USA und Europa?

Ja, mein Eindruck ist, dass die Amerikaner das Museum als den öffentlichen Platz ansehen, an dem sich ihr kulturelles, geistiges Leben zeigt. Weil die USA eine sehr junge Nation sind, haben sie ein aktiveres Verhältnis zur Stiftung und Fortschreibung von kulturellen Traditionen als die Europäer. In den USA habe ich immer das Gefühl, die Museen seien populärer. Natürlich ist der Einfluss einzelner Trustees auf amerikanische Institute zweischneidig, aber auf jeden Fall merke ich, dass da eine Nation ist, für die Kultur und kulturelle Tradition sehr wichtig sind, die aber immer wieder viel für die Erhaltung und Entwicklung ihrer Traditionen tun muss, weil sie so jung ist. Amerikaner hätten vielleicht gerne eine weiter zurückreichende Nationalgeschichte. Ich fand das so verrückt, wie bei der Versteigerung des Nachlasses von Jackie Kennedy ganz einfache Leute Unsummen für ein paar Ohrringe ausgegeben haben, nur für etwas Teilhabe an American Royalty.

Wie macht sich der Unterschied zwischen den USA und Europa, von dem du sprichst, im Kunstbetrieb bemerkbar?

Wenn ich eine Ausstellung in Amerika vorbereite, wie z.B. 1993 im Dia Center for the Arts, dann geben einem alle das Gefühl, man plant etwas Grosses und Aufregendes. Das ist für einen Künstler schmeichelhafter als bei deutschen Museumsleuten. Allerdings möchte ich jetzt damit nicht das trockene deutsche Understatement schmähen, das ja auch vieles für sich hat. Im Moment ergibt sich für mich die Spannung aus dem Wechselbad Europa-Amerika. Sich in der Öffentlichkeit zu präsentieren, hat in Amerika einfach immer etwas von Hollywood. In den USA gibt es mehr Sinn für den Auftritt, die glamouröse Inszenierung, und das passt auch zu meinen Arbeiten.

Deine «Tischgesellschaft», dieser raumgreifende Riegel, hat etwas von einem grossen, theaterhaften Auftritt.

Ja, ich inszeniere meine Arbeiten, und zwar nicht nur für bestimmte Räume, sondern auch für die Besucher. Das fängt schon beim Massstab an. Manche Sachen wie der «Rattenkönig» sind überdi-

mensional gross, andere sind verkleinert. Oder die Warengestelle mit ihrem Rückbezug auf eine Kaufhaussituation: Da gehören einfach Leute dazu. Manche Arbeiten werden erst richtig interessant mit Besuchern, z.B. das «Museum». Der Sockel ist so gemein hoch, so dass die meisten Besucher so gerade über die Kante gucken können, aber nie den grossen Überblick bekommen.

«Gemein hoch» hast du gesagt – warum baust du absichtlich ein Hindernis für den Betrachter ein?

Wenn der Sockel 5 cm tiefer wäre, kämen die Proportionen durcheinander und die Arbeit würde auseinanderfallen. Dann wäre der untere Teil ein blosser Sockel geworden. So aber ist er Teil der Skulptur. Das Ganze ist dadurch kein Architekturmodell, sondern eine Skulptur.

Aber die Höhe des Sockels behindert den Betrachter.

Keiner würde sich beschweren, dass er die Figuren am Kirchturm nicht erkennen kann. Oder eine grosse Skulptur von Richard Serra kann man auch nicht von oben betrachten, wenn man davor steht. Man soll das «Museum» schon als Inszenierung von Unerreichbarkeit betrachten, ein Bild von Ferne, nicht nur ein architektonisches, sondern auch ein gedankliches Modell, eine Erscheinung, die deutlich vor einem steht, aber nicht zu fassen ist.

Täuscht denn der Eindruck, dass der Betrachter nicht unbedingt an die Hand genommen wird, sondern dass er Schwierigkeiten überwinden muss, wenn er deine Arbeiten verstehen will?

Es geht mir nicht um eine Provokation als Selbstzweck, sondern die Provokation ergibt sich als Nebenprodukt daraus, dass meine Arbeiten auch immer Schwellenerfahrungen für den Betrachter sind. Wenn ich etwas gut hinkriegen will, dann ist meine Erfahrung, dass das selten leicht geht. Und ich glaube auf der anderen Seite, dass es für den Betrachter genausowenig eine einfache Angelegenheit ist, Kunst zu verstehen. Der Moment, in dem ich den Dingen unverstellt begegne, erschrecke, staune, den Sog eines Raumes empfinde, einer Leere begegne – das ist einfach nichts Populäres. Oder Dinge, Vasen z.B., ausserhalb ihrer Alltagsfunktion zu betrachten, da muss sich ein Betrachter schon etwas Mühe geben. Manche Betrachter sind natürlich zu zerstreut oder sie weichen der Irritation ins Didaktische, ins direkt Benennbare aus. Mir geht es aber um Rätsel wie: Wo befinden wir uns überhaupt? Was ist das für ein Raum um uns herum? Was machen wir darin?

simply have to have people. A lot of works aren't interesting until there are some visitors around, *Museum*, for example. The base is so unreasonably high that most visitors can just look over the edge, but never get an overall impression.

You say "unreasonably high." Why do you deliberately build in obstacles for viewers?

If the base were 5 centimeters lower the proportions would be all wrong and the work would lose its cohesion. Then the lower part would be just a base. But it is part of the sculpture. This means that the whole thing is not an architect's model, but a sculpture.

But the height of the base hinders the viewer.

No one would complain about not being able to make out the figures on a church tower. And you can't look down at a big sculpture by Richard Serra if you're standing in front of it. *Museum* should be seen as staging inaccessibility, as an image of distance: It is clearly in front of the viewer but difficult to grasp.

So is it wrong to say that viewers are not necessarily led by the hand, but that they have to overcome difficulties if they want to understand the works?

I do not see provocation as an end in itself, but provocation emerges as a by-product of the fact that my works are always threshold experiences for the viewer. If I want to bring something off properly I find that it's seldom easy. And I think on the other hand that it is equally little a simple matter for the viewer to understand art. The moment when I come across things in their genuine state, when I'm afraid, astonished, when I experience the pull of a space, of a vacuum – that is just not a popular thing. Or if viewers are to look at things, vases for example, outside their everyday function, then they have to make a bit of an effort. Of course a lot of viewers are too distracted or they retreat from being disturbed into didacticism, taking refuge in something that can be named directly. But I'm interested in puzzles like: where are we anyway? What sort of space is this around us? What are we doing in it?

When I think of Rattenkönig *(Rat-King) or* Mann und Maus *(Man and Mouse) – surely you're trying to give the viewer a bit of a fright?*

It isn't about treating viewers badly, I'm simply letting them be involved in my fear or astonishment, and that's ambivalent. It's

simply something that makes me an artist, and I think viewers should understand that in the best cases when they go into a museum. But only a tiny number do.

Why?

Because access is usually blocked by acquired bourgeois notions, by didactic impositions of language. And because most viewers aren't used to seeing and feeling contradictions pictorially.

What exactly do you mean by bourgeois notions?

The usual: that thing hanging on the wall there is worth so much and symbolizes this and that. But how are you supposed to look at a work by, say Donald Judd, from that point of view, when he's concerned with emptiness, when you can practically feel the empty space in his work, the void. I think these are elements that you can't explain but you can experience, if you are drawn into them quite genuinely and, if possible, without a lot of prior thought.

And what did you mean by viewers' lack of ability to feel contradictions pictorially?

Well, in the first place, it's certainly about ambivalent subjects that are often treated in clichés and superficially in public. It's like that in America for example: every evening there's something on television that gets people worked up about children being ill-treated, child abuse, or sexual harassment at work. They go on about it right down to the last detail because the public finds it provocative. "And what did he do then, and what then? Oh that's really disgusting, really nasty!"

After Mike Kelley's 1993 exhibition at the Whitney, there were voices in the New York press who insisted that the aggressive and ambivalent quality of his installations must stem from abuse in Kelley's early childhood. Conversely, an apparently harmless expression like "clean fun" seems a far more oppressive idea than anything Kelley shows.

Why does everything have to come back to concepts? Being disturbed visually, experiencing ambivalence – why does that have to go straight into the language cage? It's just an escape into didacticism. A very important element in my work is that you come in, experience an image, allow yourself to be drawn into it,

Wenn ich an den «Rattenkönig» oder an «Mann und Maus» denke – einen kleinen Schrecken willst du dem Betrachter schon einjagen?

Das ist keine Gemeinheit gegen den Betrachter, das ist einfach ein Teilhabenlassen an meinem Erschrecken oder Erstaunen, das ist ambivalent. Das ist einfach etwas, was mich dazu bringt, Künstlerin zu sein, und ich denke, das sollte der Betrachter im besten Falle, wenn er in ein Museum geht, nachvollziehen. Das tun aber die wenigsten.

Warum?

Weil der Zugang meistens verstellt ist von angelernten bürgerlichen Vorstellungen, von didaktischen Versprachlichungen. Und weil die meisten Betrachter nicht gewohnt sind, Widersprüche bildhaft zu sehen und zu empfinden.

Was meinst du genau mit bürgerlichen Vorstellungen?

Das Übliche: Was da an der Wand hängt, ist soundso teuer, und das symbolisiert das und das. Aber wie soll man sich unter so einem Aspekt z.B. eine Arbeit von Donald Judd angucken, bei der es um Leere geht, bei der man den leeren Raum praktisch spüren kann, das Nichts. Ich meine, das sind die Momente, die man nicht erklären kann, die man aber erleben kann, wenn man sich ganz unverstellt und möglichst ohne viele Vorgedanken auf diesen Moment einlässt.

Und was meintest du eben mit der mangelnden Betrachterfähigkeit, Widersprüche bildhaft zu empfinden?

Naja, es hat zunächst sicher damit zu tun, dass ambivalente Themen in der Öffentlichkeit oft in Schlagworten und oberflächlich abgehandelt werden. In Amerika z.B. ist es doch so: Jeden Abend ist irgendetwas im Fernsehen, wobei man sich über Kindesmisshandlung, Kindesmissbrauch oder sexuelle Belästigung am Arbeitsplatz aufregt. Das wird dann bis ins letzte Detail breitgetreten, weil das Publikum das im Grunde genommen aufreizend findet. «Und was hat er dann gemacht, und was dann? Oh, das ist richtig unanständig, richtig fies!»

Nach Mike Kelleys Ausstellung im Whitney 1993 gab es in der New Yorker Presse Stimmen, die die Aggressivität und Ambivalenz seiner Installationen unbedingt auf einen Missbrauch in Kelleys früher Kindheit zurückführen wollten. Umgekehrt erscheint mir ein scheinbar harmloser

Ausdruck wie «clean fun» eine viel zwangvollere Vorstellung zu sein als alles, was Kelley zeigt.

Warum muss alles auf Begriffe gebracht werden? Visuelle Irritationen, die Erfahrung von Ambivalenz – warum muss das immer gleich in den Sprachkäfig? Das ist die Flucht ins Didaktische. Bei meinen Arbeiten ist ein ganz wichtiger Moment der, dass du hereinkommst, ein Bild erlebst, dich darauf einlässt, es direkt wahrnimmst. Bei meiner Ausstellung der Lexikonzeichnungen bei Matthew Marks in New York war ich überrascht, plötzlich mit Naziästhetik in Verbindung gebracht zu werden. Einige professionelle Betrachter konnten sich nicht darauf einlassen, dass da etwas an der Wand hängt, was nicht sofort erklärt werden kann oder muss, etwas, das einen vom Gefühl her einerseits anzieht und andererseits abstösst.

Wie wurde die Assoziation an Naziästhetik begründet?

Die Vorlagen zu meinen «Zeichnungen» sind Abbildungen aus dem deutschen Bildwörterduden von 1936. Das Buch gehörte meinem Vater, und ich habe es mir als Kind oft fasziniert angesehen. Da sind eigentlich alle Themen des Lebens von Geburt bis Tod in einer trockenen, standardisierten Form in kleinen Bildern dargestellt. Mir kam es auf diesen Standardtyp von Zeichnung an. Was ist eine Zeichnung? Eine Zeichnung ist für mich erstmal ein weisses Papier mit schwarzen Linien drauf, die irgendetwas darstellen, und das einen Rahmen hat.

Dir ging es um die Zeichnung als Standard oder Schema, so wie bei Artschwager?

Ja, nur anders. Es gibt dieses Wörterbuch auch auf Englisch und der Stil dieser Illustration war damals, denke ich, keineswegs allein deutsch. Wenn da ein Volksfest abgebildet ist, z.B. «Sonnenwendfeier», verstehe ich die Assoziation an die Nazizeit schon, weil die Nazis solche Volkstraditionen missbraucht haben. Allerdings gibt es heute in Schweden immer noch Sonnenwendfeiern. Natürlich geben die Zeichnungen etwas von der Zeit wieder, in der sie entstanden sind. Aber diese Seherfahrung auf das Schlagwort Naziästhetik zu reduzieren, verfehlt das unterschwellige Befremden, auf das es mir ankam. Mir ging es um das Anheimelnde, Vertraute, aber auch um das Deprimierende, Befremdende und Enge, das von diesen Zeichnungen ausgeht. Man sieht eine standardisierte Idealwelt der dreissiger Jahre, die ich meine als Kind noch in den fünfziger und frühen sechziger Jahren erlebt zu haben. Das war aber schon

perceive it directly. At my lexicon drawings exhibition at Matthew Marks's gallery in New York, I was surprised to be suddenly linked with Nazi aesthetics. Some professional viewers could not accept that there's something hanging on the wall there that can't or doesn't have to be explained immediately, something that is emotionally both attractive and repellent.

> *What reasons were given for the association with Nazi aesthetics?*

My "drawings" were based on illustrations from the 1936 edition of the Duden pictorial lexicon. The book belonged to my father, and always fascinated me as a child. It actually shows every aspect of life from birth to death in a dry, standardized form in little pictures. I was interested in this kind of standard drawing. What is a drawing? For me a drawing is first of all a sheet of white paper with black lines on it that represent something, and a frame.

> *You were interested in drawing as a standard or a scheme, as in Artschwager's work?*

Yes, but in a different way. This lexicon is published in English as well, and I don't think that this illustration style was by any means exclusively German at the time. If a popular festival like "Summer Solstice" is shown, for example, I can understand the association with the Nazi period, because the Nazis abused popular traditions like this. But they still have Summer Solstice Festivals in Sweden. Of course the drawings reflect something of the period in which they came into being. But to reduce this visual experience to the cliché of Nazi aesthetics misses the subliminal disturbance I was aiming at. I was interested in the element that these drawings emanate, of things that were cozy and familiar, but also depressing and disturbing. You see a standard, idealized 1930s world that I think I experienced as a child in the 1950s and early 1960s. But even at the time that was a total illusion. What is shown is a strong, firmly fixed world order borrowed from a nineteenth-century Romantic Germany that didn't exist at the time either. That is the second plane of these drawings for me: black lines on a white background, hanging on the wall in a silver frame and representing a completely intangible illusion.

> *You were talking just now about a flight into didacticism. That sounds like avoiding confrontation.*

Overly hasty explanations of clichés take away the viewer's chance to recognize something new with and through an image. At the moment viewers come into the space, the important thing is that they are drawn into something that perhaps does not seem so "clean" at first. Nothing in the whole of life is unambiguous. There are the famous two sides to everything. The sooner you accept that, the more clearly you can think. I have the impression that there is even greater pressure in the American art market than in the German to make images explicable in words, to force the meaning of a work of art into discourse form. It seems to me that this constant urge for conceptual explanation also contains an obsessive attempt to maintain order or to make things look more ordered than they are. If the Nazi aesthetics cliché is applied to me because I used 1936 lexicon illustrations, that at the same time creates a little corner for all the misery in the world. Undoubtedly Nazism represents a terrible extreme in terms of contempt for human beings. But misery was and is everywhere. Even today and in many places there are people who torture other people. The politically correct reflex of insinuating that the first thing about my drawings is a link with the Nazis is one-dimensional and in fact much too harmless. In any case political correctness can only condemn any cultural approach to everything that is ambivalent, and thus all good artists. Politically correct arguments also have something totalitarian about them in a middle-class sort of way.

> *It is also possible to argue that the contradictory quality of the obsessive, illusionistically romantic ideal world of 1930s Germany is a historical or political subject, but actually not an artistic one. Why do you take it up?*

I'm surprised at the moment by the most recent anti-German tendencies in America, for instance Daniel Goldhagen's book *Hitler's Willing Executioners*. This can be seen as anti-German because of its provocative language and propositions, even though Goldhagen himself perhaps didn't intend it. It would perhaps be more in keeping with the times to write a book about people rather than about the Germans. But the book certainly reflects the situation in Germany as well – the way in which my generation of forty-somethings analyzes the past. In the Nazi period our parents were children or young people, and many also suffered a great deal as Germans. Every generation of historians and every generation of artists have analyzed it in its own way. I hope that our generation will not withdraw into

damals eine totale Illusion. Gezeigt wird eine starke, fest gefügte Weltordnung in Anlehnung an ein romantisches Deutschland des 19. Jahrhunderts, das es auch damals nicht so gegeben hat. Das ist für mich die zweite Ebene dieser Zeichnungen. Schwarze Linien auf weissem Grund, die in einem silbernen Rahmen an der Wand hängen und eine völlig ungreifbare Illusion darstellen.

Eben hast du von der Flucht ins Didaktische gesprochen. Das hört sich an wie: einer Konfrontation ausweichen.

Vorschnelle Erklärungen oder Schlagwörter bringen den Betrachter um seine Möglichkeit, mit und durch ein Bild etwas Neues zu erkennen. In dem Moment, in dem der Betrachter den Raum betritt, kommt es darauf an, dass er sich auf etwas einlässt, das vielleicht zunächst nicht so «clean» erscheint. Im ganzen Leben ist nichts eindeutig. Alles hat die berühmten zwei Seiten. Je eher man das akzeptiert, um so klarer kann man denken. Ich habe den Eindruck, dass der Druck im amerikanischen Kunstbetrieb noch grösser ist als im deutschen, Bilder in Worten erklärbar zu machen, den Sinn eines Kunstwerks in eine Diskursform zu pressen. Mir kommt es so vor, als steckte in diesem dauernden Drang zur begrifflichen Erklärung, auch ein zwanghafter Versuch, Ordnung zu halten oder Dinge viel geordneter erscheinen zu lassen, als sie sind. Wenn mir, weil ich Lexikonillustrationen von 1936 benutzt habe, das Schlagwort Naziästhetik entgegengehalten wird, ist damit zugleich so eine kleine Ecke für alles Elend dieser Welt benannt. Der Nationalsozialismus steht ohne jeden Zweifel für ein schreckliches Extrem an Menschenverachtung. Aber das Elend war und ist überall. Es gibt bis heute und an vielen Orten Menschen, die Menschen quälen. Der politisch korrekte Reflex, meinen Zeichnungen als erstes einen Nazi-Bezug zu unterstellen, ist eindimensional und eigentlich viel zu harmlos. Mit politischer Korrektheit kann man sowieso jede künstlerische Annäherung an alles, was ambivalent ist, und damit alle grossen Künstler nur noch verurteilen. Auf eine kleinbürgerliche Weise hat das politisch korrekte Argumentieren auch etwas Totalitäres.

Man könnte auch argumentieren, dass die Widersprüchlichkeit der zwanghaften, illusionär romantischen Idealwelt der dreissiger Jahre in Deutschland ein historisches oder politologisches, aber eigentlich kein künstlerisches Thema ist. Warum befasst du dich damit?

Ich finde, das kann und soll man nicht so scharf trennen. Es ist ja z.B. im Grunde ein politischer Aspekt, dass Nationalismus in der

73

Kunst überholt ist. Und in der Geschichtsschreibung ist der Nationalsimus eigentlich auch überholt. Dann aber wundere ich mich über die neuesten antideutschen Tendenzen in Amerika zur Zeit, z.B. das Buch von Daniel Goldhagen «Hitlers willige Vollstrecker». Das kann man, obwohl Goldhagen das vielleicht selbst gar nicht will, wegen seiner provokanten Sprache und Thesen als antideutsch auffassen. Es wäre vielleicht zeitgemässer, nicht ein Buch über die Deutschen zu schreiben, sondern über die Menschen. Das Buch spiegelt sicher aber auch die Situation in Deutschland wieder – die Auseinandersetzung meiner Generation um die Vierzig mit der Vergangenheit. Unsere Eltern waren zur Nazizeit Kinder oder Jungendliche, und viele haben auch als Deutsche schwer gelitten. Jede Historikergeneration und jede Künstlergeneration hat sich auf ihre Weise damit auseinandergesetzt. Ich hoffe, in unserer Generation findet kein Rückzug in nationalistische Gefilde statt. Konfrontation finde ich wichtig, aber der Schwerpunkt sollte auf Austausch und Versöhnung liegen.

Ein anderes Thema: Bezogen auf die jüngeren deutschen Künstler hat Gunter Reski geschrieben, im Augenblick gäbe es eine «schleichende Alphabetisierungskampagne», eine starke Anlehnung an Diskurs und Theorie. Gibt es in Deutschland zur Zeit so etwas wie eine Vertextung von Kunst?

Ich glaube, dass das von einigen Künstlern und Schreibern im Moment versucht wird, dass das aber nicht richtig funktioniert. Vielleicht ist das auch eine Gegenreaktion oder der Versuch einer Gegenreaktion auf die achtziger Jahre, in denen das Bild tragend und tragfähig war. Thomas Ruff, Jeff Wall, Martin Honert, Robert Gober, Jeff Koons, Fischli/Weiss und noch viele andere, die in den achtziger Jahren bekannt geworden sind: die stellen künstlerisch und oft auch technisch sehr, sehr gute Bilder her. Und dagegen gibt es dieses etwas diffuse, nennen wir es siebziger Jahre Revival, in dem Text und Diskurs eben eine besondere Rolle spielen. Aber das ist nostalgisch und in einem schlechten Sinn immateriell. Manche von den Jüngeren befassen sich kaum noch mit Material, sondern nur mit Meinungen und angerissenen Fragmenten. Das ist eine Reaktionsweise, wie man auf seine Eltern reagiert. Das heisst nicht, dass ich die offene, environmenthafte Art zu arbeiten wie bei Beuys oder Nauman uninteressant finde. Es lohnt sich sicher, daran anzuknüpfen. Das muss dann aber mit authentischen Inhalten gefüllt sein und nicht als modischer Abklatsch erscheinen. Ich denke, dass z.B. Robert Gober ein gutes Beispiel für eine Fortführung dieser

romanticized nationalism. I think confrontation is important, but we should emphasize exchange and reconciliation.

Another subject: in terms of the younger German artists, Günter Reski has written that at the moment there is a "creeping literacy campaign," a marked reliance on discourse and theory. Is something like a textualization of art happening in Germany at the moment?

I think some artists and writers are trying to do that at present, but it's not working properly. Perhaps it's just a counter-reaction or an attempt at a counter-reaction to the 1980s, in which images led and were able to take the load. Thomas Ruff, Jeff Wall, Martin Honert, Robert Gober, Jeff Koons, Fischli/Weiss, and a lot of others who became well known in the 1980s: they produce images that are very, very good artistically and often technically as well. And yet there is this somewhat diffuse – shall we call it a 1970s-revival, in which it is text and discourse that have a particular part to play. But that is nostalgic and immaterial in a bad sense. A lot of the younger artists hardly bother with material any more, but only with opinions and fragments that are touched upon. That's a way of reacting, just as you react to your parents. That isn't to say that I find an open, environmental way of working like Beuys's or Nauman's uninteresting. It's certainly worth taking it up. But it then has to be filled with authentic content and not appear as fashionable yet pale imitation. I think that Robert Gober, for instance, is a good example of a continuation of this tradition. But I see the development of art as a continuous process, and not so much as a sequence of anti-reactions.

Authenticity, continuity – that sounds conservative. Your proposition was that all artistic expression, everything that a work of art has to communicate, all the assertions that it contains, have to be conveyed by the image itself, not by additional explanations that are added to the work of art in textual form. Roughly right?

Absolutely.

But that requires a very broad consensus of understanding from the public and traditions of art understanding that have been in place for a long time.

Yes, and that is perhaps not the way sociologists and art historians intend it, perhaps it is un-American, it is certainly not didactic. There is a long tradition in painting and sculpture of working

in the way that I do. All the effect derives from the work itself. Otherwise it is merely a place holder, a substitute, and then you need a great deal of text to talk up some meaning that the work itself doesn't embody. It's just occurred to me that insisting on the sculptural object itself is definitely an American position as well, adopted by the Minimalists, for example.

Who should actually be your audience then? In the text by Heinrich von Kleist that you've selected, Kleist praises the marionette theatre, which was invented "for the crowd," and so definitely not for an audience of educated experts.

Anyone should be the audience. Anyone should be able to look at my images and I think that anyone can understand them as well. Anyone who sees my green *Elefant* (Elephant), *Rattenkönig* (Rat-King) or *Mann und Maus* (Man and Mouse), surely they're going to be interested in a very direct way from the outset. Of course there are more profound and continuing links with art history that emerge only when people read something about it or have been involved with art for longer. But it is wrong to look for a pictorial language from the start that only a few people can understand and that is restrictive. If you say, "I'm going to produce art for art historians from now on," then the end is in sight.

On the other hand, the so-called general public is by no means unbiased about contemporary art.

That's true, of course. For example, one question that people who don't have very much to do with art always ask is, "Did you make all that yourself, with your own hands?" Of course not, it's just not possible. But essentially that's a secondary reaction that fends off the first spontaneous, speechless astonishment. I find being speechless when you see one of my works for the first time much more important, and I think that has a lot more to do with art. And that's something absolutely anybody can experience.

Why are you so bothered with Kleist's "crowd," the general public, in the case of a work like Museum that contains a utopia of cultural policy? You're successful personally, and anyway there's a lot of response to art from the general public nowadays.

There certainly is on a superficial plane. But I still clearly remember the time before the art boom in the early 1980s when I was still a student in Düsseldorf. You went to exhibition openings and there wasn't a soul there, an aching void. Of course I asked

Tradition ist. Ich sehe die Kunstentwicklung aber als kontinuierlichen Prozess, nicht so sehr als Abfolge von Antireaktionen.

Authentizität, Kontinuität – das klingt konservativ. Deine These wäre: Aller künstlerischer Ausdruck, alles, was in einem Kunstwerk mitgeteilt werden soll, alle Behauptungen, die es enthält, müssen sich im Bild selber mitteilen, nicht durch zusätzliche Erklärungen, die dem Kunstwerk in Textform hinzugefügt werden. So ungefähr?

Genau.

Aber das setzt doch beim Publikum einen breiten Verständniskonsens und lang bestehende Traditionen von Kunstverständnis voraus.

Ja, und vielleicht ist das nicht im Sinne von Soziologen und Kunsthistorikern, vielleicht ist es unamerikanisch, jedenfalls ist es undidaktisch. Es ist in der Malerei und der Bildhauerei eine alte Tradition, so zu arbeiten, wie ich das tue. Alle Wirkung geht vom Werk selber aus. Sonst ist es nur ein Platzhalter, ein Ersatz, und es braucht viel Text, um irgendeinen Sinn, den das Ding selber nicht verkörpert, herbeizureden. Mir fällt gerade ein, auf das skulpturale Ding selber zu beharren, ist durchaus auch eine amerikanische Position, die der Minimalisten zum Beispiel.

Wer soll eigentlich dein Publikum sein? In dem Text von Heinrich von Kleist, den du ausgewählt hast, lobt Kleist das Marionettentheater, das «für den Haufen», also keineswegs für ein gebildetes Expertenpublikum erfunden worden sei.

Das Publikum soll jeder sein. Meine Bilder soll jeder ansehen können und ich glaube, jeder kann sie auch verstehen. Wer meinen grünen «Elefanten» sieht, den «Rattenkönig» oder «Mann und Maus» – das kann doch jeden erst einmal auf eine sehr direkte Weise interessieren. Natürlich gibt es über den ersten Anblick hinaus tiefer und weitergehende Bezüge zur Kunstgeschichte, die sich nur ergeben, wenn die Leute dazu etwas lesen oder sich schon länger mit Kunst befasst haben. Aber von Anfang an eine Bildsprache zu suchen, die nur wenig Eingeweihte verstehen und die ausgrenzt, das ist falsch. Wenn man sagt: Ich mache ab jetzt Kunst für Kunsthistoriker, dann ist man doch am Ende.

Andererseits ist das sogenannte breite Publikum ja keineswegs frei von Vorurteilen gegen die zeitgenössische Kunst.

Das stimmt natürlich. Eine Frage z.B., die Leute, die wenig mit Kunst zu tun haben, immer wieder stellen, ist: Hast du das alles selber, mit deinen Händen hergestellt? Natürlich nicht, das geht ja gar nicht. Aber das ist im Grunde so eine sekundäre Reaktion, die das erste spontane, sprachlose Staunen abwehrt. Das Sprachlos-Sein, wenn man eine von meinen Arbeiten das erste Mal sieht, das finde ich viel wichtiger und das hat meiner Meinung auch viel mehr mit Kunst zu tun. Das kann wirklich jeder erleben.

Warum bemühst du dich mit einer Arbeit wie «Museum», die ja auch eine kulturpolitische Utopie enthält, so sehr um den «Haufen», die allgemeine Öffentlichkeit? Du persönlich hast doch Erfolg, und ausserdem findet Kunst doch heute in der allgemeinen Öffentlichkeit viel Resonanz.

Auf einer oberflächlichen Ebene durchaus. Aber ich erinnere mich noch sehr genau an die Zeit vor dem Kunstboom der achtziger Jahre, als ich noch Studentin in Düsseldorf war. Du gingst zu Ausstellungseröffnungen, kein Mensch war da, gähnende Leere. Natürlich habe ich mich da gefragt: Warum will ich eigentlich Künstlerin werden? Besteht überhaupt ein allgemeines Interesse? In den Achtzigern schien das Interesse an Kunst in Deutschland sehr gross zu sein. Wenn du allerdings mit jemandem gesprochen hast, der nicht zur Kunstwelt gehörte, war da immer die Frage: Wie, Bildhauerin? Unter jedem anderen Beruf kann man sich alles vorstellen, ein Taxifahrer ist ein Taxifahrer, ein Arzt ein Arzt. Aber unter einem Bildhauer kann sich heute keiner etwas vorstellen. Künstler sein ist eine dauernde Balance. Einerseits willst du wirklich etwas besonders Konzentriertes machen, etwas ganz Anderes, als du in allen anderen Berufen machen würdest. Andererseits wird das Konzentrierte und Reduzierte in guter Kunst oft als elitär missverstanden, und dir wird die soziale Anerkennung verweigert, die du nämlich als Künstler auch brauchst, weil du ja tatsächlich für die Öffentlichkeit arbeitest. Eine Kunst nur für Fachleute, als Exotenecke ohne Anspruch auf ganz allgemeine Bedeutung für alle, das ist verfehlt. Deshalb habe ich diese Vorstellung von einem Kunstmuseum, das in Eigeninitiative von den Bürgern getragen werden würde. Ein Ansatz in diese Richtung sind natürlich die Kunstvereine in Deutschland oder die Art und Weise, wie für amerikanische Kunstmuseen der Gemeindegedanke eine Rolle spielt, die Verantwortung der Bürger vor Ort. Im Ganzen gesehen, geht es mir um eine Öffentlichkeit, die sich nicht in der Banalität erschöpft, die Teil jedes Alltags ist. Es geht um eine Öffentlichkeit mit auratischen Punkten. Mein «Museum» nimmt bewusst Bezug auf die

myself, why do I want to become an artist? Is there any general interest at all? In the 1980s there seemed to be a lot of interest in art in Germany. But if you were talking to someone who wasn't in the art world the question was always "what, a sculptor?" With any other job you can imagine everything: a taxi driver is a taxi driver, a doctor is a doctor. But nowadays no one can imagine what a sculptor does. Being an artist is a permanent balancing act. On the one hand you really want to do something concentrated, something quite different from anything you'd do in other jobs. On the other hand, things that are concentrated and reduced in good art are often misunderstood as elitist, and you don't get any social recognition, which you actually do need as an artist because in fact you are working for the public. Art that is only for experts, without any claim to a general meaning for everyone, that is just wrong. For that reason I have this notion of an art museum that would be supported by citizens on their own initiative. Kunstvereine – art associations – in Germany are of course a move in this direction, or the way in which community thinking has a part to play in American art museums, citizens taking responsibility on the spot. Seen overall, I am concerned about a public that does not exhaust itself in the banality that is part of every day. I want a public with auratic points. My *Museum* consciously relates to the pilgrimage church of *Vierzehnheiligen* with its excessive, unreal spatial feeling. We do live in a post-religious age, and artists are not the same as priests, but that does not mean that we have to go without concentration, powerful and binding images, and auratic objects. We artists have the job of concentrating experience, not just letting everything rush past, but summing things up contemplatively. That is a legacy of religion.

I have always been fascinated by the way your work combines religious elements with aspects of minimal art and pop art. But when you talk of priesthood, aren't you in danger of self-mystification?

No, I'm not interested in self-mystification. I'm suspicious of everything to do with art that's explained in terms of genius. It's much more about humility on the one hand and a professional working attitude on the other. Sensing emptiness, confronting naked existence, the modern perception of nothing, this sense of being thrown into certain circumstances against which we artists set our work, inevitably means beginning with a certain helplessness. And all the solutions we find as artists are always fleeting and concrete. They are always valid only for the one piece of work with which you are occupied at the time. The state of wordless unknowing is a great freedom, but is also a source of fear. It is ambivalent. I believe that it is possible to find elements of existential angst and darkness in my work that quite clearly result from this life without religion, without God. The moment when one confronts this being alone artistically simply is an individual and dark experience. Trying to make this experience into the loneliness of genius is nonsense, of course, precisely because what artists are doing is to convey their own experiences to other people in their work. If you concentrate yourself as an artist you do not meet an artist, but yourself. And every viewer who looks at a good work meets himself there as well.

"I have tried in my art to concentrate experiences as much as possible. This satisfies my needs, and I scarcely think that I am a person with needs that other people do not have." Carl Andre said that.

Yes, you could put it like that.

Good. But why do you link it with religion?

Because I see the artist's profession against a background of concentration, lonely concentration as well. There is a monastic aspect to this, as well as the working attitude. This means that I am privileged as an artist because I can address these existential things intensively and with concentration, like a monk, and thus have a special status as a medium who makes these things visible. But that should be combined with a modest attitude: ultimately every human being lives in awareness of death, "in anxiety." Everyone meets the "black hole" in his or her own way. For this reason the profession of artist should not be mystified and played out like Mister Genius. The moment it is used to fabricate a star image, then the concentration I've been talking about changes into its opposite, the entertainment industry. I think that something that does not go down well at all in the U.S.A. is this slightly dusty self-image that many German artists of my generation carry around with them: I am the genius of old Europe, I am unique and mysterious, and you should pay court to me.

When you relate so closely to religious thinking, it raises the question of moral derivatives. Do you not very quickly become involved in a link between morality and art that ultimately paralyzes artistic imagination?

Wallfahrtskirche Vierzehnheiligen mit ihrem überhöhten, unwirklichen Raumgefühl. Wir leben zwar in einer nachreligiösen Zeit, und Künstler sind nicht dasselbe wie Priester, aber das heisst doch nicht, dass wir auf Konzentration, starke und verbindliche Bilder und auratische Gegenstände verzichten müssen. Wir Künstler haben die Aufgabe, Erfahrungen zu konzentrieren, nicht nur alles vorbeirauschen zu lassen, sondern Sachen kontemplativ auf den Punkt zu bringen. Das ist ein Erbe aus der Religion.

An deiner Arbeit hat mich die Verbindung von religiösen Elementen mit Aspekten von Minimal Art und Pop Art immer fasziniert. Aber wenn du von Priestertum sprichst, siehst du da nicht die Gefahr der Selbstmystifizierung bei dir?

Nein, es geht mir nicht um Selbstmystifizierung. Alles, was bei der künstlerischen Arbeit mit Genie erklärt wird, ist mir verdächtig. Es geht vielmehr um Demut einerseits und eine professionelle Arbeitshaltung andererseits. Die Empfindung von Leere, die Begegnung mit nackter Existenz, die moderne Wahrnehmung von Nichts, dieses Geworfensein in bestimmte Umstände, denen wir als Künstler unsere Arbeit entgegensetzen – sich mit diesen Aspekten auseinanderzusetzen, heisst zwangsläufig, immer wieder in einer gewissen Ratlosigkeit zu beginnen. Und alle Lösungen, die man als Künstler findet, sind immer momentan und konkret. Sie gelten immer nur für die eine Arbeit, mit der man gerade beschäftigt ist. Dieses wortlose Nichtwissen ist eine grosse Freiheit, macht aber auch Angst. Es ist ambivalent. Ich glaube schon, dass man in meinen Arbeiten Momente von Existenzangst und Abgründigkeit finden kann, die ganz klar Folge dieses Lebens ohne Religion, ohne Gott sind. Der Augenblick der künstlerischen Konfrontation mit diesem Alleinsein ist eben eine individuelle und dunkle Erfahrung. Aus dieser Erfahrung dann einen genialischen Einsamkeitskult zu machen, ist natürlich Unsinn, weil man als Künstler ja gerade versucht, die eigenen Erfahrungen in seinen Arbeiten anderen mitzuteilen. Wenn du dich als Künstler konzentrierst, begegnest du keinem Genie, sondern dir selber. Und jeder Betrachter, der eine gute Arbeit anguckt, begegnet sich da auch selber.

«In meiner Kunst habe ich versucht, Erfahrungen so stark wie möglich zu konzentrieren. Dies befriedigt meine Bedürfnisse, und ich glaube kaum, dass ich eine Person mit solch einzigartigen Bedürfnissen bin, die andere Leute nicht haben.» Das hat Carl Andre gesagt.

Ja, so kann man das sagen.

Gut. Aber warum bringst du das mit Religion in Verbindung?

Weil ich den Künstlerberuf vor dem Hintergrund von Konzentration, auch einsamer Konzentration sehe. Das hat, rein von der Arbeitshaltung, auch einen Mönchsaspekt. Das heisst, dass ich als Künstler priviligiert bin, weil ich mich intensiv und konzentriert wie ein Mönch mit diesen existentiellen Dingen beschäftigen kann und dabei als Medium, das diese Dinge sichtbar macht, einen Sonderstatus habe. Das sollte sich jedoch mit einer demütigen Haltung verbinden. Denn letztendlich lebt jeder Mensch ein Leben im Bewusstsein des Todes, «in Sorge». Jeder begegnet auf seine Weise dem «schwarzen Loch». Deshalb sollte man den Künstlerberuf nicht mystifizieren und sich nicht aufspielen wie Markus Grössenwahn. In dem Augenblick, in dem er dazu benutzt wird, ein Star-Image zu fabrizieren, schlägt natürlich die Konzentration, von der ich spreche, um in ihr Gegenteil, in Unterhaltungsindustrie. Ich glaube, was z.B. in den USA überhaupt nicht ankommt, ist dieses leicht verstaubte Selbstbild, das manche deutsche Künstler meiner Generation mit sich herumtragen: Ich bin das alteuropäische Genie, ich bin einmalig und geheimnisvoll, und ich möchte hofiert werden.

Wenn du dich so deutlich auf religiöses Denken beziehst, stellt sich schnell die Frage nach moralischen Ableitungen. Gerätst du da nicht schnell in eine Verknüpfung von Moral und Kunst, die zum Schluss die künstlerische Phantasie lahmlegt?

Für mich ist das eine schwierig zu beantwortende Frage. Man muss, glaube ich, zwei Sachen auseinanderhalten. Für mich gehört zur Kultur, dass man einfach bestimmte Regeln beachtet, z.B. dass man nicht pfuscht, andere nicht betrügt oder fertigmacht und, in schlimmster Konsequenz, andere nicht tötet. Das sind einfach soziale Spielregeln. Das ist die eine Seite. Etwas anderes ist diese Begegnung mit der nackten Existenz, von der wir eben gesprochen haben, die Ratlosigkeit, die du als Künstler dabei empfindest. Die ist eigentlich vor jeder Moral oder jenseits von Gut und Böse. Dass man etwas wahrnimmt, dass man über etwas staunt, bevor man den Namen oder den Begriff dafür sagen kann – diese Erfahrungen sind vorsprachlich und vormoralisch. Und das ist die zweite Seite. Aus diesen Begegnungen mit der «anderen Seite» ergibt sich erstaunlicherweise eine Moral, die dann sichtbar wird, wenn ich eine Arbeit realisiere. Da gibt es bei der Arbeit an einer Skulptur ständig

That's a difficult question for me to answer. There are two things that I think have to be kept apart. For me it is part of culture that you simply hold by certain rules, for example that you don't botch things, betray other people or grind them down, and as the worst consequence, that you don't kill other people. These simply are social rules. That is one side. This confrontation with naked existence we've been talking about is something else, the helplessness that you feel as an artist here. This is actually outside any morality or beyond good and evil. The fact that you perceive something, that you are astonished about something before you can identify its name or concept – these experiences are outside language and morality. And that is the second side. But astonishingly enough, a morality does emerge from these confrontations with the "other side," and that becomes visible when I produce a work. Then there are constant decisions to be made when working on a sculpture – the right scale, the right color, a clear solution for the details, etc. – which have to be visible for others. That can also be seen as an image of a social structure.

You spoke earlier of the 1980s art boom. How do you rate current conditions for young artists in Germany?

The generation after me? It has definitely gotten more difficult, because there is less money available, both in the institutions and on the art market. But people are still very interested in becoming artists, the Düsseldorf Academy had over a thousand applicants this year. And the public continues to be interested in images as well. A great deal is perceived through images today, and less through reading. In purely theoretical terms that would be a sphere of activity for artists. But the flood of images in advertising and on television produces scarcely any new ideas for images. Most of what you can see on MTV or VIVA just repeats firmly established image types. Human types are fixed as well, how you should look, what you should wear, colors, movements. Most of it is frighteningly shallow. In the meantime the layout for most newspapers is done on the computer using graphics programs. This means that people no longer develop their own layout from first principles, but increasingly turn to stock material. It looks more and more boring. We artists should work hard to make images complex and surprising, whatever technique we use. It is simply a great deal to do with work and concentration, I find.

Perhaps digitally preserved things are not so much labor-saving devices as an involuntary loss of access to what is ostensibly available in the preserved matter. No renewal of pictorial ideas takes place, existing set-pieces are actually used only because no one has to take the trouble of first constructing the set-pieces again and then working through the precise relationship of the set-pieces to each other, the composition.

Yes. At the moment we know that it is coming, but so far is hasn't produced any new and powerful metaphors. Here a lot more could actually come out of it. The unreal phantasms associated with virtual space today remind me of Matthias Grünewald and Hieronymus Bosch, infinite spaces, this strange fitting together of disparate elements that produces monsters. Many visions of the future have these hybrid, monstrous undertones. These are the visions that constantly assail modern human beings: our idea of the world after the Middle Ages and after religion also means being lost, being at the mercy of a chaotic space. But things like that often can't be expressed as images by duplicating everything digitally.

But in the case of your Madonnas, your poodles, and your company at table, it is precisely the duplication of figures that has a large part to play. The tablecloth in Tischgesellschaft *(Company at Table) looks like a computer design. Were you aiming to translate the metaphor of virtual space into real sculptural space?*

That's coincidence. The pattern on the tablecloth in *Tischgesellschaft* (Company at Table) actually is a quite common tablecloth pattern. I drew the enlarged pattern onto one-millimeter-square graph paper by hand. The little steps were already there in the original. But a teacher once told me about his class looking at *Tischgesellschaft* (Company at Table) in the Frankfurt Museum. The children flipped out completely because they saw the pull into the depths exercised by this long table as a computer image, but it was quite real, there in front of them. I was interested in the nightmare quality of an individual figure suddenly sitting there in large numbers. You have to look, but at the same time your gaze slips away because of the large numbers. That is a horrifying image for me, too, identity dissolving in an infinite space.

You often work with duplications. You put the holy Mother of God, in other words that Catholic figure who is even more singular than the God of the Trinity, onto a shelf as a mass-produced article. Here the duplication seems to have a funny side to it.

Entscheidungen: das richtige Mass, die richtige Farbe, die klare Lösung der Details und so weiter, die für andere sichtbar sein müssen. Das kann man auch als Bild für ein soziales Gebilde sehen.

Du hast vorhin vom Kunstboom der achtziger Jahre gesprochen. Wie schätzt du die heutigen Bedingungen für junge Künstler in Deutschland ein?

Die Generation nach mir? Es ist auf jeden Fall schwieriger geworden, weil sowohl bei den Institutionen als auch im Kunstmarkt weniger Geld zur Verfügung steht. Das Interesse, Künstler zu werden, ist weiterhin gross, die Düsseldorfer Akademie hatte dieses Jahr über 1000 Bewerbungen. Und auch das Publikumsinteresse an Bildern ist weiterhin gross. Vieles wird heute über Bilder wahrgenommen, weniger durch Lesen. Das wäre rein theoretisch ein Betätigungsfeld für Künstler. Aber die Bilderflut in der Reklame und im Fernsehen bringt kaum irgendwelche neuen Bildideen hervor. Das meiste, was auf MTV oder VIVA zu sehen ist, wiederholt nur fest geprägte Bildtypen. Auch Menschentypen werden geprägt, wie man aussehen soll, was man anhat, Farben, Bewegungen. Das meiste ist erschreckend platt. Die Layouts der meisten Zeitschriften werden inzwischen mit Grafikprogrammen am Computer gemacht. Das führt dazu, dass die Leute gar nicht mehr von Grund auf ihr eigenes Layout entwickeln, sondern immer mehr auf Konserven zurückgreifen. Das sieht immer langweiliger aus. Wofür wir Künstler arbeiten müssen, ist, dass die Bilder, egal in welcher Technik, vielschichtig und überraschend sind. Es hat einfach viel mit Arbeit und Konzentration zu tun, finde ich.

Vielleicht sind digitale Konserven weniger eine Arbeitserleichterung als vielmehr ein unfreiwilliger Verlust des Zugriffs auf das, was angeblich in der Konserve vorrätig gehalten wird. Es findet keine Erneuerung der Bildideen statt, bestehende Versatzstücke werden eigentlich nur benutzt, weil sich niemand die Arbeit machen will, die Versatzstücke erst einmal wieder herzustellen und dann das genaue Verhältnis der Versatzstücke zueinander, die Komposition, durchzuarbeiten.

Ja. Im Moment ist es angesagt, aber es bringt bis jetzt keine neuen starken Metaphern hervor. Dabei könnte eigentlich mehr daraus werden. Die surrealen Phantasmen, die heute mit dem virtuellen Raum verbunden werden, erinnern mich an Matthias Grünewald und Hieronymus Bosch, endlose Räume, dieses seltsame Zusammenfügen disparater Elemente, das Monster entstehen lässt. Viele

Zukunftsvisionen haben ja diesen hybrid monströsen Unterton. Das sind die Visionen, die den neuzeitlichen Menschen immer wieder befallen: Unsere Vorstellung von der Welt nach dem Mittelalter und nach der Religion heisst auch Verlorensein, einem chaotischen Raum ausgeliefert sein. Aber so etwas lässt sich oft nicht dadurch als Bild ausdrücken, dass alles digital vervielfacht wird.

Andererseits spielt bei deinen Madonnen, bei den Pudeln und bei der Tischgesellschaft doch gerade die Vervielfältigung der Einzelfigur eine grosse Rolle. Die Tischdecke der «Tischgesellschaft» sieht aus wie ein Computerdesign. Ging es dir darum, die Metapher des virtuellen Raumes in den skulpturalen Realraum zu übersetzen?

Das ist Zufall. Das Muster der Tischdecke in «Tischgesellschaft» ist tatsächlich das Muster einer ganz normalen Tischdecke. Ich habe das Muster von Hand vergrössert auf Millimeterpapier gezeichnet. Die Treppchen gab es schon im Original. Aber mir hat einmal ein Lehrer erzählt, wie seine Schulklasse die «Tischgesellschaft» im Frankfurter Museum angeguckt hat. Die Schüler sind völlig ausgeflippt, weil sie den Sog in die Tiefe bei diesem langen Tisch wie ein Computerbild aufgefasst haben, das aber ganz real vor ihnen steht. Mir ging es um das Alptraumhafte, wenn plötzlich eine einzelne Figur vervielfacht dasitzt. Man muss hingucken, aber zugleich gleitet der Blick an dieser Vielzahl ab. Für mich selber ist das ein Schreckensbild, die Auflösung der Identität in einen unendlichen Raum.

Du arbeitest ja oft mit Vervielfältigung. Die heilige Muttergottes, also diejenige Gestalt im Katholizismus, die noch singulärer ist als der dreifaltige Gott, hast du als Massenartikel auf ein Regal gestapelt. Da scheint mir die Vervielfältigung eher etwas Witziges zu haben.

Erstmal ist die Madonna ja nur eine Gipsfigur, nicht Maria. Insofern ist die Gipsfigur genauso ein Ding wie eine Vase. Natürlich symbolisiert die Gipsfigur etwas, sogar etwas sehr Einmaliges. Die Einmaligkeit verschwindet in meiner Arbeit, aber im Grunde ist sie schon lange vorher verschwunden, in jedem Andenkenladen. Und das Seltsame ist jetzt, dass jeder einzelnen Gipsfigur auch in der Menge eine gewisse Aura erhalten bleibt.

Das wäre ja so etwas wie multiplizierte Aura.

Mir ging es um die Atmosphäre, die dieser strenge Typus des kleinen Götzenfigürchens einzeln oder als Massenprodukt erzeugt.

First, the Madonna is just a plaster figure, not Mary herself. To that extent the plaster figure is just as much a thing as a vase is. Of course the plaster figure symbolizes something, even something unique. The uniqueness disappears in my work, but essentially it disappeared long before, in every souvenir shop. And the strange thing now is that every individual plaster figure does retain a certain aura, even in quantity.

That would be something like a multiplied aura.

I was interested in the atmosphere that this austere type of small idol produces individually or as a mass product. Gary Garrels writes about Edward Hopper in his essay, and he asked me to choose one of Hopper's pictures. One that I mentioned was *August in the City*. It has such a peculiar light on a still summer's afternoon. You look into a window, and there is a small figure, lit in gold. The mood in this picture was one of the things that triggered me to work with this little porcelain figure. My Madonna figures with their matte, light yellow paint are banal objects, and at the same time they aren't. You can put five of them together and you can still see that this isn't the same as a Pritt Stick. You can see from the concrete form that it is also a spiritual structure.

A spiritual structure, but one that is also countered. On your department store display stand all those Marys look like an Ascension that is not taking off. In places like this I have the impression that the humorous is no longer funny, but grotesque. Your duplications, circular structures, and the frequent use of black also seem to me like metaphors for futility and hopelessness. One's eye is caught by this dense, black mass of trees in Museum, *a sort of crown of thorns. Does this black circle perhaps stand for entanglement or a subliminal threat as well?*

Well, that is true in the case of *Tischgesellschaft* (Company at Table) – that is a symbol of hopelessness for me. But *Museum* is an image of hope for me. The wood is black at the top but underneath there are paths. What this sculpture shows would be in reality that you are going through a dark wood and then see something gold glittering beyond the dark bushes. You are attracted by this point, you come into the open space and then see *Museum* as a phenomenon.

What about the poodles? They are an unpleasant pack, but they look ridiculous at the same time.

No, for me that is one of the tragic works that don't offer a solution, but an experience.

It's strange how you recycle Christian iconography – Mary or the Christ Child among the poodles don't stand for hope, but for disturbance and a feeling of insecurity.

If you wish you can see my works as metaphors for certain fundamental experiences in life. There are situations in which you think you are completely in a fix and then you get out of it again. The Christ Child with star amidst the poodles shows a moment at being completely at the mercy of others. There are moments like this in my life, moments when you feel quite powerless, and have become constrained. The possibility of threat starts at birth. The child with a circle of poodles around it is a claustrophobic, negative image.

I find it easier to characterize the black poodles spontaneously as hostile or insolent than I do to describe the rats in Rattenkönig (Rat-King) *at all. Why do animals crop up so frequently in your work?*

A certain symbolism or general idea is associated with many animals: mice are smart, elephants are majestic and do not forget anything for decades, etc. This addresses behavior patterns and qualities that can be used to characterize human beings as well. But when I use animals to avoid any sort of individualizing psychology and to still make more profound atmospheric elements visible. A second aspect is that animals are perhaps not comic in themselves, but because we think we can see human qualities in animals their behavior seems funny to us. All those poodles around the newborn child do not represent a threat, but, if you look at individual poodles in the group for cowardice, this is again comic. Something else that appeals to me is the idea that you could change yourself into an animal. This idea is also my access to the animals as I show them. I never show them as biological entities, as a genus. I am very fond of animals as natural creatures, and here there is absolutely no element of psychological insecurity for me. But if I take the idea of a human being changing into an animal, or the character qualities and symbolism that human beings ascribe to them, then that becomes interesting for a sculpture. I don't find rats at all repulsive as animals. But when I thought about my project for the Dia Center in New York, it was clear to me that the symbolism of the rat – the will to survive, aggressiveness, a

Gary Garrels schreibt in seinem Text über Edward Hopper, und er hat mich gebeten, ein Bild von Hopper auszusuchen. Ich habe ihm u.a. «August in the City» genannt. Es hat so ein merkwürdiges Licht an einem stillen Sommernachmittag. Man guckt in ein Fenster hinein, und da steht eine kleine, golden beleuchtete Figur. Die Stimmung in diesem Bild war einer der Auslöser für mich, mit dieser kleinen Nippesfigur zu arbeiten. Meine Madonnenfiguren mit ihrem matten hellgelben Anstrich sind banale Gegenstände, und zugleich sind sie es nicht. Man kann auch fünf nebeneinanderstellen, und man sieht immer noch, das ist nicht dasselbe wie ein Pritt-Stift. Der konkreten Gestalt sieht man an, es ist auch ein geistiges Gebilde.

Ein geistiges Gebilde, das aber konterkariert wird. Auf ihrem Kaufhausgestell sehen die vielen Marias aus wie eine Himmelfahrt, die nicht abhebt. An solchen Stellen habe ich den Eindruck, das Komische ist plötzlich nicht mehr lustig, sondern grotesk. Mir kommen die Vervielfältigungen, Ringstrukturen und das häufige Schwarz bei dir auch wie Metaphern für Vergeblichkeit und Ausweglosigkeit vor. In dieser dichten schwarzen Masse von Bäumen beim «Museum», so einer Art Dornenkrone, bleibt man mit dem Blick hängen. Steht dieser schwarze Ring vielleicht auch für Verstrickung oder unterschwellige Bedrohung?

Also, bei der «Tischgesellschaft» trifft das zu, die ist für mich ein Symbol der Ausweglosigkeit. Aber das «Museum» ist ein Hoffnungsbild für mich. Der Wald ist oben schwarz, aber unten gibt es die Wege. Was diese Skulptur zeigt, wäre in Wirklichkeit so, dass man durch einen dunklen Wald geht und dann hinter den dunklen Büschen schon etwas Goldenes glitzern sieht. Man wird angezogen von diesem Punkt, man kommt auf die Freifläche und sieht dann das «Museum» wie eine Erscheinung, das ist mir wichtig.

Wie ist das bei den Pudeln? Sie sind eine unangenehme Meute, aber zugleich wirken sie lächerlich.

Nein, «Kind mit Pudeln» ist für mich eine der traurigen Arbeiten, die keine Lösung anbieten, sondern eine Erfahrung wiedergeben.

Seltsam, wie du die christliche Ikonographie recyclest – Maria oder das Christuskind inmitten der Pudel stehen nicht für Hoffnung, sondern für Irritation und Verunsicherung.

Wenn man will, kann man meine Arbeiten als Metaphern für bestimmte Grunderfahrungen im Leben ansehen. Es gibt die Situation, in der du denkst, du sitzt total in der Klemme, und dann kommst du doch wieder heraus, und es gibt Situationen, aus denen kommst du nicht wieder heraus. Das Christkind mit dem Stern inmitten der Pudel zeigt den Moment des völligen Ausgeliefertseins. Solche Momente gibt es manchmal in meinem Leben, Momente, in denen man Ohnmacht empfindet, in Zwänge geraten ist. Mögliche Bedrohung beginnt bei der Geburt. Das Kind umzingelt von den Pudeln ist ein klaustrophobisches, negatives Bild.

Die schwarzen Pudel spontan als feindlich oder frech zu charakterisieren finde ich leichter als die Ratten in «Rattenkönig» überhaupt zu beschreiben. Warum kommen in deiner Arbeiten so häufig Tiere vor?

Mit vielen Tieren ist eine bestimmte Symbolik oder allgemeine Vorstellung verbunden: die Maus ist pfiffig, der Elefant ist majestätisch und vergisst über Jahrzehnte nichts usw.. Damit sind Verhaltensweisen und Eigenschaften angesprochen, mit denen man auch Menschen charakterisieren kann. Wenn ich aber Tiere nehme, vermeide ich jede individualisierende Psychologie und kann trotzdem tieferliegende atmosphärische Momente sichtbar machen. Der zweite Aspekt ist: Tiere sind vielleicht nicht von selber komisch, aber weil wir menschliche Eigenschaften in Tieren wiederzuerkennen glauben, wirkt ihr Verhalten komisch für uns. Die vielen Pudel um das Neugeborene herum stehen nicht für Bedrohung, sondern, wenn man den einzelnen Pudel in dieser Riesenanzahl betrachtet, für Feigheit, die dann wieder eher komisch ist. Was mich ausserdem reizt, ist die Vorstellung, dass man sich in ein Tier verwandeln könnte. Diese Vorstellung ist eigentlich auch mein Zugang zu den Tieren, so wie ich sie zeige. Ich zeige sie ja nie als biologische Wesen, als Gattung. Als natürliche Lebewesen mag ich Tiere sehr gerne und da fehlt für mich jedes Element von psychischer Verunsicherung. Wenn ich aber die Vorstellung der menschlichen Verwandlung in ein Tier nehme, oder die Charaktereigenschaften und die Symbolik, die der Mensch ihnen zuordnet, dann wird das für eine Skulptur interessant. Eine Ratte ist für mich überhaupt kein Ekeltier. Aber als ich in New York über mein Projekt für das Dia Center nachgedacht habe, wurde mir klar, dass die Symbolik der Ratte – Überlebenswille, Aggressivität, eine gewisse Ruchlosigkeit – gut zu New York passt. Für den «Rattenkönig» war diese Symbolik der Ausgangspunkt, aus dem sich die skulpturalen

certain ruthlessness – suits New York very well. For *Rattenkönig* (Rat- King) this symbolism was the starting point from which the sculptural figures then emerged: the strict circular shape, the knot at the center of the circle.

Why do the rats not have genitals?

It's difficult to see whether a rat is male or female in nature. It all disappears into the fur.

But you are not relating to rats as natural creatures. And so why is there no sign of sexuality on this symbolic "rat"?

Even if the genitals were easily recognizable in rats in nature I would have left them out in my sculpture because formally it would have weighted things wrongly to depict the biological anatomy literally. I was lucky enough to get hold of a mold of a cow elephant for the Krefeld elephant that seemed considerably more discreet to me than a bull elephant. Emphasizing the genitals would have given the whole work a completely different theme, and one in which I was not at all interested. Even the baby surrounded by poodles is, in fact, sexless. I find hermaphrodites interesting. The contrasting roles of "man" and "woman" soon bring one into contexts of meaning that simply drown out the vague qualities of atmosphere and situation with which I work. I am concerned with basic ideas, and here I am certainly in the minimal art tradition. A vase is first and foremost an object, not a man and not a woman. And with animals I am interested in the ambivalent symbolism in which we reflect our human qualities. Unambiguous membership of a particular sex would reduce this ambivalence, make the mirror smaller, as it were. If the viewer makes a distinction between male and female at the first or second glance that's all right, it's just that I don't lay that down definitely. The viewer can perhaps see the baby as a threatened creature and therefore female, and the pack of dogs perhaps as male. But with the poodles the large numbers were more important, this hairy, black, nasty mass. I was definitely thinking of pubic hair in the case of these black, tousled poodles' coats, and of course this contrasts with the small, smooth, innocent white baby, but it doesn't separate "male" and "female," it just brings them into play.

The animals seem funny to me as well. In Mann und Maus *(Man and Mouse) you enlarged the mouse. That seems threatening, but you have to laugh at the same time.*

Yes, the enlargement is important, and so is the fact that the roles are reversed in terms of the tradition of this motif. Normally the woman is lying in or on the bed. In Füssli's case a hairy, essentially male monster is sitting on the woman's chest. In *Mann und Maus* (Man and Mouse) the man is lying underneath, but the whole thing remains an image of despair, of the kind of oppressive nightmare that I sometimes have. You wake up because you feel that something is weighing you down, sitting on top of you. The giant mouse is a joke, of course, but I think that it has a lot to do with the way in which relationships between men and women work in my generation. To that extent the whole image has something to do with relationships between men and women, with failed relationships involving love. Often men are very passive in this respect, and women very active – and women suffer from the men's passivity. The men wait, while the women run after them. That is of course an unfortunate aspect of our society; the men withdraw increasingly, and the whole thing is funny in a sad sort of way. The man lies in bed, awake, with his eyes closed: I am white and innocent and I'm also not making an effort – actually pretty mean. The poor, heavy, fat mouse is sitting on him with its little eyes open, wide awake, and could actually crush him to bits, but it doesn't want to. What the mouse is, its size and superior strength, in contrast with the man's feeble condition – that is an image of a completely unbalanced relationship in which two people are missing each other completely. It's a terrible image, but I find it funny as well.

Laughter often expresses the fact that we don't know what we are supposed to think about something.

Yes, exactly, and that amuses me, too. We say "little mouse" or "mousikins," but then the little mouse is a great monster like this. I've just changed the scale, and suddenly the whole thing tilts, and it is funny, but disturbing as well. Actually a "little mouse" is sweet and cute, and then it crushes you to death. I was very pleased with the way Bice Curiger reacted when she saw the work in my studio for the first time. She shouted out, half laughing, "Help, mummy, get down!" That was a wonderful reaction, it hit the nail on the head. There are dear creatures that can be pretty oppressive.

You've chosen an essay by Heinrich von Kleist for the catalogue, About the Marionette Theater, *dating back to 1810. Why?*

Fragen dann ergeben haben: die strenge Kreisform, der Knoten in der Mitte des Kreises.

Warum haben die Ratten keine Geschlechtsteile?

In Natura ist es sehr schwierig zu sehen, ob eine Ratte männlich oder weiblich ist. Das veschwindet im Fell.

Aber du beziehst dich doch gar nicht auf die Ratte als natürliches Lebewesen. Warum fehlt dem Symboltier «Ratte» jedes Geschlechtsmerkmal?

Selbst wenn bei Ratten in der Natur die Geschlechtsmerkmale gut zu erkennen wären, hätte ich sie für meine Skulptur weggelassen, weil es formal eine falsche Gewichtung erzeugt hätte, die biologische Anatomie wörtlich abzubilden. Für den Elefanten in Krefeld habe ich günstigerweise eine Gussform von einer Elefantenkuh auftreiben können, was mir viel diskreter erschien als ein Abguss von einem Elefantenbullen. Betonte Geschlechtsteile hätten der ganzen Arbeit ein neues Thema gegeben, um das es mir überhaupt nicht ging. Sogar das Baby inmitten der Pudel ist eigentlich geschlechtslos. Ich finde Zwitter interessant. Mit den Rollengegensatz «Mann» und «Frau» kommt man schnell in Bedeutungszusammenhänge, die das vage Atmosphärische und Situative, an dem ich arbeite, einfach übertönen. Mir geht es um Grundvorstellungen, da stehe ich sicher in der Tradition von Minimal Art. Eine Vase ist erst einmal ein Gegenstand, keine Frau und kein Mann. Und bei Tieren interessiert mich die ambivalente Symbolik, in der wir unsere menschlichen Eigenschaften spiegeln. Eine eindeutige Geschlechtszugehörigkeit würde diese Ambivalenz reduzieren, den Spiegel sozusagen verkleinern. Wenn der Betrachter auf den zweiten oder dritten Blick in männlich oder weiblich unterscheidet, ist das in Ordnung, nur gebe ich das von mir aus nicht eindeutig vor: Das Baby als bedrohtes Wesen kann ein Betrachter vielleicht als weiblich ansehen, die Pudelmeute vielleicht als männlich. Bei den Pudeln war mir aber die Menge wichtig, diese haarige, schwarze, fiese Masse. Bei diesem schwarzen, gekräuselten Pudelfell, das in der Skulptur angedeutet ist, habe ich durchaus an Schamhaar gedacht und das kontrastiert natürlich mit dem kleinen, glattweissen, unschuldigen Baby, aber es trennt nicht «männlich» oder «weiblich», sondern bringt das ins Spiel.

Auf mich wirken die Tiere auch komisch. Bei «Mann und Maus» hast du die Maus vergrössert. Das wirkt bedrohlich und zugleich muss man lachen.

Ja, die Vergrösserung ist wichtig, und dass die Rollen gegenüber der Tradition dieses Motivs vertauscht sind. Normalerweise liegt die Frau im oder auf dem Bett. Bei Füssli sitzt dann so ein haariges, eher männliches Ungeheuer auf der Brust der Frau. Bei «Mann und Maus» liegt der Mann unten, aber das Ganze bleibt ein Bild der Verzweiflung, des Alpdrucks, den ich nachts manchmal empfinde. Man wacht auf, weil man das Gefühl hat, irgend etwas lastet auf einem, sitzt auf einem drauf. Diese Riesenmaus ist natürlich ein Witz, aber ich denke, dass sie viel mit der Art und Weise zu tun hat, wie Beziehungen zwischen Mann und Frau in meiner Generation funktionieren. Insofern hat das ganze Bild natürlich mit den Beziehungen zwischen Mann und Frau zu tun, mit gescheiterten Liebesbeziehungen. Oft sind die Männer in Beziehungen sehr passiv, die Frauen sehr aktiv – und die Frauen leiden unter der Passivität der Männer. Die Männer warten ab, die Frauen laufen den Männern hinterher. Das ist in unserer Gesellschaft natürlich ein Unglück, die Männer entziehen sich immer mehr, das Ganze ist auf eine traurige Art witzig. Der Mann liegt im Bett, wach, hat die Augen zu: ich bin weiss und unschuldig, und ausserdem strenge ich mich nicht an – eigentlich ziemlich gemein. Die arme, dicke, fette Maus sitzt mit aufgerissenen Äuglein auf ihm, hellwach, und könnte ihn eigentlich zerquetschen, aber das will sie ja gar nicht. Was sie ist, ihre Grösse und Übermacht, dagegen der schlappe Zustand, in dem der Mann ist – das ist das Bild einer völlig unausgewogenen Beziehung, in der zwei Leute einander total verfehlen. Das ist ein schreckliches Bild, aber ich finde es auch zum Lachen.

Lachen ist oft einfach der Ausdruck dafür, dass man nicht weiss, was man von einer Sache halten soll.

Ja, genau, und das macht mir selber auch Spass. Man sagt «kleine Maus» oder «Mausi», aber dann ist die Mausi so ein grosses Ungeheuer. Ich habe nur den Massstab verändert, und auf einmal kippt die ganze Sache, es ist irgendwie zum Lachen, aber auch irritierend. Eigentlich ist eine «Mausi» süss und niedlich, und dann drückt sie dich tot. Mir hat gut gefallen, wie die Bice Curiger reagiert hat, als sie die Arbeit zum ersten Mal bei mir im Atelier gesehen hat. Sie hat halb lachend aufgeschrien: «Hilfe, Mutti, geh´ runter!» Das war eine tolle Reaktion, genau ins Schwarze. Es gibt liebe Wesen, die ziemlich erdrückend sein können.

Für den Katalog hast du einen Text von Heinrich von Kleist ausgewählt, «Über das Marionettentheater» von 1810. Warum?

It's been said that Kleist is the first modern human being. In any case he was one of the first to verbalize our modern experience of being uprooted, this awareness of life as homelessness, that you'll never really manage to start a family, that social cohesion is breaking down completely, and that certain aims in life like jobs and having a partner are completely at odds with each other. I do not live in the place I want to live in. I have to do thousands of things that I actually don't want to do. Having a relationship and a family isn't simple anyway, but it's becoming less and less taken for granted. Kleist simply never managed to build up workable relationships. I think Kleist suffered from the illness that a lot of people have today, a profound emotional insecurity – as though he was always looking for truth in emotions and intuitions. His characters in stories and plays, e.g. Kätchen von Heilbronn, sometimes act on the basis of definite emotional certainties. And I think that Kleist did not have such certainties himself, and that is precisely what a lot of people have lost, this ability to trust one's own intuition. He was already carrying the difficulties we have today inside himself. And he made all this profound self-doubt artistically productive.

Quite apart from biographical aspects, Kleist also shows a profound mistrust of the theoretical explicability of life as we experience it, and especially of the explicability of artistic experience.

Yes, that's important to me. Kleist talks about precisely this element into which observers have to allow themselves to be drawn. Grace emerges either from total consciousness or total unconsciousness. As an artist you have to act very consciously to be able to reconstruct this unconscious moment. If I stay in the middle I'm with the people who are didactic about art. All that happens there is that everything is explained. But explaining in itself is not neutral. Art that struggles to be explicable is not natural, but "willed." And Kleist puts it so well by saying that this dancer dances so badly because her soul is in the small of her back. But the marionette does not have a soul, and so it dances much more beautifully. It does not think, it does not feel. The bear that Kleist mentions always moves properly, it always fights properly, it can do nothing wrong because unlike human beings it always reacts intuitively. Either God or animal, infinite consciousness and the completely unconscious, I find that interesting.

The astonishment and fear you keep talking about sound like a theme of original sin in Kleist. The Tree of Knowledge defines the problem of falling out with oneself at the moment at which one perceives something intensely, recognizes it, and at the same time notices that one is recognizing something. At the moment when we observe ourselves recognizing something, we are no longer at one with ourselves.

Exactly, paradise lost. And that is an artistic problem for me. In fact working artistically includes both: the naïve, powerful impulse and then the long and difficult way to reconstructing the directness and immediacy of the first impulse very artificially. I see something, that is the moment of vision, of forgetting yourself totally. But then comes the artistic work, which is a reconstruction. How do I reconstruct the image? How do I make my experiences comprehensible to others? I have pulled a thorn out of the sole of my foot, I wasn't thinking about it much while I was doing it, but it was the moment. How do I reconstruct that? That is the actual work, that every dancer, actor, or fine artist has to do. Reconstructing so consciously that it again seems uninhibitedly immediate and natural, acquiring the greatest possible naturalness from the greatest possible artificiality, acquiring a quality of being taken for granted that means an image is correct within itself again. That is how I would describe my working method, and I think the working method of other artists as well, Jeff Wall, for example. There are always protracted periods of thought, concealed quotations, long motif traditions, a great deal of technical effort, and that leads to sights that seem natural straight away. Of course for me as for other artists there is always the one or the other work where this natural expressiveness simply hasn't come off, but that doesn't change anything about the fundamental working method. It's wonderful to bring off this quality of directness in a work.

Über Kleist ist gesagt worden, er sei der erste moderne Mensch. Jedenfalls war er einer der ersten, die unsere moderne Erfahrung von Entwurzelung zur Sprache gebracht haben, dieses Lebensgefühl von Heimatlosigkeit, dass man es nicht schafft, wirklich eine Familie zu gründen, dass sich der soziale Zusammenhalt überhaupt auflöst, dass verschiedene Lebensziele wie Beruf und Partnerschaft so scharf gegeneinander stehen. Ich wohne nicht an dem Ort, an dem ich wohnen will. Tausend Sachen muss ich erledigen, die ich eigentlich nicht machen will. Eine Beziehung und eine Familie zu haben ist sowieso nicht einfach, aber in unserer Generation ist das noch weniger selbstverständlich geworden. Kleist hat es einfach nie geschafft, tragfähige Beziehungen aufzubauen. Ich glaube, Kleist hatte die Krankheit, die heute viele Leute haben, eine tiefe emotionale Unsicherheit. Also suchte er immer in den Emotionen, in der Intuition den Punkt der Wahrheit. Seine Figuren in den Erzählungen und Dramen, z.B. das Kätchen von Heilbronn, handeln manchmal aus ganz festen emotionalen Gewissheiten heraus. Und ich glaube, solche Gewissheiten hatte Kleist selber nicht, und das ist eben das, was vielen Menschen verloren gegangen ist, dieses Vertrauen-Können auf die eigene Intuition. Er hat die Schwierigkeiten von uns Heutigen schon in sich getragen. Und er hat alle diese tiefen Selbstzweifel künstlerisch produktiv gemacht.

Abgesehen von biographischen Aspekten gibt es bei Kleist auch eine starkes Misstrauen gegen die theoretische Erklärbarkeit unseres Erfahrungslebens und besonders gegen die Erklärbarkeit künstlerischer Erfahrung.

Ja, das ist mir wichtig. Kleist redet genau über diesen Moment, auf den sich der Betrachter einlassen muss. Grazie entsteht entweder durch das total Unbewusste oder das total Bewusste. Als Künstler muss man sehr bewusst vorgehen, um diesen unbewussten Moment rekonstruieren zu können. Wenn ich in der Mitte stehen bleibe, dann bin ich bei den Kunstdidaktikern. Da wird nämlich alles nur erklärt. Aber das Erklären selber ist nicht neutral. Eine Kunst, die sich abmüht, erklärbar zu sein, ist misslungen. Und da sagt Kleist so schön, diese Tänzerin tanzt so schlecht, denn ihr sitzt die Seele im Kreuz. Die Marionette dagegen hat keine Seele, die tanzt deshalb viel schöner. Sie denkt nicht, sie fühlt nicht. Der Bär, den Kleist erwähnt, bewegt sich immer richtig, er fechtet einfach immer richtig, der kann nichts falsch machen, weil er anders als der Mensch immer intuitiv reagiert. Entweder Gott oder Tier, unendliches Bewusstsein und das völlig Unbewusste, das finde ich interessant.

Das Staunen und Erschrecken, von dem du immer wieder sprichst, klingt bei Kleist als Erbsündenthema an. Der Baum der Erkenntnis bezeichnet das Problem der Selbstentzweiung in dem Moment, in dem man etwas intensiv wahrnimmt, erkennt und dabei bemerkt, dass man etwas erkennt. In dem Moment, in dem man sich selber beim Erkennen beobachtet, ist man nicht mehr bei sich.

Genau, der Verlust des Paradieses. Und das ist für mich ein künstlerisches Problem. Das künstlerische Arbeiten umfasst nämlich beides: den naiven, starken Impuls und dann den langen mühevollen Weg, die Direktheit und Unmittelbarkeit des ersten Impulses sehr künstlich zu rekonstruieren. Ich sehe etwas, das ist der Moment der Vision, des total sich selbst Vergessens. Dann kommt aber die künstlerische Arbeit, die eine Rekonstruktion ist. Wie rekonstruiere ich das Bild in allen kleinen formalen Entscheidungen? Wie mache ich meine Erfahrungen für andere nachvollziehbar? Ich habe mir einen Dorn aus der Fusssohle gezogen, mir währenddessen nicht sehr viel gedacht, es war aber der Moment. Wie rekonstruiere ich das? Das ist die eigentliche Arbeit, die jeder Tänzer, Schauspieler oder bildende Künstler hat. So bewusst rekonstruieren, dass es wieder unbefangen unmittelbar und natürlich wirkt, und über die grösste Künstlichkeit zur grössten Natürlichkeit finden, zu einer Selbstverständlichkeit, dass ein Bild in sich wieder stimmt. So würde ich meine Arbeitsweise beschreiben, und ich glaube auch die Arbeitsweise von anderen Künstlern, z.B. Jeff Wall. Da gibt es immer langwierige Überlegungen, verdeckte Zitate, längere Motivtraditionen, einen sehr grossen technischen Aufwand und das führt zu Anblicken, die auf Anhieb selbstverständlich erscheinen. Natürlich gibt es bei mir wie bei anderen Künstlern immer die eine oder die andere Arbeit, wo das Selbstverständliche des Ausdrucks einfach nicht geglückt ist, aber das ändert nichts an der grundsätzlichen Arbeitsweise. Wenn einem diese Direktheit in einer Arbeit gelingt, das ist toll.

Theodora Vischer

Des Pudels Kern –
the Heart of the Matter*
Thoughts on the work of
Katharina Fritsch

Des Pudels Kern
Überlegungen zum Werk
von Katharina Fritsch

AN IMAGE OF DISTANCE[1]

The first public presentation of works by Katharina Fritsch was in 1981, in the form of *Werbeblatt I* (Advertising Leaflet I). In the previous year she had taken part in the Düsseldorf Academy's annual exhibition of students' work, called *Rundgang* (Walk Round), for which she set up a few objects on and around a table (fig. 8).[2] But with *Werbeblatt I* the 25-year-old artist had created a platform for herself that she could handle precisely as she wished. She had been asked by friends from the music scene if she would make a contribution to their magazine. She designed the *Werbeblatt* (pl. 1, cat. 24), with the intention of having it stapled into the magazine as a four-page, black-and-white insert. Two works were depicted on each page, together with short descriptions, prices and order numbers.[3]

The occasion for the second carefully prepared presentation was her first individual exhibition in the Galerie Rüdiger Schöttle in Munich, which took place in 1984. By this time a substantial group of objects was in existence, but they were all on a very small scale, so Katharina Fritsch designed *Warengestell* (Display Stand, pl. 2, cat. 40). This was a round stand with four aluminium supports and five glass shelves, on which she arranged a total of twelve objects. The way in which the objects were allotted to shelves turned out to be just as carefully thought through as their precise placing on the sheets of glass.[4] The open arrangement and the transparency of the shelves meant that all the objects were easy to see.

While working on *Warengestell*, Katharina Fritsch was invited to take part in the major group exhibition called *von hier aus* (from here onward), in which Kasper König investigated contemporary artistic work in Germany (the former West Germany), and evaluated its current position. The exhibition was held in a trade fair hall in Düsseldorf, for which interior designer Hermann Czech designed different pavilions, not unlike the exhibition architecture for the first World Fairs. The work *Acht Tische mit acht Gegenständen* (Eight Tables with Eight Objects), which Katharina Fritsch conceived for this exhibition (pl. 3, cat. 48) looks like a companion piece – but a companion piece adapted for a public place – to *Warengestell*. Eight objects created since 1981 were placed on the octagonal surface created by pushing the tables together, all clearly larger and apparently more bulky than the objects on *Warengestell*. The table is only about 30 in. high, so that it is possible to take everything in easily despite its large area.

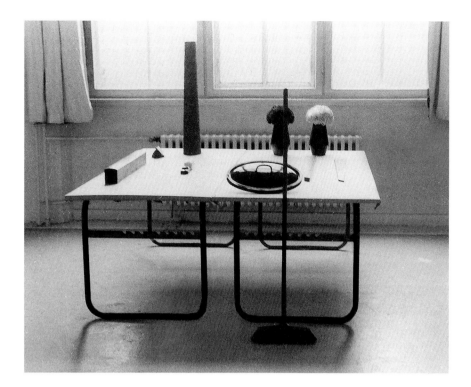

EIN BILD VON FERNE[1]

Die erste öffentliche Präsentation von Werken von Katharina Fritsch erfolgte 1981 in Form des «Werbeblattes I». Ein Jahr zuvor hatte sie im Rahmen der Düsseldorfer Akademie an der jährlichen, «Rundgang» genannten Ausstellung der Studentenarbeiten teilgenommen, anlässlich der sie einige Gegenstände auf und um einen Tisch aufgebaut hatte (Abb. 8).[2] Mit dem «Werbeblatt I» dagegen hatte sich die junge, 25-jährige Künstlerin eine Plattform geschaffen, die sie ganz und gar selber inszenieren konnte. Sie war von Freunden aus der Musikszene angefragt worden, für deren Zeitschrift eine Beilage beizusteuern. Sie entwarf darauf das «Werbeblatt I» (Taf. 1, Kat. 24), das als vierseitiges, schwarz-weisses Faltblatt in die Zeitschrift eingeheftet werden sollte. Auf jeder Seite waren zwei Arbeiten abgebildet und mit Kurzangaben, Preis und Bestellnummer versehen.[3]

Anlass für die zweite, sorgfältig inszenierte Präsentation war die erste Einzelausstellung in der Galerie Rüdiger Schöttle in München, die 1984 stattfand. Bis zu diesem Zeitpunkt war eine stattliche Gruppe von Objekten entstanden, von denen jedes jedoch nur geringe Ausmasse besass. Katharina Fritsch entwarf darauf das «Warengestell» (Taf. 2, Kat. 40), ein rundes Gestell aus vier Aluminiumstützen und fünf Glasetagen, auf denen sie insgesamt zwölf Gegenstände ausbreitete. Die Aufteilung der Gegen-

stände in die Regale erwies sich dabei als ebenso durchdacht wie ihre präzise Plazierung auf den Glasplatten.[4] Die lockere Auslegung und die Transparenz der Regale bewirkten eine optische Verfügbarkeit der Gegenstände.

Während der Arbeit am «Warengestell» erhielt Katharina Fritsch die Einladung zur Teilnahme an der wichtigen Gruppenausstellung «von hier aus», in der Kasper König eine Untersuchung und Standortbestimmung des zeitgenössischen Kunstschaffens in Deutschland (der ehemaligen BRD) unternahm. Ort der Ausstellung war eine Messehalle in Düsseldorf, für deren Innenarchitektur Hermann Czech verschiedenartige Pavillons entwarf, nicht unähnlich den Ausstellungsarchitekturen der ersten Weltausstellungen. Wie ein Pendant – allerdings ein dem öffentlichen Ort angepasstes Pendant – zum «Warengestell» nimmt sich die Arbeit «Acht Tische mit acht Gegenständen» aus, die Katharina Fritsch für diese Ausstellung konzipiert hat (Taf. 3, Kat 48). Auf der achteckigen, zusammengesetzten Tischfläche stehen acht Objekte, die seit 1981 entstanden waren und von denen fast alle deutlich grösser sind und massiger wirken als die Gegenstände auf dem «Warengestell». Der Tisch ist nur 75 cm hoch, so dass er trotz seiner Grösse gut überblickt werden kann.

Mit dem «Werbeblatt», dem «Warengestell» und den «Acht Tischen mit acht Gegenständen» hat Katharina Fritsch Möglichkeiten

Werbeblatt I, Warengestell and *Acht Tische mit acht Gegenständen* are opportunities that Katharina Fritsch has created for showing individual objects in a visitor-friendly way. The design and titles of the works demonstrate in an even more concrete way that this showing involves offering goods for sale. The fact that Katharina Fritsch's works were goods was also repeatedly discussed. But as well as being a way of presenting work attractively, these devices were demarcation devices as well. Thus the *Werbeblatt I* takes the contribution by and about Katharina Fritsch away from the context of the magazine. *Warengestell* and the *Acht Tische mit acht Gegenständen* represent a kind of exhibition in an exhibition, and they do this so effectively that the artist decided to do without an exhibition pavilion of her own in *von hier aus*: she placed her work in a zone between the clearly defined exhibition galleries. Establishing boundaries between art and reality using three-dimensional objects has been a frequent and fertile subject for discussion in 20th century art since Duchamp. Suddenly, boundaries that had hitherto been undisputed were negotiable, opened up, extended, redrawn or completely blurred. The idea of extending boundaries became central again in the eighties, in the work of artists like Jeff Koons, Haim Steinbach, Sherrie Levine or Fischli/Weiss. And so it is all the more striking when Katharina Fritsch creates new forms of drawing borders for her objects from the very beginning, and very definitely.

Ten years after *Acht Tische mit acht Gegenständen* (Eight Tables with Eight Objects) Katharina Fritsch started work on a project that was once more based on the concept of an octagonal basic area for presenting objects. I mean *Museum, Modell 1:10* (Museum, Model 1:10), which was set up at the 1995 Venice Biennale in the main gallery in the German Pavilion (pl. 21, cat. 100).[5] It is true that Biennale participants come from all over the world and that the exhibition is on a much larger scale than in Düsseldorf in 1984, but the two situations are comparable. As it had been ten years before, the occasion was a group exhibition with various unpredictable contributions and, as then, the exhibition architecture in Venice was made up of individual pavilions. In *Museum, Modell 1:10* the area, which is about 1 3/4 yards high and over eleven yards in diameter, cannot be taken in all at once. With some persistence it is possible to gain an impression of what is happening in this area and at the center of it. In the early examples the demarcation process (in the form of the advertising leaflet, the glass shelves and the table) went hand in hand with the

fact that all the objects could be assimilated, but in *Museum, Modell 1:10* it is immediately clear how difficult it is even to imagine what the work is actually about. *Museum, Modell 1:10* is not an architectural model in the classical sense, showing the design to be realized in a readily understandable way. It is a sculpture whose statement is experienced in contemplation. Hence the enormous dimensions, which can have been realized only with great effort. If this were an ordinary model its size would make no sense, but it is only through that size that the sculptural potential of the model can become reality (fig. 9).

When standing in front of the base one can imagine that the difficulty presented by its height is not dissimilar to the difficulty in which you would find yourself when going into the woods. The absolute uniformity of the trees and the darkness of the wood would make it more difficult to establish a sense of direction and find the way to the center after a certain amount of effort. The place of presentation is to be found only in the center; once it was called a display stand, now it is defined as a museum. Just as octagons and the number 8 have repeatedly cropped up in Katharina Fritsch's work since 1982,[6] the museum's color design also relates to the artist's previous output in a concrete way. For example, the glass, gold, and silver of the outer skin are also found in *Warengestell* (glass shelves), in the series of color paintings (gold frames, cat. 82-93) or in the *Lexikonzeichnungen* (Lexicon Drawings: silver frames, cat. 104-112) as design devices that frame or create boundaries. The colors of the glass walls inside the upper floor of the museum take up the colors of the *Acht Bilder in acht Farben* (Eight Paintings in Eight Colors, 1990/91, cat. 93) in the same sequence; Katharina Fritsch brought all the colors she had used so far together in this work. The museum is empty, and has to be, as here the artist is emphatically concerned with the difficulty of reaching the objects – she is talking about "staging inaccessibility" here, and about an "image of distance"[7] – not about the objects themselves.[8] Something that began to appear in the early examples in the early eighties, the desire to create demarcated zones, has become a wonderful and daring manifesto in *Museum, Modell 1:10*, in which the wish appears as a necessity.[9]

An essay by Katharina Fritsch on the *Museum* was published in the small brochure that appeared for the Biennale.[10] This also discusses the kind of objects and works of art that can be shown in a place of this kind: they are works of art by "artists interested in identity, not in art-historical, in-house speculations, in cynicism, in overdrawn egomaniacal self-representation. [...] Artists who try to

geschaffen, einzelne Objekte besucherfreundlich vorzuzeigen. Die Gestaltung und die Titel der Werke beschreiben den Aspekt des Vorzeigens noch konkreter als Feilhalten oder Anbieten von Waren. Immer wieder wurde denn auch vom Warencharakter der Werke von Katharina Fritsch gesprochen. Ebenso sehr wie ein Mittel der gefälligen Präsentation stellen diese Vorrichtungen aber auch Formen der Abgrenzung her. So hebt das «Werbeblatt» den Beitrag von und über Katharina Fritsch aus dem Kontext der Zeitschrift heraus. Das «Warengestell» und die «Acht Tische mit acht Gegenständen» stellen eine Art Ausstellung in der Ausstellung dar, und dies so wirkungsvoll, dass die Künstlerin in «von hier aus» auf ein eigenes Ausstellungspavillon verzichten und ihr Werk in einer Zone zwischen den klar definierten Ausstellungsräumen plazieren konnte. In der Kunst des 20. Jahrhunderts ist die Grenzziehung zwischen Kunst und Wirklichkeit am Gegenstand des plastischen Objektes spätestens seit Duchamp ein viel und fruchtbar diskutiertes Thema geworden. Plötzlich standen die bisher unangefochtenen Grenzen zur Disposition, wurden geöffnet, erweitert, neu gezogen oder gänzlich verunklärt. In den achtziger Jahren war das Thema der Grenzerweiterung mit Künstlern wie Jeff Koons, Haim Steinbach, Sherrie Levine oder Fischli/Weiss erneut ins Zentrum der Aufmerksamkeit gerückt. Umso mehr muss man aufhorchen, wenn Katharina Fritsch für ihre Objekte von Anfang an und mit aller Bestimmtheit neue Formen der Grenzziehung schafft.

Zehn Jahre nach den «Acht Tischen mit acht Gegenständen» nahm Katharina Fritsch die Arbeit an einem Projekt auf, dem noch einmal das Konzept einer achtseitigen Grundfläche zur Präsentation von Gegenständen zugrundeliegt. Die Rede ist vom «Museum, Modell 1:10», das an der Biennale von Venedig 1995 im Hauptraum des deutschen Pavillons aufgebaut war (Taf. 21, Kat. 100).[5] Zwar sind die Teilnehmer einer Biennale international und die räumliche Ausbreitung der Ausstellung grösser als 1984 in Düsseldorf, dennoch sind die beiden Situationen vergleichbar. Wie vor zehn Jahren war der Anlass eine Gruppenausstellung mit unterschiedlichen und unvorhersehbaren Beiträgen und wie damals wird in Venedig die Ausstellungsarchitektur von einzelnen Pavillons gebildet.

Im «Museum, Modell 1:10» ist die Fläche, die auf einer Höhe von 160 cm liegt und deren Durchmesser über zehn Meter beträgt, nicht überschaubar. Mit einiger Beharrlichkeit kann man sich eine Vorstellung von dem verschaffen, was sich auf dieser Fläche und in deren Zentrum abspielt. Ging in den frühen Bei-

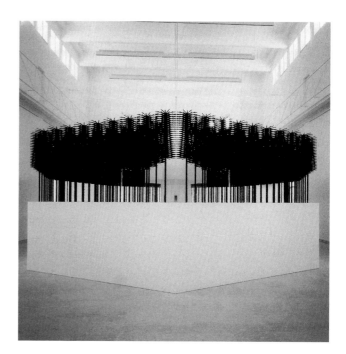

Fig./Abb. 9
Museum, Modell 1:10, 1995

spielen die Grenzziehung (in Form des Faltblattes, des Glasregals und des Tisches) mit einer optimalen Überschaubarkeit der Gegenstände einher, so wird im «Museum, Modell 1:10» die Schwierigkeit unmittelbar erlebbar, das, worum es eigentlich geht, auch nur zu erahnen. Das «Museum, Modell 1:10» ist kein Architekturmodell im klassischen Sinn, das den zu realisierenden Entwurf gut nachvollziehbar vor Augen führt. Es ist eine Skulptur, deren Aussage in der Anschauung zum Erlebnis wird. Daher die enormen Dimensionen, hinter deren Realisierung eine gewaltige Anstrengung stehen muss, die – wenn es sich um ein gewöhnliches Modell handeln würde – ohne Sinn wären, durch die erst jedoch das skulpturale Potential des «Modells» sich verwirklichen kann (Abb. 9).

Vor dem Sockel stehend kann man sich vorstellen, dass die Schwierigkeit, die die Sockelhöhe bietet, nicht unähnlich der Schwierigkeit ist, in der man sich beim Betreten des Waldes befinden würde. Die absolute Gleichförmigkeit der Bäume und die Dunkelheit des Waldes würden die Orientierung erschweren und einen nach einiger Anstrengung den Weg ins Zentrum finden lassen. Erst im Zentrum befindet sich der Ort der Präsentation, der früher einmal Warengestell hiess und jetzt als Museum bezeichnet ist. So wie das Oktagon und die Zahl 8 überhaupt seit 1982 immer wieder im Werk von Katharina Fritsch auftritt,[6] so

Fig./Abb. 10
7. Serie Familienfeste, 1996

develop accessible imagery that draws on our archetypal heritage, but also creates new pictorial means of addressing contemporary problems, fears, hopes. Instead of opting for the easy way out, namely nihilism, they work at finding a new ethic; for us that means finding a new form in an attempt to challenge chaos and disintegration, without falling back on rigid, traditional forms."[11] Let us now glance at Katharina Fritsch's objects and figures themselves and see how her own works stand up to these artistic ideas.

THE MOMENT OF BEING SURPRISED

For some months Katharina Fritsch has been working on a series of silk-screen prints called *Lexikonzeichnungen* (pl. 23 and fig. 10, cat. 104-112). They are monochrome black screen prints in wooden frames covered with silver foil. The images are taken from an old Duden Pictorial Lexicon.[12] So far she has produced images of fairy tales, scenes of superstition, of Christian rituals, popular festivals and family celebrations. Work in preparation includes images of human physiognomy, scenes of urban life, and animal species. The images are taken from the book with slight changes and enlarged many times as screen prints on paper. The outline, which makes it possible for the images to be so clear in the small format of the dictionary, is strikingly simple when enlarged. The standardized outline, which records the various, emotionally highly differentiated scenes in monotonous uniformity, is given a deliberately neutralizing character. This means that the known and familiar features in the images are "dressed" in a generalizing and alienating fashion that makes us see them as if they were new. The tension that this produces between the familiar and the strange is a phe-

nomenon that has characterized the effect of Katharina Fritsch's work from an early stage.[13] It is fascinating to discover, on the design plane, how deliberately, and yet with what sophistication, she pushes neutralizing the subjective and generalizing the individual forward in these works.

This begins for example in the form of the objects and figures selected for presentation. Whether they are *Schüssel* (Bowl, 1984, cat. 45) or *Schwarze Vase* (Black Vase, 1984, cat. 47), *Schwarzer Tisch mit eineiigen Zwillingen* (Black Table with Identical Twins, 1985, cat. 53) or *Mann und Maus* (Man and Mouse, 1991/92, cat. 96) – it is always possible to observe reduction of a conceivably specific form that leads away from the illustrative and instead contains a tendency to abstraction. The objects seem clear and simple, and in terms of proportion they turn out to be carefully thought through, complex structures. The figures seem to be allotted as little as possible individually and specifically to a gender or species. It is not an individual or several individuals sitting at the black table, but identical twins whose individuality is cancelled in the person sitting opposite in each case. The man in bed is defined exclusively by the mouse sitting on top of him, and conversely the excessive size and position of the mouse is based on the predetermined metaphor of the nightmare.

Every object and every figure by Katharina Fritsch is perfectly fashioned. When passing an eye over *Madonnenfigur* (Madonna Figure) or one of the *Warengestelle* (cat. 69, 70, 77), there are no irregularities or details that stand out from the whole to provide an interruption. There are no signs of personal handwriting or of

90

stellt auch die farbliche Gestaltung des Museums einen konkreten Bezug zum bisherigen Schaffen der Künstlerin her. Das Glas, Gold und Silber der Aussenhaut trifft man zum Beispiel im «Warengestell» (Glasregale), in der Serie der farbigen Bilder (Goldrahmen, Kat. 82-93) oder in den «Lexikonzeichnungen» (Silberrahmen, Kat. 104-112) als rahmende bzw. abgrenzende Gestaltungsmittel. Die Farben der Glaswände im Innern des Obergeschosses des Museums nehmen in der gleichen Abfolge die Farben der Arbeit «Acht Bilder in acht Farben» von 1990/91 (Kat. 93) auf, in der Katharina Fritsch die von ihr bisher verwendeten Farben zusammengefasst hat. Das Museum ist leer, muss es sein, da es hier so ausdrücklich um die schwierige Erreichbarkeit der Gegenstände geht – Katharina Fritsch spricht hier von einer «Inszenierung von Unerreichbarkeit» und einem «Bild von Ferne»[7] –, und nicht um die Gegenstände selbst.[8] Was sich in den frühen Beispielen zu Anfang der achtziger Jahre abgezeichnet hat: der Wunsch, ausgegrenzte Orte zu schaffen, ist im «Museum, Modell 1:10» zu einem wunderbaren und wagemutigen Manifest geworden, in dem der Wunsch als Notwendigkeit aufscheint.[9]

In der schmalen Katalogbroschüre, die zur Biennale erschienen ist, wurde ein Text von Katharina Fritsch zum «Museum» publiziert.[10] Darin ist auch von der Art der Gegenstände und Kunstwerke die Rede, die an einem solchen Ort gezeigt werden könnten: Es sind Kunstwerke, von «Künstlern, denen es um Identität geht, nicht um Spekulationen innerhalb der Kunstgeschichte, Zynismen oder überzogene egomanische Selbstdarstellung. [...] Künstler,

die versuchen eine verständliche Bildersprache zu entwickeln, die einerseits auf überlieferten Archetypen beruht, andererseits den Zeitbezug zu den Problemen, Ängsten, Hoffnungen durch neue Bildfindungen sichtbar macht. Die versuchen, den ach so bequemen Nihilismus zu überwinden, im Wissen darum eine neue Ethik, das heisst für uns eine neue Form finden, ein Versuch dem Chaos und der Auflösung etwas entgegenzusetzen, ohne in starre, überkommene Formen zurückzufallen.»[11] Werfen wir nun einen Blick auf Katharina Fritschs Gegenstände und Figuren selbst und schauen wir, wie ihre eigenen Werke sich gegenüber diesen künstlerischen Vorstellungen ausnehmen.

DER PUNKT DES SICHWUNDERNS

Seit einigen Monaten arbeitet Katharina Fritsch an einer Serie von Siebdrucken, die den Titel «Lexikonzeichnungen» tragen. (Taf. 23 und Abb. 10, Kat. 104-112) Es handelt sich um einfarbige schwarze Siebdrucke, die mit von Silberfolie ummantelten Holzrahmen gefasst sind. Die Darstellungen sind einem alten Bildwörterlexikon entnommen.[12] Bisher sind Darstellungen von Märchen, von Szenen aus dem Bereich des Aberglaubens, von christlichen Ritualen, von Volksfesten und von Familienfesten entstanden. In Vorbereitung sind unter anderem Darstellungen zur menschlichen Physiognomie, Szenen aus dem Stadtleben und Tiergattungen. Die Darstellungen werden von der Vorlage mit leichten Veränderungen übernommen und vom Kleinformat um ein Vielfaches vergrössert im Siebdruck aufs Papier gebracht. Die Kontur, die im Kleinformat der Lexikonzeichnung den Darstellungen die notwendige Klarheit ermöglicht, wirkt in

a technical manufacturing process. The objects and figures are simply there, taken for granted and effortless.

Their structure as such and – in the case of works with several parts – their arrangement and their combination are characterized by simple rules of order and basic stereometric forms. They are all based on the order of symmetry and the basic shape of the circle. They produce closed bodies and systems both outward and inward, which refer to and reflect themselves. No temporal movement with a beginning and an end develops within them; on the contrary, they have an eerie tendency to cancel themselves out or to repeat themselves *ad infinitum*.

The works are often deliberately placed so that the viewer approaches them head on, like a picture. However large their three-dimensional scale may be, their plasticity and materiality recede to an equal extent. One suspects that walking round a work will add nothing to the head-on perception that is crucial or that completely changes the first impression.

The color quality of the works constantly forces itself to the center of attention. It is inseparable from the perception of the "neutralizing" tendencies that have been described on the plane of formal design, but in presentation it works like a bright counterpoint. It became impossible to overlook this striking use of color for the first time in 1987, when the green *Elefant* (Elephant, pl. 12, cat. 64) and shortly afterwards the large yellow *Madonnenfigur* (pl. 13, cat. 67) appeared on the scene. The lemon-yellow of the Madonna and the rich dark green of the elephant make their effect without any mimetic or iconographic function. Nor do they have any modeling effect on the three-dimensional body. The colors are expressed within themselves in just such a saturated form as they are presented, indeed celebrated, in the 1990/91 work *Acht Bilder in acht Farben* (pl. 15, cat. 93). As pure colors, they have become one with the figures.

Color in a particular work by Katharina Fritsch can seldom be explained, but it always seems, as Julian Heynen so beautifully put it, "indisputably correct."[14] One is tempted to imagine that these colors condense and express the tone, the sound that is part of the newly made object. There is a group of works in which Katharina Fritsch does in fact work with the sound of objects and everyday phenomena, with the sound of color or the color of sound, and once even with the smell of a place. These are the four records *Unken* (Toads, 1982/88, cat. 32), *Regen* (Rain, 1987, cat. 63), *Krankenwagen* (Ambulance) and *Mühle* (Mill, 1990, cat. 79 and 80),

whose tone is always allotted a certain color by the record sleeve, the installation *Roter Raum mit Kamingeräusch* (Red Room with Chimney Noise, 1991, cat. 94) and the action *Parfüm im Hausflur* (Perfume in the Hallway, 1984, cat. 41), which is documented only by a photograph. This fascinating group of ephemeral works – it also includes *Spaziergänger mit Hund* (Man out for a Walk with Dog, 1986, cat. 60) – throws light on the breadth with which Katharina Fritsch explores the relative value of all phenomena that have an effect and allows us to realize that she leaves nothing to chance, but works on the basis that the inexplicable is calculable by intuition. But the group also indicates a comprehensive understanding of color for three-dimensional objects and figures, a grasp of color as a medium that can be permeated by sensual effects not normally attributed directly to color effects that lie in the realm of prelinguistic cognition.[15] This use of color plays a crucial part in transforming objects and figures from individuals into types.

The interplay of all design devices that constitutes Katharina Fritsch's objects and figures raises them above the everyday and random, gives them a distance and a prototypical order, and makes them alien. In this alien quality, beyond the familiar, can be seen an unexpected and indefinable "liveliness", with a mysterious radiance. It demands a moment's pause, a moment of concentrating on what we have in front of us. It is not a breathless pause at a moment of the highest possible tension. It is a timeless pause, in which we ask ourselves in amazement why something as familiar as a bowl or an elephant can possess such a quality of strangeness or otherness. The experience when confronted with these works has been compared with the experience that can be invoked within us by memory or dreams, the two realms in which the flow of real events is stopped and in which individual objects, figures, and situations can contain quite new values that are consistent within themselves.

TO CHALLENGE DISINTEGRATION

Can the sphere into which Katharina Fritsch's works abduct us be characterized more precisely in terms of content – beyond a first understanding of the visible, something that is always possible?

If we keep the early works in mind, Katharina Fritsch seems to proceed according to a clearly definable scheme when selecting her objects. It has been repeatedly noticed that a large proportion of the objects – like for example the *Anturien* (Anthurium). the *Tapetenmuster* (Wallpaper Pattern), the *Töpfe* (Pans), the

der Vergrösserung in ihrer Einfachheit auffällig. Die standardisierte Kontur, der die vielfältigen, emotional äusserst unterschiedlichen Szenen in monotoner Gleichförmigkeit aufzeichnet, erhält einen absichtsvoll neutralisierenden Charakter. Dadurch erscheint das Bekannte und Vertraute der Darstellungen in einem verallgemeinernden, befremdlichen «Kleid», das sie einen wie neu wahrnehmen lässt. Die daraus hervorgehende Spannung zwischen Vertrautem und Fremdem ist ein Phänomen, das die Wirkung der Arbeiten von Katharina Fritsch von früh an prägt.[13] Es ist faszinierend zu entdecken, wie gezielt und dabei wie differenziert in den Arbeiten die Neutralisierung des Subjektiven, die Verallgemeinerung des Individuellen auf der Ebene der Gestaltung vorangetrieben wird.

Das beginnt zum Beispiel in der Ausprägung der zur Darstellung ausgewählten Gegenstände und Figuren. Seien es die «Schüssel» oder die «Schwarze Vase» (beide von 1984, Kat. 45 und 47), der «Schwarze Tisch mit eineiigen Zwillingen» (1985, Kat. 53) oder «Mann und Maus» (1991/92, Kat. 96) – immer lässt sich eine Reduktion einer denkbaren spezifischen Ausprägung beobachten, die vom Illustrativen wegführt und stattdessen eine abstrahierende Tendenz enthält. Die Gegenstände wirken klar und einfach, in ihren Proportionen erweisen sie sich als sorgfältig durchdachte, komplexe Gebilde. Die Figuren scheinen so wenig wie möglich individuell und geschlechts- bzw. gattungsspezifisch ausdefiniert. Am schwarzen Tisch sitzt nicht eine Einzelperson oder mehrere Einzelpersonen, sondern eineiige Zwillinge, deren Individualität sich im jeweiligen Gegenüber aufhebt. Der Mann im Bett ist ausschliesslich über die auf ihm sitzende Maus definiert, und umgekehrt ist die Übergrösse und Position der Maus in der vorgegebenen Metapher des Alptraums begründet.

Jeder Gegenstand und jede Figur von Katharina Fritsch ist perfekt ausgearbeitet. Der Blick, der über die «Madonnenfigur» oder eines der «Warengestelle» (Kat. 69, 70, 77) gleitet, bleibt an keiner Unregelmässigkeit, keinem aus dem Ganzen herausfallenden Detail hängen. Keine Spuren sind zu bemerken, die eine Handschrift oder einen technischen Herstellungsprozess in Erinnerung rufen. Die Gegenstände und Figuren sind einfach da, selbstverständlich und ohne Anstrengung.

Ihr Aufbau in sich sowie – bei mehrteiligen Arbeiten – ihre Anordnung und ihre Konstellationen sind von einfachen Ordnungsregeln und stereometrischen Grundformen geprägt. Ihnen allen zugrunde liegt die Ordnung der Symmetrie und die Grundform des Kreises. Sie erzeugen nach aussen und nach innen geschlossene Körper und Systeme, die auf sich selbst verweisen und sich spiegeln. In ihnen entfaltet sich keine zeitliche Bewegung mit Anfang und Ende, vielmehr haben sie die unheimliche Tendenz, sich aufzuheben bzw. sich ins Unendliche zu wiederholen.

Die Werke sind mit Bedacht oft so plaziert, dass man sich ihnen frontal, wie einem Bild, nähert. So gross ihre dreidimensionale Ausdehnung auch ist, so sehr tritt durch die beschriebenen Massnahmen ihre Plastizität und Materialität zurück. Man ahnt, dass das Umgehen eines Werkes die frontale Wahrnehmung nicht um entscheidende, den ersten Eindruck völlig verändernde Merkmale ergänzen wird.

Untrennbar von der Wahrnehmung der beschriebenen «neutralisierenden» Tendenzen auf der Ebene der formalen Gestaltung, dabei aber in der Vorstellung wie ein heller Kontrapunkt wirkend, drängt sich die Farbigkeit der Werke immer wieder ins Zentrum der Aufmerksamkeit. Zum ersten Mal unübersehbar geworden war der auffällige Einsatz der Farbe 1987, als der grüne «Elefant» (Taf. 12, Kat. 64) und kurz darauf die grosse gelbe «Madonnenfigur» (Taf. 13, Kat. 67) auftraten. Das Zitronengelb der Madonna und das satte Dunkelgrün des Elefanten wirken frei von jeder mimetischen oder ikonographischen Funktion. Ebensowenig wie sie mimetisch gebunden sind, modellieren sie den plastischen Körper. Die Farben kommen so in sich gesättigt zum Ausdruck wie sie in der Arbeit «Acht Bilder in acht Farben» von 1990/91 (Taf. 15, Kat. 93) vorgeführt, ja zelebriert werden. Als reine Farben sind sie mit den Figuren eins geworden.

Die jeweilige Farbe eines Werkes von Katharina Fritsch lässt sich selten begründen, aber sie erscheint immer, wie Julian Heynen es so schön formulierte, «fraglos richtig».[14] Man ist versucht sich vorzustellen, dass sich in diesen Farben der Ton, der Klang, der zum neu gemachten Gegenstand gehört, verdichtet und ausdrückt. Es gibt eine Gruppe von Werken, in denen Katharina Fritsch tatsächlich mit dem Klang von Gegenständen und alltäglichen Phänomenen, mit dem Klang von Farbe oder der Farbe von Klang, und einmal auch mit dem Geruch eines Ortes arbeitet. Es sind die vier Schallplatten «Unken» (1982/88, Kat. 32), «Regen» (1987, Kat. 63), «Krankenwagen» und «Mühle» (1990, Kat. 79 und 80), deren Ton mit der Plattenhülle jeweils eine bestimmte Farbe zugeordnet wird, die Installation «Roter Raum mit Kamingeräusch» (1991, Kat. 94) und die Aktion «Parfüm im Hausflur» (1984, Kat. 41), die nur als

Kerze (Candle), the *Schwarzer Tisch mit Geschirr* (Black Table with Table Ware), the *Bücherregal* (Bookcase) – could be allotted to the everyday household world, that in other words the immediate environment is the first object of Katharina Fritsch's creative work. This classification was broken off abruptly in 1987 with the appearance of *Elefant* and *Madonnenfigur*. They were followed in 1988 by *Tischgesellschaft* (Company at Table, pl. 17, cat. 75) and *Gespenst und Blutlache* (Ghost and Pool of Blood, pl. 18, cat. 76), in 1991-1992 by *Mann und Maus* (Man and Mouse, pl. 19, cat. 96), in 1991-1993 by *Rattenkönig* (Rat-King, pl. 20, cat. 97) and in 1996-1996 by *Kind mit Pudeln* (Child with Poodles, pl. 22, cat. 102). Unlike the objects of the early years, these do not identify a certain sphere of life, as the objects of the early years seem to do. And works like *Warengestell mit Vasen* (Display Stand with Vases) and *Warengestell mit Madonnen* (Display Stand with Madonnas) dating from 1987/89 (pls. 11 and 10, cat.

69 and 70), *Wühltisch* (Bargain Counter, 1987/89, cat. 71) and *Geldkisten* (Money Chests, 1988, cat. 74), which may still contain elements of everyday domestic life, cannot be said to belong there entirely. They are all individual images that stand for themselves and do not have a common denominator, unless their wonderful and remarkably alienating, and their increasingly eerie quality could be called a common denominator. This aspect of the works, of which we perhaps became properly aware because of the size and exposed quality of *Elefant* and *Madonnenfigur*, also places the early works in a different light in retrospect. Classification in the domestic sphere becomes questionable, or better: less interesting. It is not always as striking as it is in the case of *Katzen im Körbchen* (Cats in a Little Basket, 1980, fig. 11, cat. 13), the plan for a *Friedhof mit Reihengräbern* (Cemetery with Rows of Graves, 1980/82, cat. 17) or *Selbstklebendes Kreuz* (Self-Adhesive Cross, 1982, cat. 30), but in fact the early works

94

Photographie dokumentiert ist. Diese hochinteressante Gruppe von ephemeren Arbeiten – dazu gehörte auch der «Spaziergänger mit Hund» (1986, Kat. 60) – wirft ein Licht auf die Breite, mit der Katharina Fritsch die Wertigkeit aller Wirkungsphänomene erforscht und lässt erahnen, dass sie nichts dem Zufall überlässt, sondern von einer intuitiven Kalkulierbarkeit des Unerklärbaren ausgeht. Die Gruppe ist aber auch ein Indiz für ein umfassendes Verständnis von Farbe an den plastischen Gegenständen und Figuren. Für eine Auffassung von Farbe als Medium, das durchlässig ist für sinnliche Wirkungen, die man gewöhnlich nicht direkt der Farbe zuschreibt und die im Bereich der vorsprachlichen Erkenntnis liegen.[15] Diese Verwendung der Farbe hat entscheidenden Anteil an der Transformation der Gegenstände und Figuren vom Individuellen ins Typenhafte.

Das Zusammenspiel aller Gestaltungsmittel, das die Gegenstände und Figuren von Katharina Fritsch konstituiert, hebt sie aus dem Alltäglichen und Zufälligen heraus, verleiht ihnen eine Distanz und prototypische Ordnung und macht sie fremd. In diesem Fremden, jenseits des Vertrauten, zeigt sich eine unerwartete und undefinierbare «Lebendigkeit» von rätselhafter Ausstrahlung. Sie fordert auf zu einem Moment des Innehaltens, der Konzentration auf das, was vor einem steht. Es ist nicht das atemlose Innehalten in einem Moment der höchsten Anspannung. Es ist ein Innehalten ohne Zeit, bei dem man sich verwundert fragt, warum etwas so Bekanntem wie einer Schüssel oder einem Elefanten eine derartige Fremdheit oder Andersheit eigen sein kann. Man hat die Erfahrung vor diesen Werken mit den Erfahrungen verglichen, die die Erinnerung oder der Traum in einem wachrufen können, die beiden Bereiche, in denen der Fluss des realen Geschehens ausgesetzt ist, und in denen die einzelnen Gegenstände, Figuren und Situationen ganz neue, dabei in sich stimmige Wertigkeiten erhalten können.

95

DER AUFLÖSUNG ETWAS ENTGEGENSETZEN

Lässt sich der Bereich, in den die Werke von Katharina Fritsch einen entführen, auch inhaltlich näher charakterisieren – über ein immer mögliches erstes Verständnis des Sichtbaren hinaus?

Wenn man sich die Arbeiten der ersten Jahre vor Augen hält, scheint Katharina Fritsch in der Auswahl ihrer Gegenstände nach einem klar definierbaren System vorzugehen. Immer wieder wurde festgestellt, dass sich ein grosser Teil der Gegenstände – wie z.B. die «Anturien», das «Tapetenmuster», die «Töpfe», die «Kerze», der

«Schwarze Tisch mit Geschirr», das «Bücherregal» – dem Bereich des häuslichen Alltags zuordnen lasse, dass also die nächste Umgebung erstes Objekt des Schaffens von Katharina Fritsch sei. Diese Klassifizierung wurde 1987 abrupt aufgebrochen mit dem Erscheinen des «Elefanten» und der «Madonnenfigur». Ihnen folgten 1988 die «Tischgesellschaft» (Taf. 17, Kat. 75) und «Gespenst und Blutlache» (Taf. 18, Kat. 76), 1991-1992 «Mann und Maus» (Taf. 19, Kat. 96), 1991-1993 «Rattenkönig» (Taf. 20, Kat. 97) und 1995-1996 «Kind mit Pudeln» (Taf. 22, Kat. 102). Sie alle bezeichnen nicht einen bestimmten Lebensbereich wie die Gegenstände der ersten Jahre dies zu tun scheinen. Und auch Werke wie «Warengestell mit Vasen» und «Warengestell mit Madonnen» von 1987/89 (Taf. 11 und 10, Kat. 69 und 70), «Wühltisch» (1987/89, Kat. 71) und «Geldkisten» (1988, Kat. 74), die noch Elemente des häuslichen Alltags enthalten mögen, lassen sich als Ganze nicht dazu zählen. Es sind alles Einzelbilder, die für sich stehen und keinen gemeinsamen Nenner haben, ausser man möchte das Wunderbare und merkwürdig Befremdliche und je länger je mehr das Unheimliche, das in ihnen zum Ausdruck kommt, als gemeinsamen Nenner bezeichnen. Diese Seite der Werke, die vielleicht durch die Grösse und Exponiertheit des «Elefanten» und der «Madonnenfigur» so richtig bewusst wurde, lässt im Rückblick auch das frühere Schaffen mit anderen Augen sehen. Die Zuordnung zum Bereich des Häuslichen wird fragwürdig oder besser: verliert an Interesse. Nicht immer so auffällig wie zum Beispiel die «Katzen im Körbchen» (1980, Abb. 11, Kat. 13), der Plan für einen «Friedhof mit Reihengräbern» (1980/82, Kat. 17) und andere Pläne oder das «Selbstklebende Kreuz» (1982, Kat. 30) enthalten nämlich auch die früheren Arbeiten vielfältige inhaltliche Andeutungen und Hinweise in Richtung des Wunderbaren und Befremdlichen, das später immer unverdeckter manifest wird.

Die neueren Werke – vom «Elefanten» über «Gespenst und Blutlache» bis zu «Kind mit Pudeln» und den «Lexikonzeichnungen» – verweisen in ihrer Bildlichkeit auf die kollektiven Erfahrungsbereiche der Religion und des Volksglaubens, der Mythen und Märchen. Die inhaltliche Anlage dieser Bilder ist trivial – wie es ja auch die Objekte der früheren Werke sind –, insofern komplexe emotionale Erfahrungen auf einfach verständliche, stereotype Grundmuster reduziert werden. Es ist die Welt der Schauerromantik und Billigromane, der Vulgärpsychologie und der medialen Simplifizierung, die hier anklingt. Gerade in dieser trivialen Qualität scheint jedoch das Potential zu liegen, aus dem Katharina Fritsch

also contain numerous hints and pointers in terms of content that direct us toward the wonderful and the strange, things that are increasingly less concealed later on.

The more recent works – from *Elefant* (Elephant) via *Gespenst und Blutlache* (Ghost and Pool of Blood) to *Kind mit Pudeln* (Child with Poodles) and *Lexikonzeichnungen* (Lexicon Drawings) – refer in their pictorial quality to the collective spheres of experience of religion and popular belief, of myths and fairytales. The content element of these pictures is trivial – as are the objects in the early works – to the extent that complex emotional experiences are reduced to readily comprehensible, stereotypical basic patterns. It is the world of Gothic romance and cheap novels, of popular psychology and media simplification that is starting to emerge here. But it is precisely in this trivial quality that the potential seems to lie from which Katharina Fritsch draws appropriate impetus for finding her images. Let us try to examine some works in this light.

In our imagination the elephant is the epitome of a large, strong and archaic animal. From our childhood we become familiar with them above all as culturally domesticated miraculous beasts, rather than as biological creatures. We look at them in amazement in the zoo, for example, and admire their skill and patience at the circus, and we learn from a number of stories that they are good-natured but incredibly strong and are scarcely ever impressed by any human attempts to approach them. Katharina Fritsch presents us with this elephant in its actual size. (pl. 12) The model for the cast was a stuffed animal from a museum. But in the case of Katharina Fritsch's elephant the atmosphere of preserved life that one feels in the natural history museum is missing. He is saved from this by the fact that his hide is green. And this animal is equally little reminiscent of a real elephant in the wild state. He stands – at peace with himself in his attitude – on an oval, very high plinth, so that we look up to him with an exaggerated view from below. But his own gaze is directed into a far and unknown distance. Katharina Fritsch's *Elefant* appears as a complete image of the creature, as it exists in our collective imagination – strong and inviolable, in a state of pre-conscious innocence.

Gespenst und Blutlache (pl. 18) takes us into other realms: into the world of 19th century novels, into the world of ghosts, vampires, and other phenomena of the night, a world in which real and half-real dangers lurk. We do not know what a ghost looks like. Katharina Fritsch has represented it as we see it in the

theater and old films as well: as a faceless figure covered in a white cloth. But a ghost as a motionless sculpture, as a statue two yards high, does not have the credibility of a film ghost, as one crucial ghostly quality is missing completely: its ephemeral nature. The pool of blood on the floor opposite the ghost is also remarkable. It is the same size as a recumbent figure, its surface gleams juicily, and it seems to be almost overflowing. The ghost and the pool of blood do not relate actively and yet seem to be attached to each other: on the one hand is the pure white ghost, as if turned into a pillar of salt, and opposite the dark red, almost black pool of blood, suggesting uncertain danger, impurity and injury. The lack of a linking action means that the two parts grow together into a vivid double figure, in which purity and impurity, guilt and innocence, danger and harmlessness are linked closely and yet strikingly without emotion.

The core of the installation *Kind mit Pudeln* (pl. 22) is a scene of adoration, but it has acquired a perverse form here. A doll-like, white, sexless infant is lying on an octagonal golden star. It is surrounded by 224 black miniature poodles, arranged regularly in four closed circles. The poodles stand body to body. They are rubbing together and thrusting towards the center, where they are held as if by an invisible spell. The protagonists of this work do not come from the world of the imagination like the ghost and the pool of blood, but refer to concrete reality. In the early sixties a poodle was an essential accessory for a smart nuclear family. The child is reminiscent of cheap reproductions of Philipp Otto Runge's *Morgen* (Morning), for example, which hung in thousands of German homes as a sign of a religious faith that had long been lost. But in Katharina Fritsch's image, child and poodles have changed into quite different, independent beings that carry their origins with them as a pale shadow. As in the work *Gespenst und Blutlache*, a double figure has been created in *Kind mit Pudeln*, in which innocence and evil, purity and impurity seem indissolubly linked. But here the image is charged with threatening aggression and sexual energy. These are all the more powerfully effective as the double figure is paralysed in a set pose, and so are the active negative energies. The destructive potential that is almost tangible within it hangs threateningly over the perverse order of this image.

Let us finally remember the project *Lexikonzeichnungen* (pl. 23 and fig. 10). The task of a lexicon is to classify and to create order. It transforms an enormous amount of heterogeneous knowledge and experience into a clearly defined leveling system

die adäquaten inhaltlichen Impulse für ihre Bildfindungen gewinnt. Versuchen wir einige Werke daraufhin anzusehen.

Der Elefant ist in unserer Vorstellung der Inbegriff eines grossen, starken und archaischen Tieres. Von Kind an lernt man ihn vor allem als kulturell domestiziertes Wundertier kennen, weniger als biologisches Wesen. Man bestaunt ihn z.B. im Zoo, man bewundert sein Geschick und seine Geduld im Zirkus, und man erfährt aus vielen Geschichten, dass er gutmütig, aber unglaublich stark ist und sich von menschlichen Annäherungsversuchen verschiedenster Art kaum je beeindrucken lässt. Katharina Fritsch stellt diesen Elefanten in Originalgrösse vor uns hin. (Taf. 12) Modell für den Abguss war ein ausgestopftes Museumstier. Beim Elefanten von Katharina Fritsch fehlt jedoch die Atmosphäre konservierten Lebens, die man im naturhistorischen Museum antrifft. Die grüne Färbung seiner Haut bewahrt ihn davor. Ebensowenig lässt dieses Tier an einen wirklichen Elefanten aus der Wildnis denken. Er steht – in seiner Haltung in sich ruhend – auf einem ovalen, sehr hohen Sockel, so dass man in stark gesteigerter Untersicht zu ihm aufsieht. Sein eigener Blick hingegen ist in eine weite, unbekannte Ferne gerichtet. Der «Elefant» von Katharina Fritsch erscheint als vollkommenes Bild des Tieres, wie es in unserer kollektiven Vorstellung existiert – stark und unantastbar in einem Zustand vorbewusster Unschuld.

«Gespenst und Blutlache» (Taf. 18) führt in andere Bereiche: in die Welt von Romanen des 19. Jahrhunderts, in die Welt von Gespenstern, Vampiren und anderen nächtlichen Erscheinungen, in der echte und halbechte Gefahren lauern. Von einem Gespenst weiss man nicht, wie es aussieht. Katharina Fritsch hat es so dargestellt, wie es auch im Theater oder in alten Filmen zu sehen ist: als mit einem weissen Tuch verhüllte, gesichtslose Figur. Ein Gespenst als unbewegte Skulptur, als zwei Meter hohe Statue, hat aber nicht die Glaubwürdigkeit eines Filmgespenstes, denn die ein Gespenst konstituierende Eigenschaft: seine Flüchtigkeit, fehlt hier gänzlich. Merkwürdig ist auch die Blutlache, die sich dem Gespenst gegenüber auf dem Boden ausbreitet. Sie hat die Ausdehnung einer liegenden Figur, ihre Oberfläche glänzt saftig und sie scheint fast überzulaufen. Das Gespenst und die Blutlache stehen nicht in einem Handlungszusammenhang und scheinen doch einander zugeordnet: auf der einen Seite das reine, weisse, wie zur Salzsäule erstarrte Gespenst, gegenüber die dunkelrote, fast schwarze Blutlache, ungewisse Gefahr, Unreinheit und Verletzung suggerierend. Der fehlende Handlungszusammenhang lässt die beiden Teile zu einer bild-

haften Doppelgestalt zusammenwachsen, in der Reinheit und Unreinheit, Schuld und Unschuld, Gefahr und Harmlosigkeit eng und dabei auffällig emotionslos verbunden sind.

Kern der Installation «Kind mit Pudeln» (Taf. 22) ist eine Anbetungsszene, die hier jedoch eine pervertierte Form erhalten hat. Auf einem achteckigen goldenen Stern liegt ein puppenhaftes, weisses, geschlechtsloses Neugeborenes. Es ist umringt von 224 schwarzen Zwergpudeln, die in vier geschlossenen Kreisen regelmässig angeordnet sind. Die Pudel stehen Körper an Körper, reiben sich aneinander, drängen gegen das Zentrum, wo sie wie von einem unsichtbaren Bann aufgehalten werden. Die Protagonisten dieser Arbeit kommen nicht aus der Welt der Vorstellung wie das Gespenst und die Blutlache, sondern sie verweisen auf konkrete Wirklichkeit. Der Pudel galt einst als festes Zubehör der properen Kleinfamilie der frühen sechziger Jahre. Das Kind erinnert zum Beispiel an Billigreproduktionen von Philipp Otto Runges «Morgen», die als Zeichen einer längst verlorenen Gläubigkeit zu Tausenden in deutschen Heimen hingen. Kind und Pudel haben sich in Katharina Fritschs Bild jedoch in ganz andere, selbständige Wesen verwandelt, die ihre Herkunft als blassen Schatten mit sich tragen. Wie im Werk «Gespenst und Blutlache» ist in «Kind mit Pudeln» eine Doppelgestalt entstanden, in der Unschuld und Böses, Reinheit und Unreinheit unauflösbar aufeinander bezogen scheinen. Hier aber ist das Bild aufgeladen von bedrohlicher Aggression und sexueller Energie. Diese wirken umso stärker, da die Doppelgestalt in Pose erstarrt ist und mit ihr die aktiven negativen Energien. Das darin fast greifbar werdende zerstörerische Potential hängt bedrohlich über der pervertierten Ordnung dieses Bildes.

Erinnern wir uns schliesslich an das Projekt der «Lexikonzeichnungen». (Taf. 23) Aufgabe eines Lexikons ist es, zu klassifizieren und Ordnung zu schaffen. Es verwandelt unübersehbares und heterogenes Wissen und Erleben in ein klar definiertes, egalisierendes und vermittelbares System. Katharina Fritsch verwendet als Vorlage ein populäres Bildwörterbuch. Sie wählt für ihre Darstellungen Szenen aus, die eine Wirklichkeit entstehen lassen, die von Märchen, Mythen, Bräuchen und Populärwissen strukturiert ist. Die Ordnung, die ein Lexikon und damit auch die Lexikonzeichnungen entwerfen, ist eine doppelt trügerische: Zum einen kann keine Ordnung, ob wissenschaftlich begründet oder auf kultureller Überlieferung beruhend, objektiv richtig sein. Zum anderen verdrängt jede Ordnung, je präziser sie ist, umso nachhaltiger die von ihr nicht erfassbaren und nicht benennbaren Bereiche.

that can be communicated. Katharina Fritsch uses a popular illustrated dictionary as her model. She selects scenes for her images that create a reality structured by fairytales, myths, customs, and popular knowledge. The order designed by a lexicon, and thus also by lexicon drawings, is doubly deceptive: on the one hand order, whether it is scientifically based or draws on cultural tradition, can be objectively correct. On the other hand any order, the more precise it is, all the more lastingly forces out areas that it cannot record or name.

This short consideration of the content of four works by Katharina Fritsch stands as an example for other comparable works. A similar look at them would show that the same basic human experience becomes a metaphor in different form and with a different interpretation: guilt and innocence, good and evil, order and chaos, purity and impurity are indissolubly bound together.

Katharina Fritsch stages this metaphor with the high degree of creative precision and deliberateness described above. She so refines its latent triviality and simplicity, by formal design and shifts in content, that these qualities become artificial and striking, so that the images demand that we pause, and their content can be reconsidered.

CONCLUSION

It is now clear that the devices of distancing, neutralizing and generalizing do not simply take Katharina Fritsch's objects and figures into a strange order with a seductively radiant quality that makes us perceive them in a different way. The creative order established here – and the longer it is considered the clearer this is – also betrays its function of capturing the threatening potential of unnameable and chaotic things that accumulate underneath ordinary things and experiences. This perhaps explains the slight melancholy that is peculiar to the early sculptures in particular. A sign that the pressure is rising is given by the new figurative works in which Katharina Fritsch allows chaos to express itself all the more clearly – not without a humor that inclines toward self-irony.

*   In the study scene in Goethe's *Faust Part One*, Faust is pestered by a barking, snarling poodle he had met while walking outside the city gates. He tries in various ways to discover what lies behind the creature's persistence, and finally conjures up Mephistopheles. As Mephistopheles enters, Faust says: "Das also war des Pudels Kern!" (Literally: "So that was the poodle's core!").

1. The three titles in this essay are taken from quotations by Katharina Fritsch. "An image of distance": see p. 70, "The moment of being surprised": Matthias Winzen, "Katharina Fritsch - Ein Gespräch", in: *Das Kunst-Bulletin*, no. 1/2, Jan./Feb. 1994, p. 14; "To challenge disintegration": Katharina Fritsch, *Museum*, ex.cat., German Pavillon, Venice Biennale 1995, p. 12.

2. These are the works numbered 3 - 11 in the catalogue.

3. K. Fritsch on the insert: "When I designed the insert I wasn't looking for a big gesture and a great deal of luxury. The simplest thing to do was to print a list of my work to date, cheaply. But it had to meet my ideas of a printed work. For example, I chose a quite particular typeface, which I have used for all printed material since. I could print the leaflet as an insert in a magazine published by friends of mine, like an advertising supplement. I thought to myself: If I now sell ten of these multiples at 100 marks each every month . . . that would be quite something. I hadn't any money at all at the time, and could see myself getting rich." Matthias Winzen, "Katharina Fritsch – Ein Gespräch", see note 1, p. 20.

4. In his contribution, Gary Garrels calls the *Warengestell* (Display Stand) "a kind of anthropomorphic cosmos", see p. 20.

5. Detailed description of the model under cat. 100, and on p. 26, where a description by Katharina Fritsch is quoted.

6. See for example *Friedhof mit Urnengräbern* (Cemetery for Urn Graves, cat. 26), *Stern* (Star, cat. 34), *Treppenhaus mit achtzig Stufen* (Staircase with Eighty Steps, cat. 37), *Rasenplatz mit achtzig Bäumen* (Lawn with Eighty Trees, cat. 38), *Schlüsselring* (Key Ring, cat. 44), *Acht Tische mit acht Gegenständen* (Eight Tables with Eight Objects, cat. 48), *Acht Bilder in acht Farben* (Eight Painting in Eight Colours, cat. 93).

7. See p. 70.

8. *Museum, Modell 1:10* was conflictingly received at the Biennale, and if you read the reviews, not very productively. One reason was that the work was received completely without reference to the rest of the artist's work. Constantly recurring approaches to criticism were the monumental quality of the sculpture and the fact that it could not all be taken in at once, in other words two elements that – if the *Museum* is put into its context in Katharina Fritsch's output – are of constituent importance. One principal direction of argument was to discuss the work within an architectural rather than an artistic tradition. This is based on the assumption that any architectural model is intended only for the technical execution, and cannot be an ideal model for spatial concepts as well. However, as we know, a model can convey irreplaceable experiences; this is regardless of whether it is only in the mind, or is to be realized, as is the case with Katharina Fritsch.

9. The weight the artist attaches to Heinrich von Kleist's essay *On the Marionette Theater* (see pp. 32-38) and statements in this catalogue (p. 82) and in the 1994 interview (see note 1, p. 20 ff.) provide a discursive framework for these observations.

10. Katharina Fritsch, *Museum*, ex.cat., German Pavillon, Venice Biennale 1995, pp. 10-12.

11. As in note 10, p. 12.

12. *Der grosse Duden*, Vol.: "Bildwörterbuch", Bibliographische Institut AG (ed.), Leipzig 1936.

13. This has for a long time been an important element that is discussed and captured in reception. For this see Julian Heynen, "Familiarity – Alienation – Realization. (Fragments on the work of Katharina Fritsch)", in: *Katharina Fritsch 1979-1989*, ex. cat., Westfälischer Kunstverein Münster/Portikus, Frankfurt am Main 1989, pp. 67-71.

14. As note 13, p. 69.

15. It would be interesting to examine this view of color and also the named group of works from the point of view of synaesthesia.

Die kurze inhaltliche Betrachtung der vier Arbeiten von Katharina Fritsch steht exemplarisch für die anderen vergleichbaren Werke. Ein entsprechender Blick auf sie würde zeigen, dass in unterschiedlicher Form und Ausdeutung dieselbe menschliche Grunderfahrung zur Metapher wird: dass nämlich Schuld und Unschuld, Gut und Böse, Chaos und Ordnung, Reinheit und Unreinheit unauflösbar ineinander verwoben sind.

Mit der oben beschriebenen hohen bildnerischen Präzision und Bewusstheit inszeniert Katharina Fritsch diese Metapher. Sie treibt ihre latente Trivialität und Simplizität durch formale Gestaltung und inhaltliche Verschiebungen so sehr auf die Spitze, dass sie künstlich wird und auffällt, so dass die Bilder zum Innehalten auffordern und ihre Inhalte neu bedacht werden können.

SCHLUSS

Es zeigt sich jetzt, dass die Massnahmen der Distanzierung, Neutralisierung und Verallgemeinerung die Gegenstände und Figuren von Katharina Fritsch nicht nur in eine fremde Ordnung von verführerischer Ausstrahlung überführen, die sie einen neu wahrzunehmen veranlasst. Die bildnerische Ordnung, die hier aufgebaut wird, verrät je länger je deutlicher auch ihre Funktion, das bedrohliche Potential an Unnennbarem und Chaotischem, das sich im Untergrund der gewöhnlichen Dinge und Erfahrungen staut, zu bannen. Vielleicht lässt sich daraus die leichte Melancholie erklären, die besonders den früheren Skulpturen eigen ist. Ein Zeichen dafür, dass der Druck sich steigert, sind die neueren figuralen Werke, in denen Katharina Fritsch das Chaos immer deutlicher – nicht ohne Humor und Selbstironie – zu Wort kommen lässt.

1. Die drei Titel in diesem Text sind Zitaten von Katharina Fritsch entnommen. «Ein Bild von Ferne»: siehe S. 69; «Der Punkt des Sichwunderns» aus: Matthias Winzen, «Katharina Fritsch – Ein Gespräch», in: Das Kunst-Bulletin, Nr. 1/2, Jan./Feb. 1994, S. 14; «Der Auflösung etwas entgegensetzen» aus: Katharina Fritsch, Museum, Ausst.kat. Deutscher Pavillon, Biennale Venedig 1995, S. 9.
2. Es sind dies die Werke mit den Katalognummern 3-11.
3. K. Fritsch zum Faltblatt: «Als ich das Faltblatt machte, wollte ich keinen grossen Gestus und keinen Luxus. Da war es das Einfachste, die Liste meiner bisherigen Arbeiten billig zu drucken. Aber es sollte meinen Vorstellungen eines Druckwerks entsprechen. Ich wählte zum Beispiel einen ganz bestimmten Schrifttypus, den ich seitdem für alles Gedruckte benutze. Das Faltblatt konnte ich als Beilage zu einer Zeitung, die Freunde von mir herausbrachten, drucken, wie so eine Werbebeilage. Ich dachte mir: Wenn ich jetzt jeden Monat zehn von diesen Multiples zu je 100 Mark verkaufe, … das wär' doch was. Ich hatte damals überhaupt kein Geld und sah mich schon reich werden.» Matthias Winzen, «Katharina Fritsch – Ein Gespräch», wie Anm. 1, S. 20.
4. Gary Garrels charakterisiert in seinem Beitrag das «Warengestell» als «eine Art anthropomorphen Kosmos», siehe S. 23.
5. Ausführliche Beschreibung des Modells unter Kat. 100 und auf S. 27, wo eine Beschreibung von Katharina Fritsch zitiert wird.
6. Siehe z.B. «Friedhof für Urnengräber» (Kat. 26), «Stern» (Kat. 34), «Treppe mit achtzig Stufen» (Kat. 37), «Rasenplatz mit achtzig Bäumen» (Kat. 38), «Schlüsselring» (Kat. 44), «Acht Tische mit acht Gegenständen» (Kat. 48), «Acht Bilder in acht Farben» (Kat. 93).
7. Siehe S. 69.
8. Die Rezeption des «Museums, Modell 1:10» an der Biennale war zwiespältig und, wenn man die Kritiken liest, wenig ergiebig. Ein Grund dafür lag darin, dass die Arbeit losgelöst vom übrigen Schaffen der Künstlerin rezipiert wurde. Immer wiederkehrende Ansatzpunkte zur Kritik waren die Monumentalität der Skulptur und ihre Unüberschaubarkeit, also zwei Momente, die – wenn das «Museum» im Kontext von K. Fritschs Schaffen betrachtet wird – von konstituierender Bedeutung sind. Eine Hauptrichtung der Argumentation verlief im Versuch, die Arbeit in einer architektonischen anstatt einer künstlerischen Tradition zu diskutieren. Dem liegt die Annahme zugrunde, dass jedes Architekturmodell nur die technische Ausführung vorwegnimmt, und nicht auch ein Gedankenmodell für räumliche Konzeptionen sein kann. Gerade das Modell kann jedoch, wie wir wissen, unersetzbare Erfahrungen vermitteln; unabhängig davon, ob es nur gedacht ist, oder, wie bei K. Fritsch, realisiert werden soll.
9. Das Gewicht, das die Künstlerin dem Text von Heinrich von Kleist «Über das Marionettentheater» beimisst (S. 32-37) und Äusserungen in diesem Katalog (S. 83 f.) und im Interview von 1994 (wie Anm. 1, S. 20f.) geben diesen Beobachtungen einen diskursiven Rahmen.
10. Katharina Fritsch, Museum, Ausst.kat. Deutscher Pavillion, Biennale Venedig 1995, S. 7-9.
11. Wie Anm. 10, S. 9.
12. Der grosse Duden, Bd.: «Bildwörterbuch», hrsg. v. d. Bilbiographischen Institut AG, Leipzig 1936.
13. Schon lange ist dieses ein wichtiges Moment, das in der Rezeption diskutiert und festgehalten wird. Vgl. dazu Julian Heynen, «Vertrauen – Verfremden – Verwirklichen. (Fragmente zu den Arbeiten von Katharina Fritsch)», in: Katharina Fritsch 1979-1989, Ausst.kat. Westfälischer Kunstverein Münster/Portikus, Frankfurt a. Main 1989, S. 61-65.
14. Wie Anm. 13, S. 63.
15. Es wäre interessant, diese Auffassung von Farbe wie auch die genannte Gruppe von Arbeiten unter dem Stichwort der Synästhesie zu untersuchen.

Valeria Liebermann

Catalogue
1979-1996

Werkverzeichnis
1979-1996

The following chronological catalogue covers Katharina Fritsch's work up to and including July 1996.

All the works were titled by the artist and titles identify only the object involved in the sculpture. The English titles are translations and do not replace the original German titles.

Dimensions follow the scheme height x width x depth. Editions vary in number between unique and unlimited. If no number is given the piece is unique, otherwise the number of existing versions is given. There may be slight variations in multiple editions. Some pieces exist in unique and multiple versions, but may also be used as a basis for new sculptures. The phrase "component of …" indicates how a particular piece was used; it refers to the artist's suggested way of presenting individual works or multiples.

Das nachfolgende, chronologische Werkverzeichnis umfasst alle bis Juli 1996 entstandenen Werke von Katharina Fritsch.

Die Titel der Arbeiten stammen ausnahmslos von der Künstlerin und bezeichnen lediglich den Gegenstand der Skulptur. Die englischen Titel sind Übersetzungen und ersetzen nicht die Originaltitel.

Die Masse werden nach dem Schema Höhe x Breite x Tiefe angeführt. Die Auflagenhöhe der einzelnen Werke variiert zwischen Unikat und unlimitiert. Ist keine Anzahl angegeben, so handelt es sich immer um ein Einzelstück, ansonsten ist die Anzahl der existierenden Ausführungen angegeben. Diese Art der Ausführung kann unterschiedlich erfolgen. Manche Arbeiten sind sowohl als Einzelstück oder Multiple ausgeführt, aber gleichzeitig auch für die Herstellung einer neuen Skulptur benutzt worden. Die Angabe «Bestandteil von …» weist auf die entsprechende Benutzung hin. Es handelt sich dabei dann um eine von der Künstlerin vorgeschlagene Art der Präsentation von Einzelwerken oder Multiples.

1.

2.

3.

4.

5.

1. **Piano,** 1979
colored wax
11 ¹³/₁₆ x 7 ⁷/₈ x 5 ⁷/₈ in.
Katharina Fritsch, Düsseldorf

The work consists of a wax block in the shape of a
stylized piano, uniformly colored black. The only fully
developed detail is the beveled front edge of the key-
board lid.

2. **Piano with Stairs,** 1979
colored wax
2 items, each 11 ¹³/₁₆ x 7 ⁷/₈ x 5 ⁷/₈ in.
Katharina Fritsch, Düsseldorf

Two pianos in black wax, equivalent to *Klavier* (cat. 1)
in their external form, are placed back to back, but
with a steep, narrow staircase between them. The
steep stairs – with steps roughly twice as high as they
are deep – are set symmetrically and precisely in the
center.

3. **Dark Green Tunnel,** 1979
colored wax
3 ¹/₈ x 3 ¹/₈ x 31 ¹/₂ in.
edition: 2
Private collection, United States
Fritz Schwegler, Düsseldorf

A relatively small channel has been left open on the
underside of a uniformly dark green block of wax in the
shape of a thick bar, curved at the top. In cross-section
the channel is in the shape of a semicircle on stilts, and
occupies about a quarter of the total volume. Looking
through the channel gives the impression of a long,
potentially infinite tunnel.

4. **Chimney,** 1979
clay, mortar
height 31 ¹/₂ in., diameter 3 ¹/₈ in.
Katharina Fritsch, Düsseldorf

A round chimney, tapering toward the top, is built of
small reddish bricks and gray mortar. The bricks are not
set close together: slight, differently sized gaps can be
made out. There are spaces between the bricks in the
individual rows and they are arranged irregularly
above each other, giving the impression of hand-built
masonry.

5. **Gray Mill,** 1979
plastic, paint
2 ³/₄ x 3 ¹/₈ x 2 ¹⁵/₁₆ in.
component of *Warengestell* (cat. 40)

Graue Mühle is a small, apparently stone building on a
square ground plan with a gabled roof, small chimney,
and a large waterwheel at the front. On the left of the
mill is a small tool-shed, and on the right a simple
wooden fence. Both the mill and the adjacent sections
are made of plastic and painted in a uniform gray color.

For this work a model of a Faller-house, a building for
a model railway system, was sprayed gray.

1. **Klavier,** 1979
eingefärbtes Wachs
30 x 20 x 15 cm
Katharina Fritsch, Düsseldorf

Die Arbeit besteht aus einem einheitlich schwarz ge-
färbten Wachsblock in Form eines stilisierten Klaviers.
An Details ist nur die abgeschrägte vordere Kante des
Tastendeckels herausgearbeitet.

2. **Klavier mit Treppe,** 1979
eingefärbtes Wachs
2 tlg., je 30 x 20 x 15 cm
Katharina Fritsch, Düsseldorf

Zwei Klaviere aus schwarzem Wachs, die in der äusseren
Form dem «Klavier» (Kat. 1) entsprechen, in deren Mitte
allerdings eine steile, schmale Treppe eingelassen ist,
sind Rücken an Rücken aufgestellt. Die steile Treppe
läuft symmetrisch genau in der Mitte, die Stufen sind
ungefähr doppelt so hoch wie tief.

3. **Dunkelgrüner Tunnel,** 1979
eingefärbtes Wachs
8 x 8 x 80 cm
Auflage 2
Privatsammlung USA
Fritz Schwegler, Düsseldorf

An der Unterseite eines einheitlich dunkelgrün gefärb-
ten Wachsblockes, der die Form eines dicken, an der
Oberkante gewölbten Balkens besitzt, wurde eine relativ kleine Rinne ausgespart. Im Querschnitt besitzt sie
die Form eines gestelzten Halbkreises und nimmt etwa
ein Viertel des gesamten Volumens ein. Blickt man
durch die Rinne, entsteht der Eindruck eines langen,
nicht enden wollenden Tunnels.

4. **Schornstein,** 1979
Ton, Mörtel
Höhe 80 cm, Durchmesser 8 cm
Katharina Fritsch, Düsseldorf

Aus kleinen, rötlichen Ziegeln ist mit grauem Mörtel ein
sich leicht nach oben verjüngender runder Schornstein
gemauert. Die Ziegel sind nicht dicht an dicht gesetzt,
sondern weisen leichte, unterschiedlich grosse Lücken
auf. Die Abstände der Ziegel zueinander in den einzelnen Reihen und die Anordnung übereinander ist nicht
streng regelmässig, so dass der Eindruck eines von
Hand hergestellten Mauerwerks entsteht.

5. **Graue Mühle,** 1979
Kunststoff, Farbe
7 x 8 x 7,5 cm
Bestandteil von «Warengestell» (Kat. 40)

Ein kleines, scheinbar aus Steinen gemauertes Gebäude mit quadratischem Grundriss, einem Giebeldach mit
einem kleinen Schornstein und einem grossen Mühlrad
an der Vorderseite. An die Mühle schliesst sich links ein
kleiner Geräteschuppen, rechts ein einfacher Holzzaun
an. Die Mühle sowie die sich anschliessenden Teile bestehen aus Kunststoff und wurden mit einer einheitlichen Graufärbung versehen.

Für die Arbeit wurde das Modell eines Fallerhauses,
eines der Gebäude für Modelleisenbahnen, grau gespritzt.

<table>
<tr>
<td>

6. **Black and White Car,** 1979
    sheet metal, plastic, lacquer
    2 ³/₈ x 9 ¹³/₁₆ x 2 ¹⁵/₁₆ in.
    edition: 2
    component of *Warengestell* (cat. 40)
    Private Collection, Switzerland

The model Mercedes was painted with a uniform coat of black lacquer, and the caravan attached to it was painted with white lacquer.

For this work Katharina Fritsch used a model of a Mercedes car with a 1970s trailer, available from toyshops.

7. **Pan Lids,** 1979
    cast iron, enameled
    height 16 ⁹/₁₆ in.
    Fritz Schwegler, Düsseldorf

This work consists of two identical black oval pan lids of enameled cast iron. They have identical irregularities in their shape and surface quality. The handle fitting on the top is visible underneath as well. The lids were fastened together by a simple hinge attached to the narrow side of the oval. This means that they cannot be used as intended, but can be presented in two states, open and closed, suggesting an association with open and closed mussels.

The shape and color of the individual lids is reminiscent of a kind of pan lid that was particularly popular in the 1940s and 1950s.

8. **Green Case,** 1979
    cardboard, lizard paper, felt
    height ³/₁₆ in., 37 ¹³/₁₆ x 3 ³/₈ in., tapering to
    1 ³/₈ in.
    edition: 3
    Katharina Fritsch, Düsseldorf
    Norbert Wehner, Düsseldorf

The trapezium-shaped shallow case was made from cardboard covered by green lizard paper. The irregular dotted pattern of the paper creates a shimmering color varying between a dark and a lighter green. The work is almost one meter long, but very narrow, and looks like a container for a valuable object. The case, which can be opened, is lined with red felt.

9. **Blue Case,** 1979
    cardboard, lizard paper
    height ¹⁵/₁₆ in., 37 ¹³/₁₆ x 3 ³/₈ in., tapering to
    1 ³/₈ in.
    Katharina Fritsch, Düsseldorf

Blaues Futteral differs from cat. 8 in that blue lizard paper was used, and in that it is two centimeters higher. Unlike *Grünes Futteral*, *Blaues Futteral* cannot be opened.

</td>
<td>

6. **Schwarz-weisses Auto,** 1979
    Blech, Kunststoff, Lack
    6 x 25 x 5 cm
    Auflage 2
    Bestandteil von «Warengestell» (Kat. 40)
    Privatbesitz Schweiz

Das Modell eines Mercedes wurde mit einer einheitlichen schwarzen Lackschicht gestrichen, der an das kleine Auto befestigte Wohnwagen mit weissem Lack.

Für die Arbeit benutzte Katharina Fritsch ein Modellauto vom Typ Mercedes mit Anhänger aus den siebziger Jahren, das in Spielwarengeschäften erhältlich war.

7. **Topfdeckel,** 1979
    Gusseisen, emailliert
    Höhe 42 cm
    Fritz Schwegler, Düsseldorf

Die Arbeit besteht aus zwei gleichen, schwarzen, ovalen Topfdeckeln aus emailliertem Gusseisen. Sie weisen identische Unregelmässigkeiten in Form und Oberflächenbeschaffenheit auf. Die Befestigung des Henkels an der Oberseite des Deckels ist an der Unterseite sichtbar. Die Deckel wurden mit einem einfachen Scharnier, das an der Schmalseite des Ovales angebracht ist, miteinander befestigt. Diese Montage macht sie unbenutzbar und erlaubt die Präsentation in zwei verschiedenen Zuständen: geschlossen und geöffnet. Dadurch entsteht gleichzeitig die Assoziation von geöffneten und geschlossenen Muscheln.

Der einzelne Deckel erinnert in seiner Form und Farbigkeit an Topfdeckel, die vor allem in den vierziger und fünfziger Jahren benutzt wurden.

8. **Grünes Futteral,** 1979
    Pappe, Eidechsenpapier, Filz
    Höhe 4 mm, 96 x 8,5 cm, zulaufend auf 3,5 cm
    Auflage 3
    Katharina Fritsch, Düsseldorf
    Norbert Wehner, Düsseldorf

Das trapezförmige, flache Etui wurde aus mit Pappe bezogenem grünen Eidechsenpapier hergestellt. Durch das unregelmässig gepunktete Muster des Papiers entsteht eine changierende Farbigkeit, die zwischen einem dunklen und einem helleren Grün variiert. Fast einen Meter lang, dafür aber sehr schmal, scheint das Etui ein Behältnis für einen kostbaren Gegenstand zu sein. Das Futteral lässt sich öffnen und ist innen mit rotem Filz ausgekleidet.

9. **Blaues Futteral,** 1979
    Pappe, Eidechsenpapier
    Höhe 2,4 cm, 96 x 8,5 cm, zulaufend auf 3,5 cm
    Katharina Fritsch, Düsseldorf

Das «Blaue Futteral» unterscheidet sich von dem «Grünen Futteral» durch die Farbigkeit – es wurde blaues Eidechsenpapier benutzt –, durch die Grösse – es ist zwei Zentimeter höher – und durch die Unbenutzbarkeit. Im Gegensatz zum «Grünen Futteral» lässt sich das blaue nicht öffnen.

</td>
</tr>
</table>

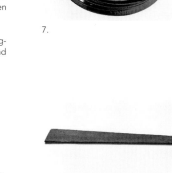

7.

8.

10.

10. **Bouquets in Vases,** 1979
    plastic, lacquer
    13 3/8 x 16 9/16 x 7 7/8 in.
    Thomas Huber, Düsseldorf

Each of two black lacquered vases contains a bouquet of fifteen to twenty plastic carnations, red blooms in one and white in the other. The body of each vase, whose upper conclusion cannot be seen, at first becomes constantly wider but narrows down again toward the base, so that the widest part is in the lowest quarter of the vase.

Simple plastic milk containers painted with black lacquer were used as vases. For the flowers, store-bought artificial carnations were lacquered white or red.

10. **Sträusse in Vasen,** 1979
    Kunststoff, Lack
    34 x 42 x 20 cm
    Thomas Huber, Düsseldorf

In zwei schwarzlackierten Vasen befindet sich jeweils ein Strauss aus 15 – 20 Kunststoffnelken, der eine mit weissen Blüten, der andere mit roten. Der Körper der Vasen, deren oberer Abschluss nicht zu sehen ist, verbreitert sich zunächst beständig, verjüngt sich aber im unteren Teil wieder, so dass sich die breiteste Stelle im untersten Viertel der Vase befindet.

Einfache Milchbehälter aus Kunststoff, die mit schwarzem Lack versehen wurden, dienten als Vasen. Für die Nelken wurden im Handel erhältliche künstliche Nelken mit rotem bzw. weissem Lack bemalt.

11.

11. **Broom,** 1979
    wood, bristles, paint
    50 3/8 x 12 5/8 x 4 3/4 in.
    Katharina Fritsch, Düsseldorf

This work is a simple household broom with a red, rounded handle and black, hard bristles. In color, shape, and size it is exactly the same as the everyday domestic article. The wooden parts glow with intense color, contrasting with the deep, rich black of the bristles. No trace of cracks or sign of use is evident.

For this work the handle and bristle holder of a household broom were painted red, and the bristles sprayed black.

11. **Besen,** 1979
    Holz, Borsten, Farbe
    128 x 32 x 12 cm
    Katharina Fritsch, Düsseldorf

Ein einfacher Haushaltsbesen mit rotem, rundem Stiel und schwarzen, harten Borsten. Er entspricht sowohl in Farbe, Form und Grösse genau dem täglich benutzten Haushaltsartikel. Die Holzteile besitzen eine intensive, leuchtende Farbigkeit, die im Kontrast zum satten Schwarz der Borsten steht. Sie weisen keinerlei Kratzbzw. Benutzerspuren auf.

Für diese Arbeit wurde ein normaler Haushaltsbesen an Stiel und Borstenhalter rot lackiert, die Borsten schwarz gespritzt.

12. **Armchair with Cotton Reels,** 1980
    armchair, cardboard box, 32 black-lacquered cotton reels
    armchair: 31 1/2 x 24 7/16 x 29 1/2 in.
    cardboard box: 2 9/16 x 4 15/16 x 7 11/16 in.
    Katharina Fritsch, Düsseldorf

A small, gray cardboard box is placed on the floor beside a simple wooden armchair with an upholstered seat and back. In the box are thirty-two black-lacquered, chunky, unused cotton reels. The armchair comes from a garage-sale and its brownish upholstery is covered with a typically 1950s furnishing fabric. The pattern of the fabric shows threads crossing each other.

12. **Sessel mit Garnrollen,** 1980
    Sessel, Pappkarton, 32 schwarz lackierte Garnrollen
    Sessel: 80 x 62 x 75 cm
    Pappschachtel: 6,5 x 12,5 x 19,5 cm
    Katharina Fritsch, Düsseldorf

Neben einem einfachen, hölzernen Sessel mit Sitz- und Rückenpolstern steht eine kleine, graue Pappschachtel auf dem Fussboden. In ihr befinden sich 32 schwarz lackierte, dicke Garnrollen, die noch nicht benutzt wurden. Der Sessel stammt vom Sperrmüll und besitzt bräunliche Polster, die mit einem Dekorationsstoff bezogen sind, wie er für die fünfziger Jahre typisch ist. Das Muster zeigt sich überkreuzende aufgelöste Fäden.

12.

13. **Cats in a Little Basket,** 1980
    wire, lacquer, colored silicone
    wire basket: 2 9/16 x 10 5/8 x 7 1/2 in.
    80 cats, each: 2 9/16 x 2 9/16 x 9/16 in.
    Katharina Fritsch, Düsseldorf

Eighty small black silicone cats are placed randomly in a shallow rectangular basket made of white-lacquered wire mesh. Each small cat has a narrow body, thin legs, and a delicate head. The slender body is hunched and ends in an inward-curling tail. The legs are joined together in pairs; they incline inward and stand on a low truncated cone.

Katharina Fritsch took a small bronze cat used for stubbing out cigarettes as a pattern for the cat. In 1981/89 she made an enlarged version of the cat in plastic (see cat. 25).

13. **Katzen im Körbchen,** 1980
    Draht, Lack, eingefärbtes Silikon
    Drahtkorb: 6,5 x 27 x 19 cm
    80 Katzen je: 6,5 x 6,5 x 1,5 cm
    Katharina Fritsch, Düsseldorf

In einem rechteckigen, flachen Korb aus weisslackiertem Drahtgeflecht sind ungeordnet achtzig kleine schwarze Silikonkätzchen gelegt. Die kleine Katze besitzt einen schmalen Körper, dünne Beine sowie einen zierlichen Kopf. Der schlanke Körper ist zum Katzenbuckel gerundet und endet in einem nach innen geringelten Schwanz. Die Beine, die paarweise zusammengefasst wurden, laufen zueinander und enden auf einem niedrigen Kegelstumpf.

Als Muster für die Katze benutzte Katharina Fritsch eine kleine Bronzekatze, die als Glutlöscher für Zigaretten benutzt wurde. 1981/89 liess sie die Katze in vergrösserter Form aus Kunststoff herstellen (siehe Kat. 25).

14. **Wall Vase,** 1980
    plastic, water
    11 x 5 $^7/_8$ x 3 $^{15}/_{16}$ in.
    edition: 25 + 10 artist's proofs

Wandvase features a dark green, cone-shaped plastic vase tapering toward the bottom to a blunted tip. The top of the vase is bent slightly outward and thin seams are visible. The vase is suspended in a black iron ring in such a way that the bent-out edge fits precisely onto the ring. Attached to the ring is an iron bar with a screw thread, so that the vase can be fixed to a wall. The vase is filled to the brim with clear water.

The work is reminiscent in shape, size, and color of vases used to decorate graves in cemeteries.

The wall vase was made in 1980 in an edition of twenty-five with an additional ten artist's proofs as the Bonner Kunstverein's annual gift.

14. **Wandvase,** 1980
    Kunststoff, Wasser
    28 x 15 x 10 cm
    Auflage 25 + 10 AP

Eine konisch geformte, sich nach unten verjüngende Vase mit abgestumpfter Spitze aus dunkelgrünem Kunststoff. Der obere Abschluss der Vase ist leicht nach aussen gebogen und weist dünne Nähte auf. Die Vase wird so in einen schwarzen Eisenring eingehängt, dass der nach aussen gebogene Rand genau auf dem Ring aufliegt. An den Ring ist ein Eisenstab mit Schraubgewinde angebracht, mit dessen Hilfe man die Vase an der Wand befestigen kann. Die Vase ist bis zum Rand mit klarem Wasser gefüllt.

Die Arbeit erinnert in ihrer Form, Grösse und Farbe an Vasen, wie sie auf Friedhöfen für den Blumenschmuck auf Gräbern benutzt werden.

Die Wandvase wurde 1980 als Jahresgabe des Bonner Kunstvereins in einer Auflage von 25 Exemplaren zuzüglich 10 AP hergestellt.

14.

15. **Anthurium,** 1980
    plastic, wire, lacquer
    14 $^1/_{16}$ x 13 $^3/_8$ x 12 $^5/_8$ in.
    edition: 8
    component of *Warengestell* (cat. 40)
    Katharina Fritsch, Düsseldorf
    Matthew Marks Gallery, New York
    Birgit Müller, Cologne
    Private Collection, Switzerland
    Walker Art Center, Minneapolis

Three plain, clean preserving jars of white glass each serve as a vase for three glowing red plastic anthurium with yellow inflorescence. The three glasses are arranged in a triangle and the three flowers in them each point in a different direction. The flowers, supported by simple, thin florist's wire that represents the flower stem, are precise replicas and even have the typical waxy sheen of natural blooms.

For this work Katharina Fritsch used industrially manufactured plastic anthurium, and further heightened the intensity and the luminosity of their colors with an additional coat of high-gloss lacquer.

15. **Anturien,** 1980
    Kunststoff, Draht, Lack
    36 x 34 x 32 cm
    Auflage 8
    Bestandteil von «Warengestell» (Kat. 40)
    Katharina Fritsch, Düsseldorf
    Matthew Marks Gallery, New York
    Birgit Müller, Köln
    Privatbesitz Schweiz
    Walker Art Center, Minneapolis, USA

Drei schlichte, gereinigte Einmachgläser aus weissem Glas dienen jeweils drei leuchtend roten Anturien mit gelben Blütenständen aus Kunststoff als Vase. Angeordnet wurden die drei Gläser in einem Dreieck, so wie die sich in ihnen befindlichen Blumen jeweils in eine andere Richtung zeigen. Die Blüten, auf einen einfachen, dünnen Blumendraht gesteckt, der den Blumenstengel darstellt, sind der Natur identisch nachempfunden und besitzen den gleichen, wächsernen Glanz.

Für diese Arbeit hat Katharina Fritsch industriell hergestellte Kunststoff-Anturien benutzt, auf deren Oberseite der Rot- und Gelbton sowie die Leuchtkraft der Farben durch eine zusätzliche hochglänzende Lackierung noch intensiviert wurde.

15.

16. **Wallpaper Pattern,** 1980
    wall paint
    size: variable
    Katharina Fritsch, Düsseldorf

Tapetenmuster was formed by rolling paint onto plaster in a small to midsize room. Applied to a gray background, the pattern comprises red, green, and blue wedges featuring uneven edges; irregular lines in the same colors; and white wedges and lines reminiscent of bamboo canes.

At first glance, the pattern seems rather haphazard, but a clear serial order emerges upon further inspection. The colored lines and wedges run horizontally and form groups such that the red and green wedges always point to each other and the blue wedges always point downward. The colored lines relate to the white pattern beneath them, vaguely resembling an upright pair of compasses. The horizontal tripes are continued vertically and are consistently staggered.

16. **Tapetenmuster,** 1980
    Wandfarbe
    Grösse: variabel
    Katharina Fritsch, Düsseldorf

In einem kleinen bis mittelgrossen Zimmer wird ein Muster direkt auf Putz ausgerollt. Das Muster, das auf einen grauen Untergrund aufgebracht wird, setzt sich aus roten, grünen und blauen Keilen mit unregelmässigem Rand, aus scheinbar unregelmässigen Strichen in den genannten Farben und aus weissen Keilen und Strichen, die an Bambusrohre erinnern, zusammen. Scheint das Muster auf den ersten Blick sehr unregelmässig, zeigt sich auf den zweiten Blick eine klare, serielle Ordnung. Horizontal fortlaufend sind jeweils die farbigen Striche und Keile zu einer Gruppe zusammengefasst: Die roten und grünen Keile weisen aufeinander, die blauen jeweils nach unten; die farbigen Striche beziehen sich auf das darunterliegende weisse Muster, das vage an einen aufrecht stehenden Zirkel denken lässt. In der Vertikalen werden die horizontalen Musterstreifen jeweils versetzt fortgeführt.

17.

17. Cemetery with Row Graves, 1980/82
project
documented as ground plan and elevation on a
scale of 1:400
2 versions of the drawings:
a) ink drawing
31 1/2 x 31 1/2 in.
Katharina Fritsch, Düsseldorf
b) blue-print
31 1/2 x 31 1/2 in.
Kasper König, Frankfurt

Both the project's ground plan and elevation are in the
form of a square, with a Greek key pattern of double
lines and bands formed by circles or egg-shaped ovals.
The lines and bands run parallel, both beginning at the
four corners of the square, turning at the corner points
and finally forming a cross at the center. The drawing is
in the style of an architectural plan.

The project is drawn as a ground plan and an elevation
and can be implemented as follows: four asphalted
paths with anonymous graves and egg-shaped bushes
are brought together in a Greek key pattern in a square
with sides intended to be 200 yards long. The graves
are planted with grass and should be placed to the
right and left of the asphalted paths, which run to a
cruciform center from the north, south, east, and west.
From there they again lead to one of the points of the
compass. Between the graves the strips, 4 3/8 yards
wide, are densely planted with rowan bushes, which
bear orange berries in the summer.

17. Friedhof für Reihengräber, 1980/82
Projekt
dokumentiert als Grundriss und als Aufriss im
Massstab 1:400
2 Ausführungen der Zeichnungen:
a) Tuschezeichnung
80 x 80 cm
Katharina Fritsch, Düsseldorf
b) Lichtpause
80 x 80 cm
Kasper König, Frankfurt

Sowohl der Grund- als auch der Aufriss zeigen die Gestaltung einer quadratischen Fläche mit mäanderartig
geführten Doppellinien und Bändern aus Kreisen bzw.
eiförmigen Ovalen. Die parallel laufenden Linien und
Bänder beginnen jeweils an den vier Ecken des Quadrates, knicken an den Eckpunkten um und bilden
schliesslich ein kreuzförmiges Zentrum. Die grafische
Ausführung entspricht Architekturplänen.

Das als Grund- und Aufriss gezeichnete Projekt kann
wie folgt ausgeführt werden: Auf einer quadratischen
Grundfläche mit einer vorgesehenen Kantenlänge von
184 Metern werden vier asphaltierte Wege mit anony-
men Gräbern und eiförmigen Büschen mäanderartig
zusammengeführt. Die mit Rasen bepflanzten Gräber
sollen jeweils rechts und links der asphaltierten Wege
liegen, die von Süden, Westen, Norden und Osten zu
dem kreuzförmigen Zentrum laufen. Von dort führen sie
wieder in eine der vier Himmelsrichtungen hinaus. Zwischen den Gräbern werden die vier Meter breiten Streifen dicht mit Vogelbeerbüschen bepflanzt, die im Sommer orangefarbene Früchte tragen.

18.

18. Red Lorry, 1980/86
sheet metal, plastic, lacquer
2 9/16 x 11 13/16 x 1 15/16 in.
model for a lorry intended to travel through
Germany ad infinitum
Andreas Gursky, Düsseldorf

Similarly to *Schwarz-weisses Auto* (cat. 6), this toy lorry
with trailer was subsequently painted black and red.
The cab, the under-side and the wheels were painted
with slightly glossy black lacquer, the loading area and
coverings were dipped in bright red. The lorry was intended as a model for a project for a red lorry to travel
through Germany ad infinitum, with no particular des-
tination.

18. Roter Lastwagen, 1980/86
Blech, Kunststoff, Lack
6,5 x 30 x 5 cm
Modell für Lastwagen, der endlos durch
Deutschland fährt
Andreas Gursky, Düsseldorf

Ähnlich der Arbeit «Schwarz-weisses Auto» (Kat. 6) wurde hier das Spielzeugmodell eines Lastwagens mit An-
hänger nachträglich in den Farben Rot und Schwarz lak-
kiert. Das Führerhaus, der Unterboden und die Räder
wurden mit einem leicht glänzenden schwarzen Lack
angestrichen, die Ladefläche und die Abdeckungen
wurden in kräftiges Rot getaucht. Der Lastwagen soll
als Modell für ein Projekt stehen, bei dem vorgesehen
ist, einen roten Lastwagen endlos und ziellos durch
Deutschland fahren zu lassen.

19. Lübeck Picture, 1981
xerox-print, glass
7/8 x 2 3/16 in.
Katharina Fritsch, Düsseldorf

A black and white xerox copy of an old view of the city
of Lübeck – showing churches and other buildings as
well as fortifications and some of the surroundings – is
mounted between two sheets of glass.

19. Lübeck-Bild, 1981
Photokopie zwischen zwei Glasscheiben
2,2 x 5,5 cm
Katharina Fritsch, Düsseldorf

Die hartschwarz-weisse Photokopie einer alten Stadt-
ansicht von Lübeck – neben den Kirchen und der Be-
bauung werden die Befestigungsanlagen und ein Teil
des Umlandes wiedergegeben – ist zwischen zwei
Glasscheiben montiert.

19.

20. **Parrot Picture,** 1981
offset print, silkscreen print
2 versions:
a) 9 $^7/_{16}$ x 7 $^1/_{16}$ in.
b) 1986 edition by the Kunstring Folkwang, Essen,
23 $^5/_8$ x 17 $^3/_4$ in.
print run: 50

A color photograph, like a snapshot, is framed by red
passe partout with an oval opening. The photograph
shows a group of visitors at the zoo, standing outside
a concrete animal house – presumably the aviary – and
looking at a brightly colored parrot. The parrot,
perched on the remains of a dead tree, is asleep.

Papageienbild was published as an annual gift by the
Kunstring Folkwang Essen in 1986. The print run was
distributed as follows:
nos. 1 - 20: in the portfolio *5 Bildhauer als Grafiker* (5
Sculptors as Graphic Artists)
nos. 21 - 40: individual sheets
nos. 41 - 50: artist's proofs

21. **Cheese,** 1981
silicone, paint, polystyrene
height 5 $^1/_2$ in., diameter 39 $^3/_8$ in.
edition: 6
component of *Acht Tische mit acht Gegenständen* (cat. 48)
component of *Tisch mit Käse* (cat. 81)

Käse features a large, thick disk of light yellow silicone,
with rounded edges and outward-curving edge. The
smooth surface of the work reveals slight imperfec-
tions, like small indentations or bumps. The material,
shape, and surface quality recall the work's inspiration:
large cheeses typical of Switzerland or Holland.

22. **Pans,** 1981
aluminum, rubber lining
height each 16 $^9/_{16}$ in., diameter each 16 $^9/_{16}$ in.
component of *Acht Tische mit acht Gegen-
ständen* (cat. 48)

Töpfe consists of two large, polished aluminum pans.
Each has riveted handles and a simple lid. One pan
holds a red-colored rubber lining, while the other is
filled to the brim with water. The pans are placed side
by side in such a way that their handles almost touch
and the handles on the lids point in the same direction,
at right angles to the pan handles.

The shape and size of the work is reminiscent of cook-
ware used in canteens, commercial kitchens and
homes beginning in the 1950s.

23. **Double-Sided Mirror,** 1981
glass covered with a reflective surface
$^1/_8$ x 7 $^7/_8$ x 5 $^7/_8$ in.
component of *Warengestell* (cat. 40)

The work comprises an oval sheet of glass with a reflective surface on both sides and an unpolished edge. The
mirror reveals no scratches or fingerprints on either
side.

24. **Advertising Leaflet I,** 1981 (pl. 1)
paper, offset printing
11 $^{11}/_{16}$ x 8 $^1/_4$ in.
edition: 1000

Each page of the four-page *Werbeblatt I* presents illustrations of the works by the artist. The inside pages are

---

20. **Papageienbild,** 1981
Offsetdruck, Siebdruck
2 Versionen:
a) 24 x 18 cm
b) 1986 Edition des Kunstring Folkwang, Essen,
60 x 45 cm
Auflage 50

Eine Farbfotografie, einem Schnappschuss ähnlich, ist
in einem roten Passpartout mit ovalem Ausschnitt gerahmt. Das Foto darin zeigt eine Gruppe von Zoobesu-
chern, die vor einem Tierhaus – vermutlich dem Vogel-
haus – aus Beton einen bunten Papagei betrachtet. Der
Papagei sitzt auf den Resten eines abgestorbenen Bau-
mes und schläft.

1986 wurde das «Papageienbild» vom Kunstring Folk-
wang Essen als Jahresgabe herausgegeben. Die Aufla-
ge wurde wie folgt aufgeteilt:
Nr. 1 - 20: in der Mappe «5 Bildhauer als Grafiker»
Nr. 21 - 40: Einzelblätter
Nr. 41 - 50: Artist Proofs

20.

21. **Käse,** 1981
Silikon, Farbe, Styropor
Höhe 14 cm, Durchmesser 100 cm
Auflage 6
Bestandteil von «Acht Tische mit acht Gegen-
ständen» (Kat. 48)
Bestandteil von «Tisch mit Käse» (Kat. 81)

Eine grosse, dicke Scheibe mit abgerundeten Kanten
und sich nach aussen wölbendem Rand aus hellgelb
gefärbtem Silikon. Die glatte Oberfläche der Arbeit
weist kaum sichtbare Unregelmässigkeiten auf, wie kleine Vertiefungen oder Erhebungen. Das Material, die
grosse, runde Form und die Oberflächen-beschaffen-
heit weisen auf das Vorbild der Arbeit hin: grosse Käse-
laibe aus der Schweiz oder den Niederlanden.

22. **Töpfe,** 1981
Aluminium, Gummikern
Höhe je 42 cm, Durchmesser 42 cm
Bestandteil von «Acht Tische mit acht Gegen-
ständen» (Kat. 48)

Zwei grosse, hohe Töpfe aus blank poliertem Aluminium bilden die Arbeit «Töpfe». Sie besitzen jeweils mit
Nieten befestigte Henkel und einfache Deckel. Das Innere des einen Topfes ist mit einem rot eingefärbten
Gummikern gefüllt, der andere bis zum Rand mit Wasser. Die Töpfe werden so nebeneinander gestellt, dass
sich ihre Henkel fast berühren und die Griffe der Deckel
in gleicher Richtung – rechtwinklig zu den Henkeln –
ausgerichtet sind.

In Form und Grösse erinnert die Arbeit an Kochtöpfe,
die seit den fünfziger Jahren in Kantinen, Grossküchen
oder Privathaushalten benutzt werden.

22.

23. **Doppelseitiger Spiegel,** 1981
Glas, verspiegelt
0,4 x 20 x 15 cm
Bestandteil von «Warengestell» (Kat. 40)

Eine ovale, doppelseitig verspiegelte Glasscheibe mit
ungeschliffenem Rand. Der Spiegel zeigt keinerlei Krat-
zer oder Fingerspuren.

24. **Werbeblatt I,** 1981 (Taf. 1)
Papier, Offsetdruck
DIN A4
Auflage 1000

Auf vier DIN A4 Seiten, die Innenseite weiss grundig,
die Aussenseite grau, werden je zwei Arbeiten der

23.

distinguished by a white background, while the outer pages feature a gray background. The typeface and layout are unpretentious and clear: under each illustrated object is a corresponding order number, description, and price.

Printed in 1981 as an unbound insert for a newspaper published by friends of Katharina Fritsch, *Werbeblatt I* shows a selection of her work to date.

Künstlerin abgebildet. Unter den freigestellten Objekten befindet sich eine Bestellnummer, eine Kurzbeschreibung und der jeweilige Preis des Gegenstandes. Der gewählte Schrifttypus und das Layout wirken unprätentiös und klar. Das Werbeblatt wurde als Beilage einer Zeitung gedruckt, die Freunde von Katharina Fritsch herausgaben. Es zeigt wie Werbebeilagen grosser Tageszeitungen eine Auswahl der bis zu diesem Zeitpunkt entstandenen Arbeiten.

25.

25.   **Cat,** 1981/89
synthetic material
6 $^{11}/_{16}$ x 6 $^{11}/_{16}$ x 2 $^{3}/_{8}$ in.
unlimited multiple

The small, stylized cat in black synthetic material has a narrow body, thin legs, and a delicate head. The slender body is hunched and ends in an inward-curling tail. The legs were joined together in pairs; they incline inward and stand on a low truncated cone. The head is turned at ninety degrees to the body. The almond-shaped eyes, with the pupil indicated by a light dot in the middle, and the Y-shaped mouth are suggested by delicate lines. The eyes and cheeks on the head, and on the body the points at which the limbs begin, are emphasized by slight indentations. The matte coloring – the black plastic was subsequently painted with matte black lacquer – means that the details disappear in favor of the overall form.

The shape of the cat's body and head is reminiscent of the "Katjes" company's logo design, which was developed in the 1950s and 1960s. The cat was used as early as 1980 for a work, in a smaller version (see cat. 13).

25.   **Katze,** 1981/89
Kunststoff
17 x 17 x 6 cm
unlimitiertes Multiple

Die stilisierte, kleine Katze aus schwarzem Kunststoff besitzt einen schmalen Körper, dünne Beine sowie einen zierlichen Kopf. Der schlanke Körper ist zum Katzenbuckel gerundet und endet in einem nach innen geringelten Schwanz. Die Beine, die paarweise zusammengefasst wurden, laufen zueinander und enden auf einem niedrigen Kegelstumpf. Der Kopf ist um 90° zum Körper gedreht. Die mandelförmigen Augen, in deren Mitte die Pupille durch einen leichten Punkt wiedergegeben ist, und die Y-förmige Schnauze sind mit zarten Strichen angedeutet. Mit Hilfe leichter Vertiefungen wurden am Kopf die Ohren und die Wangen, am Körper der Ansatz der Gliedmassen hervorgehoben. Durch die matte Farbigkeit – der schwarze Kunststoff wurde nachträglich mit einem schwarzen Mattlack versehen – verschwinden die Details zugunsten der Gesamtform.

Die Form des Körpers und des Kopfes der Katze erinnert an die Gestaltung des Logos der Firma «Katjes», das in den fünfziger/sechziger Jahren entwickelt wurde. Bereits 1980 wurde die Katze in kleinerer Form für eine Arbeit benutzt (siehe Kat. 13).

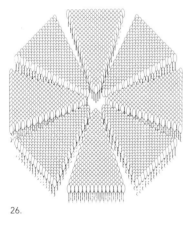
26.

26.   **Cemetery for Urn Graves,** 1982-1983
project
documented as ground plan and elevation on a scale of 1:200
2 versions of the drawings:
a) ink drawing
31 $^{1}/_{2}$ x 31 $^{1}/_{2}$ in.
Katharina Fritsch, Düsseldorf
b) blue-print
31 $^{1}/_{2}$ x 31 $^{1}/_{2}$ in.
Kasper König, Frankfurt

Both the ground plan and the elevation show an octagonal shape with triangular sections that are divided by pathways widening outward to create a stelliform center. In the ground plan the triangles are filled with small, evenly spaced circles and squares, and in the elevation with geometrically simplified trees and small squares. The drawing, which is like a geometrically produced pattern, is presented in the style of an architectural plan.

The project is drawn as a ground plan and an elevation and can be implemented as follows: a birch wood with 312 trees in rows, regularly arranged in triangles, is planted on an octagonal area with an intended diameter of 105 yards. In front of each birch tree a large 7 $^{7}/_{8}$ by 7 $^{7}/_{8}$ inch black slab is sunk into the ground, and under each of these is an urn grave. The wood with an octagonal outline thus produced has a stelliform open space in the centre from which paths radiate, widening towards the outside.

The project is documented as a ground plan and as an elevation and can be implemented at any time.

26.   **Friedhof für Urnengräber,** 1982-1983
Projekt
dokumentiert als Grund- und als Aufriss im Massstab 1:200
2 Ausführungen der Zeichnungen:
a) Tuschezeichnungen
80 x 80 cm
Katharina Fritsch, Düsseldorf
b) Lichtpause
80 x 80 cm
Kasper König, Frankfurt

Sowohl der Grund- als auch der Aufriss zeigen die Gestaltung eines Achtecks mit dreieckigen Flächen. Diese sind durch sich nach aussen verbreiternde Gassen getrennt, wodurch ein sternförmiges Zentrum entsteht. Die Dreiecke sind im Grundriss mit kleinen, regelmässig gesetzten Kreisen und Quadraten, im Aufriss mit geometrisch vereinfachten, eng aneinanderstehenden Bäumen und kleinen Quadraten versehen. Die grafische Ausführung, die einer geometrischen Musterzeichnung ähnelt, entspricht Architekturplänen.

Das als Grund- und Aufriss gezeichnete Projekt kann wie folgt ausgeführt werden: Auf einer achteckigen Grundfläche mit einem vorgesehen Durchmesser von 96 Metern wird ein Birkenwald gepflanzt, bei dem jeweils 312 Bäume in Reihen regelmässig einem Dreieck zugeordnet sind. Vor jeder Birke befindet sich eine zwanzig mal zwanzig Zentimeter grosse schwarze, in den Boden versenkte Platte, unter der sich das jeweilige Urnengrab befindet. Der so entstandene, im Umriss achteckige Wald besitzt einen sternförmigen Freiplatz in der Mitte, von dem strahlenförmig nach aussen sich verbreiternde Wege ausgehen.

Das als Grund- und Aufriss festgehaltene Projekt kann jederzeit ausgeführt werden.

27. **Green Silk Scarf**, 1982/89
printed silk
31 ¹/₂ x 31 ¹/₂ in.
component of *Warengestell* (cat. 40)
component of *Wühltisch* (cat. 71)
unlimited multiple

The work features a square of chromoxid green silk printed with a drawing of Saint Martin in the middle. The body of the figure retains the color of the background, but his horse is white and his cloak is red.

Grünes Seidentuch is a component of the works *Warengestell* and *Wühltisch*, but also stands as an unlimited multiple.

28. **White Cardboard Box**, 1982/91
Bristol board (.06 in. thick)
5 ⁷/₈ x 7 ⁷/₈ x 5 ⁷/₈ in.
component of *Warengestell* (cat. 40)
1991 multiple set with *Schafe*; edition: 80
signed, dated, and numbered in pencil (Katharina Fritsch 1982/92 serial number/80)

A plain, rectangular box with a lid was made from miter-cut, matte white Bristol board. The edges of both the body of the box and the lid are fitted together and glued very carefully, so that the joints are visible from the outside only at a very few points as thin hairlines. The height and depth of the box measure three quarters of the width; the height of the lid represents one fifth of the overall height.

The multiple is signed, dated, and numbered in pencil on the inner edge of the lid. The white cardboard box was produced as a multiple in 1991 in an edition of eighty, with the work *Schafe*.

29. **Sheep**, 1982/91
wire, plaster of Paris
2 ³/₁₆ x 15 ³/₄ x 9 ⁷/₁₆ in.
component of *Warengestell* (cat. 40)
1991 multiple set with *Weisser Pappkarton*; edition: 80
signed, dated, and numbered in pencil (Katharina Fritsch 1982/92 serial number/80)

The work consists of three pairs of small, white plaster of Paris sheep, with each pair in one of three poses: standing, grazing, or lying down. The details, like wool texture, hooves, head shape, and eyes, are developed three-dimensionally. The figures are hard-mold plaster of paris casts of crib figures from the 1950s.

In the multiple set, one of the two sheep that are lying down is signed, dated, and numbered underneath in pencil. The sheep were produced as a multiple in 1991 in an edition of eighty, with the work *Weisser Pappkarton*.

109

30. **Self-Adhesive Cross**, 1982
stainless steel, celluloid, adhesive film
¹/₁₆ x 3 ¹⁵/₁₆ x 3 ¹⁵/₁₆ in.
Katharina Fritsch, Düsseldorf

This work is a Greek cross of chromium-plated steel and light-colored celluloid, with double-sided adhesive film on the back. The shimmering celluloid, an imitation white tortoiseshell, was applied to the stainless steel in such a way that the cross is framed by a thin, shining rim.

27. **Grünes Seidentuch**, 1982/89
Seide bedruckt
80 x 80 cm
Bestandteil von «Warengestell» (Kat. 40)
Bestandteil von «Wühltisch» (Kat. 71)
unlimitiertes Multiple

Ein quadratisches, chromoxid grünes Seidentuch, das in der Mitte mit einer Zeichnung von Sankt Martin bedruckt ist. Während der Körper der Person in der Farbe des Hintergrundes bleibt, ist das Pferd weiss, der Mantel rot eingefärbt.

Das Seidentuch wurde als Teil der Arbeiten «Warengestell» und «Wühltisch» verwendet, ist aber gleichzeitig ein unlimitiertes Multiple.

27.

28. **Weisser Pappkarton**, 1982/91
Bristolkarton (1,5 mm stark)
15 x 20 x 15 cm
Bestandteil von «Warengestell» (Kat. 40)
Multiple-Set von 1991 mit «Schafe»; Auflage 80
signiert, datiert und numeriert mit Bleistift (Katharina Fritsch 1982/92 laufende Nummer/80)

Aus auf Gehrung geschnittenen, mattweissen Bristolkartonplatten wurde eine schlichte, rechteckige Kiste mit Deckel gefertigt. Die Kanten sowohl des Kistenkörpers als auch des Deckels sind sehr sauber zusammengefügt und verklebt, so dass von aussen die Nähte nur an wenigen Stellen als dünne Haarfugen sichtbar werden. Die Höhe und die Tiefe der Kiste betragen 3/4 der Breite, die Höhe des Deckels beträgt 1/5 der Gesamthöhe.

Am Innenrand des Deckels ist das Multiple mit Bleistift signiert, datiert und numeriert. 1991 wurde der weisse Pappkarton zusammen mit der Arbeit «Schafe» als Multiple in einer 80er Auflage hergestellt.

28.

29. **Schafe**, 1982/91
Draht, Gips
5,5 x 40 x 24 cm
Bestandteil von «Warengestell» (Kat. 40)
Multiple-Set von 1991 mit «Weisser Pappkarton»; Auflage 80
signiert, datiert und numeriert mit Bleistift (Katharina Fritsch 1982/92 laufende Nummer/80)

Die Arbeit besteht aus sechs kleinen, weissen Gipsschafen, von denen sich jeweils zwei in identischer Haltung befinden: stehend, grasend und liegend. Bei allen sechs Tieren sind die Einzelheiten, wie Fellbeschaffenheit, Hufe, Kopfausformung, Augen etc., plastischheraus gearbeitet. Die Figuren sind Abgüsse aus Hartformgips von Krippenfiguren, die in den fünfziger Jahren hergestellt wurden.

Bei dem Multiple-Set ist eines der beiden liegenden Schafe auf der Unterseite mit Bleistift signiert, datiert und numeriert. 1991 wurden die Schafe zusammen mit der Arbeit «Weisser Pappkarton» als Multiple in einer 80er Auflage hergestellt.

29.

30. **Selbstklebendes Kreuz**, 1982
Edelstahl, Zelluloid, Klebefolie
0,2 x 10 x 10 cm
Katharina Fritsch, Düsseldorf

Ein griechisches Kreuz aus verchromtem Edelstahl und hellem Zelluloid, auf dessen Rückseite doppelseitige Klebefolie angebracht wurde. Das schillernde Zelluloid, das weisses Schildplatt imitiert, wurde so auf den Edelstahl geklebt, dass ein dünner, glänzender Rand das Zelluloidkreuz umrahmt.

30.

31.

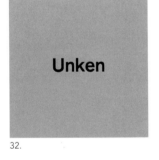

32.

33.

31. **Madonna Figure,** 1982
plaster of Paris, paint
11 ¹³/₁₆ x 3 ¹/₈ x 2 ³/₈ in.
component of *Warengestell* (cat. 40)
component of *Warengestell mit Madonnen*
(cat. 70)
unlimited multiple

The sculpture consists of a peacefully introverted Madonna figure with hands folded in prayer. Wearing a long, belted robe and a veil over head, shoulders, and arms, she hangs a long rosary over her right arm. In contrast to the brightly painted original, a Madonna statue from Lourdes, the sculpture is a uniformly matte and yet glowing yellow. The monochrome yellow somewhat reduces the figure's three-dimensional quality and renders it more pictorial.

The sculpture was cast after a replica of the Lourdes-Madonna as can be purchased in devotional shops. Katharina Fritsch made this figure with various materials in several, different sizes. For *Warengestell* (cat. 40) she painted one of the plaster figures that she had bought with lemon-yellow paint. For the unlimited multiple, of which 288 copies were used for the work *Warengestell mit Madonnen* (cat. 70), and for the hard epoxy casting for the *Skulptur Projekte in Münster 1987* (Sculpture Projects in Münster 1987) exhibition (cat. 67), she used the Madonna figure as a pattern for the mold.

32. **Toads,** 1982/88
45-inch vinyl record
Edition Philomene Magers, Bonn
new edition with *Krankenwagen* (cat. 79) and
Mühle (cat. 80) for *Parkett* 25, 1990

A single record is placed in a grass-green sleeve with the title *Unken* printed in the center in black letters. As is usually the case with records, there is a round label in the centre, also grass-green. On this is printed, alongside the details about copyright, the recording, and the record company, the instruction *Bitte leise abspielen* ("Please play softly"). The recording reproduces the high-pitched calls of courting toads, constantly repeated.

The single was published for the first time in 1983 by the Galerie Philomene Magers in Bonn, then again in 1990 as a special edition by *Parkett* magazine.

33. **Fish Ring,** 1983/93
plastic, paint
diameter 3 ¹/₈ in.
component of *Warengestell* (cat. 40)
1993 multiple set with *Stern* (cat. 34); edition: 80

Fischring is a slender, blue plastic ring made up of six identical fish, each biting into the tail of the one in front of it. Each fish has small scales on its back, a protruding fin on either its back or belly, clearly formed gills, and large, heavily bulging eyes. The ring is sprayed with a slightly metallic blue lacquer. Both the size and shape suggest that the ring could be used as an item of jewelry.

Fischring, together with the work *Stern* (cat. 34), was produced in an edition of eighty copies in 1993 for the *Das Jahrhundert des Multiple* (The Century of the Multiple) exhibition and offered with *Stern* as a set.

31. **Madonnenfigur,** 1982
Gips, Farbe
30 x 8 x 6 cm
Bestandteil von «Warengestell» (Kat. 40)
Bestandteil von «Warengestell mit Madonnen»
(Kat. 70)
unlimitiertes Multiple

Die Skulptur besteht aus einer ruhig in sich gekehrten, die Hände zum Gebet gefalteten Madonnenfigur. Sie ist in ein langes, gegürtetes Gewand gekleidet, hat einen Schleier über Kopf, Schultern und Arme gelegt und trägt am rechten Arm einen länglichen, herabhängenden Rosenkranz. Im Gegensatz zu ihrem bunt bemalten Vorbild, einer Madonnenstatue aus Lourdes, besitzt sie eine einheitlich matte und doch leuchtende Gelbfärbung. Das monochrome Gelb nimmt der Figur ansatzweise die Tiefenräumlichkeit und lässt sie bildhaft werden.

Die Madonna ist ein identischer Abguss der Madonna Typ Lourdes aus dem Devotionalienhandel. Katharina Fritsch hat diese Figur in verschiedenen Materialien und in mehreren, in der Grösse variierten Versionen ausgeführt. Für das «Warengestell» (Kat. 40) übermalte sie eine der gekauften Gipsfiguren mit zitronengelber Farbe. Für das unlimitierte Multiple, von dem jeweils 288 Exemplare für die Arbeit «Warengestell mit Madonnen» (Kat. 70) verwendet wurden, und den Epoxiharzguss für die Ausstellung «Skulptur Projekt in Münster 1987» (Kat. 67) benutzte sie die Madonnenfiguren als Vorlage für die Gussform.

32. **Unken,** 1982/88
Single
Edition Philomene Magers, Bonn
Neuauflage zusammen mit «Krankenwagen» (Kat.
79) und «Mühle» (Kat. 80) für Parkett 25, 1990

In einem grasgrünen Cover mit der in schwarzen Buchstaben mittig gesetzten Aufschrift «Unken» befindet sich eine Single-Schallplatte. Wie bei Platten üblich, ist in der Mitte ein runder, ebenfalls grasgrüner Aufkleber, auf dem neben den Angaben zum Copyright, zur Aufnahme und zum Verleger die Anweisung «Bitte leise abspielen» zu lesen ist. Die Aufnahme gibt die sich ständig wiederholenden, hohen Töne von balzenden Unken wieder.

Erstmals wurde die Single 1983 von der Galerie Philomene Magers in Bonn, 1990 erneut als Vorzugsausgabe mit zwei weiteren Singles von der Zeitschrift «Parkett» verlegt.

33. **Fischring,** 1983/93
Kunststoff, Farbe
Durchmesser 8 cm
Bestandteil von «Warengestell» (Kat. 40)
Multiple-Set von 1993 mit «Stern» (Kat. 34);
Auflage 80

Ein schmaler, blauer Kunststoffreif aus sechs identischen Fischen, die jeweils in die Schwanzflosse des vorderen beissen. Die Fische sind mit kleinen Schuppen am Rücken, jeweils einer abstehenden Flosse am Rücken bzw. Bauch, deutlich ausgebildeten Kiemen sowie grossen, stark hervortretenden Augen charakterisiert. Der Reif ist mit einem leicht metallisch wirkenden blauen Lack gespritzt. Sowohl die Grösse als auch die Form deuten darauf hin, dass der Reif als Schmuckstück dienen könnte.

1993 wurde der «Fischring» zusammen mit der Arbeit «Stern» (Kat. 34) als Objekt für die Ausstellung «Das Jahrhundert des Multiple» in einer Auflage von 80 Exemplaren hergestellt und als Set angeboten.

34. **Star**, 1983/93
    brass, lacquered
    diameter 3 $^9/_{16}$ in.
    component of *Warengestell* (cat. 40)
    1993 multiple set with *Fischring* (cat. 33);
    edition: 80

This regular, eight-pointed aluminum star features delicate rays with pointed ends. The sheet aluminum is sprayed with lemon-yellow matte lacquer, giving the star a golden tinge. A pin is affixed to the back of the star so that it can be used as a brooch.

Star, together with the work *Fischring* (cat. 33), was produced in an edition of eighty copies in 1993 for the *Das Jahrhundert des Multiple* (The Century of the Multiple) exhibition and offered with *Fischring* as a set.

35. **Chain**, 1983
    glass beads, paint
    7 $^1/_{16}$ x 5 $^1/_8$ in.
    beads diameter $^1/_2$ in.
    component of *Warengestell* (cat. 40)

Thirty-two red lacquered glass beads are arranged at regular intervals in an oval pattern to form *Kette*. Each bead is the same size as, and the same distance from, the next, so that neither beginning nor end can be discerned.

36. **Precious Stone**, 1983
    Plexiglas, paint
    5 $^1/_2$ x 39 $^3/_8$ x 23 $^5/_8$ in.
    component of *Warengestell* (cat. 40)

Edelstein features a large rectangular block with beveled corners and edges in green-tinted Plexiglas. When viewed from above, it becomes clear that the basic form is that of a precious stone in the so-called diamond-emerald cut. A rectangle with the described cut is laid on top of a second, so that the emerald form is doubled.

34. **Stern**, 1983/93
    Messing, lackiert
    Durchmesser 9 cm
    Bestandteil von «Warengestell» (Kat. 40)
    Multiple-Set von 1993 mit «Fischring» (Kat. 33);
    Auflage 80

Ein gleichmässiger, achtzackiger Aluminiumstern, dessen zierliche Strahlen in spitze Enden auslaufen. Das Aluminiumblech ist mit zitronengelbem Mattlack gespritzt, wodurch der Stern eine Goldfärbung erhält. An die Rückseite des Sternes ist eine Nadel geklebt, so dass er auch als Brosche benutzt werden könnte.

1993 wurde der «Stern» zusammen mit der Arbeit «Fischring» (Kat. 30) als Objekt für die Ausstellung «Das Jahrhundert des Multiple» in einer Auflage von 80 Exemplaren hergestellt und als Set angeboten.

35. **Kette**, 1983
    Glaskugeln, Farbe
    18 x 13 cm
    Kugeln: Durchmesser 1,2 cm
    Bestandteil von «Warengestell» (Kat. 40)

In regelmässigen Abständen wurden 32 rot lackierte Glaskugeln zu einem ovalen Kreis ausgelegt. Jede Kugel besitzt die gleiche Grösse und jeweils den selben Abstand zu der nächsten, so dass es keinen Anfang und kein Ende gibt.

36. **Edelstein**, 1983
    Plexiglas, Farbe
    14 x 100 x 60 cm
    Bestandteil von «Warengestell» (Kat. 40)

Ein grosser, rechteckiger Block mit abgeschrägten Ecken und Kanten aus grün gefärbtem Plexiglas. Blickt man von oben auf die Arbeit, erkennt man, dass die Grundform einem geschliffenen Edelstein mit sogenanntem Diamant-Smaragdschliff entspricht. Die Form mit Smaragdschliff wurde so verdoppelt, dass jeweils ein Rechteck, das den nachempfundenen Schliff besitzt, mit der flachen Seite auf das andere gelegt wurde.

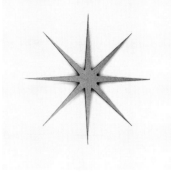

34.

35.

36.

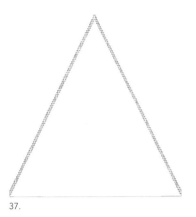

37.

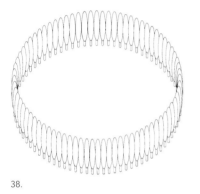

38.

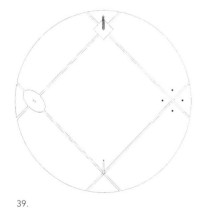

39.

37. **Staircase with Eighty Steps**, 1983-1984
project; documented as an elevation on a scale of 1:100
2 versions:
a) ink drawing
31 1/2 x 31 1/2 in.
Katharina Fritsch, Düsseldorf
b) blue-print
31 1/2 x 31 1/2 in.
Kasper König, Frankfurt

The drawing shows a design for a simple, steep, double-sided staircase with eighty steps on each side. The two sides meet at the top to form a single step, producing the shape of an isosceles triangle. The individual steps are roughly four times as wide and twice as high as they are deep. The drawing is reminiscent of an architectural plan.

The project is documented as an elevation and can be implemented at any time.

38. **Lawn with Eighty Trees**, 1983-1984
project; documented as ground plan and elevation on a scale of 1:100
2 versions:
a) ink drawing
31 1/2 x 31 1/2 in.
Katharina Fritsch, Düsseldorf
b) blue-print
31 1/2 x 31 1/2 in.
Kasper König, Frankfurt

In the ground plan, an oval pattern of eighty precisely placed small circles represents the design of a lawn, dotted with trees. The elevation suggests that the circles are trunks of tall, geometrically stylized trees. The distance between the individual trees is calculated so that their edges always touch the oval precisely.

The project is documented as a ground plan and as an elevation and can be implemented at any time. The oval area is to be planted with grass and bordered with tall poplars. The place is intended to be a housing estate of architectural and socio-cultural significance.

39. **Amusement Park**, 1983-1984
project; documented as ground plan and elevation on a scale of 1:200
2 versions:
a) ink drawing
31 1/2 x 31 1/2 in.
Katharina Fritsch, Düsseldorf
b) blue-print
31 1/2 x 31 1/2 in.
Kasper König, Frankfurt

The ground plan and elevation show a circle with a square inside it produced by double lines intersecting at right angles. The following shapes are to be found at the intersection points of the lines, working clockwise and starting at the top left: a large and a small oval, a square area with a smaller square inside, four large black dots, and a circle surrounding a black dot. In the elevation the small square area is presented as a tower standing on four tall legs, and the small circle is presented as a tall tube. The drawing, which is like a geometrically produced pattern, is in the style of an architectural plan.

This project can be implemented at any time, as follows: asphalted footpaths approximately one yard wide are laid out according to the plan in a circular patch of grass 17 7/16 yards in diameter. Four areas designed as follows are created at the intersection points: 1. an oval area with an oval, silver aluminum pool of water with a two-centimeter-high edge; 2. a square area in which there is an 8 3/4-yards-high, gray

37. **Treppe mit achtzig Stufen**, 1983-1984
Projekt; dokumentiert als Aufriss im Massstab 1:100
2 Ausführungen:
a) Tuschezeichnung
80 x 80 cm
Katharina Fritsch, Düsseldorf
b) Lichtpause
80 x 80 cm
Kasper König, Frankfurt

Die Zeichnung zeigt den Entwurf einer einfachen, steilen, doppelseitigen Treppe mit je achtzig Stufen. Die beiden Seiten der Treppe treffen in der Spitze in einer Stufe zusammen, so dass die Form eines gleichschenkligen Dreiecks entsteht. Die einzelnen Stufen sind ungefähr viermal so breit und zweimal so hoch wie tief. Die grafische Ausführung erinnert an Architekturpläne.

Das als Aufriss festgehaltene Projekt kann jederzeit ausgeführt werden.

38. **Rasenplatz mit achtzig Bäumen**, 1983-1984
Projekt; dokumentiert als Grund- und als Aufriss im Massstab 1:100
2 Ausführungen:
a) Tuschezeichnung
80 x 80 cm
Katharina Fritsch, Düsseldorf
b) Lichtpause
80 x 80 cm
Kasper König, Frankfurt

Ein ovaler Kranz aus achtzig exakt plazierten kleinen Kreisen bilden im Grundriss die Form des Rasenplatzes mit Bäumen. Dem Aufriss ist zu entnehmen, dass die Kreise als Angabe für Stämme von geometrisch stilisierten, hohen Bäumen stehen. Der Abstand der einzelnen Bäume zueinander ist so gewählt, dass sich die Ränder der Ovale immer gerade berühren.

Das als Grund- und Aufriss festgehaltene Projekt kann jederzeit ausgeführt werden. Die ovale Fläche wird dann mit Rasen bepflanzt und von hohen Pappeln begrenzt. Als Ort ist ein architektonischer und soziokultureller Raum – Wohnsiedlung – vorgesehen.

39. **Vergnügungspark**, 1983-1984
Projekt; dokumentiert als Grund- und als Aufriss im Massstab 1:200
2 Ausführungen:
a) Tuschezeichnung
80 x 80 cm
Katharina Fritsch, Düsseldorf
b) Lichtpause
80 x 80 cm
Kasper König, Frankfurt

Grund- und Aufriss zeigen die Gestaltung eines Kreises mit innen liegendem Quadrat, das durch sich rechtwinklig kreuzende Doppellinien entsteht. An den Kreuzungspunkten der Linien befinden sich folgende im Uhrzeigersinn angeführte Formen: links oben beginnend, ein grosses und ein kleines Oval, dann eine quadratische Fläche mit kleinen Winkeln, danach vier schwarze, grössere Punkte und schliesslich ein Kreis, der einen schwarzen Punkt umschliesst. Im Aufriss ist die kleine quadratische Fläche als ein auf vier hohen Beinen stehender Turm, der kleine Kreis als hohe Röhre ausgeführt. Die grafische Zeichnung entspricht Architekturplänen.

Auch dieses Projekt kann jederzeit wie folgt ausgeführt werden: Auf einer kreisrunden Rasenfläche mit einem Durchmesser von 96 Metern werden asphaltierte, ein Meter breite Gehwege entsprechend dem Plan angelegt. An den Kreuzungspunkten der Wege entstehen vier verschieden gestaltete Plätze: 1. ein ovaler Platz mit einem ovalen, silbernen Aluminiumwasserbecken, das einen zwei Zentimeter hohen Rand besitzt; 2. ein vier-

concrete tower with eight clocks, four outside and four inside at the top; 3. a junction with four black pools of water tapering to a point in the ground, each approximately 1 yard deep; 4. a circular area with a round brick chimney 8 3/4-yards- high.

40. **Display Stand,** 1979-1984 (pl. 2)
shelves: glass, aluminum
objects dating from 1979-1984:
Graue Mühle (cat. 5), *Schwarz-weisses Auto* (cat. 6), *Anturien* (cat. 15), *Doppelseitiger Spiegel* (cat. 23), *Grünes Seidentuch* (cat. 27), *Weisser Pappkarton* (cat. 28), *Schafe* (cat. 29), *Madonnenfigur* (cat. 31), *Fischring* (cat. 33), *Stern* (cat. 34), *Kette* (cat. 35), *Edelstein* (cat. 36)
height 79 15/16, diameter 47 1/4 in.
Kaiser Wilhelm Museum, Krefeld

A round set of shelves, with five sheets of glass kept twenty inches apart by four aluminum rods running continuously through them, forms the basis of the sculpture. The following objects are to be found on the different shelf levels, working from bottom to top: on the bottom shelf three preserving jars arranged in a triangle with three plastic flowers (Anthurium) on wires in each of them. On the next shelf, working clockwise, are an oval of precisely placed glass beads, a golden lacquered brass star with eight points, an oval, double-sided mirror, and a blue plastic ring made up of six fish, each biting the tail of the fish in front. In one of the two possible variants of this work, the fish ring and the star are omitted and replaced by a carefully folded green silk square laid out lengthways in the center. On the third shelf from the bottom, four white plaster of Paris sheep (two standing, two grazing), a gray plastic model of a mill, a white cardboard box, and a black toy car with a white caravan were grouped around a yellow Madonna figure in the center. On the fourth shelf is a large, green synthetic material block in the form of a cut precious stone. The top shelf is empty. The objects on the second and third levels are placed symmetrically opposite each other between the aluminum rods.

All the objects on the shelves are multiples, listed separately in the catalogue. The work in Krefeld is intended as a suggestion for presenting the multiples. Other possible ways of "presenting goods" are shown in *Acht Tische mit acht Gegenständen* (cat. 48) or the display stands each with one kind of multiple (cat. 69; cat. 70; cat. 77).

41. **Perfume in the Hallway,** 1984 (pl. 5)
perfume, hallway

A sufficient quantity of perfume (*Je reviens*) is sprayed in any hallway or stairway for the fragrance to remain perceptible in the air for a long period of time. The work is intended as an image of the inevitably familiar phenomenon of entering a hall that a freshly perfumed person has just left. A photograph published in the catalogue shows a stairway in which the work was carried out.

42. **Candle,** 1984
height 31 1/2 in., diameter 1 3/16 in.
2 versions:
a) polyester, component of *Acht Tische mit acht Gegenständen* (cat. 48)
b) wax, component of *Kerzenständer* (cat. 54)

113

eckiger Platz, auf dem ein acht Meter hoher, offener Turm aus grauem Beton steht, in dessen Spitze sich acht Uhren, vier aussen und vier innen, befinden; 3. ein Wegkreuz, bei dem vier je einen Meter tiefe, schwarze, in die Erde spitz zulaufende Wasserbecken eingelassen wurden; 4. ein runder Platz mit einem acht Meter hohen roten, gemauerten Schornstein.

40. **Warengestell,** 1979-1984 (Taf. 2)
Gestell: Glas, Aluminium
Objekte von 1979-1984:
«Graue Mühle» (Kat. 5), «Schwarz-weisses Auto» (Kat. 6), «Anturien» (Kat. 15), «Doppelseitiger Spiegel» (Kat. 23), «Grünes Seidentuch» (Kat. 27), «Weisser Pappkarton» (Kat. 28), «Schafe» (Kat. 29), «Madonnenfigur» (Kat. 31), «Fischring» (Kat. 33), «Stern» (Kat. 34), «Kette» (Kat. 35), «Edelstein» (Kat. 36)
Höhe 203 cm, Durchmesser 120 cm
Kaiser Wilhelm Museum, Krefeld

Ein rundes Regal mit fünf Glasplatten, die von vier durchgehenden Aluminiumstangen in einem Abstand von jeweils 50 cm gehalten werden, bildet die Grundform der Skulptur. Auf den einzelnen Ebenen des Regals befinden sich von unten nach oben folgende Objekte: auf der untersten Platte drei im Dreieck angeordnete Einmachgläser, in denen jeweils drei Plastikblumen an Drähten (Anturien) stecken. Auf der nächsten Platte im Uhrzeigersinn ein ovaler Kranz aus exakt gelegten roten Glaskugeln, ein golden lackierter Messingstern mit acht Zacken, ein ovaler, doppelseitiger Spiegel und ein blauer Kunststoffreif aus sechs sich jeweils in die Schwänze beissenden Fischen. Bei einer zweiten möglichen Aufbau-Variante werden der Fischring und der Stern weggelassen und durch ein sorgsam gefaltetes und länglich ausgelegtes grünes Seidentuch im Zentrum ersetzt. Auf der dritten Platte von unten vier weisse Gipsschafe (zwei stehend, zwei grasend), das Modell einer Mühle aus grauem Kunststoff, ein weisser Pappkarton und ein schwarzes Spielzeugauto mit weissem Wohnwagen um eine in der Mitte stehende gelbe Madonnenfigur gruppiert. Auf der vierten Platte liegt ein grosser, grüner Kunststoffblock, der die Form eines geschliffenen Edelsteines besitzt. Die letzte Platte ist leer. Die Objekte der zweiten und dritten Lage wurden sich symmetrisch gegenüberliegend in die Zwischenräume der Aluminiumstangen gelegt.

Alle im Gestell befindlichen Objekte sind Multiples, die im Werkverzeichnis gesondert aufgeführt sind. Die in Krefeld befindliche Arbeit soll als eine Art Vorschlag, wie die Multiples präsentiert werden könnten, dienen. Andere Möglichkeiten der «Warenpräsentation» zeigen «Acht Tische mit acht Gegenständen» (Kat. 48) oder die Warengestelle mit jeweils einer Sorte der Multiples (Kat. 69; Kat. 70; Kat. 77).

41. **Parfüm im Hausflur,** 1984 (Taf. 5)
Parfüm, Hausflur

In einem beliebigen Hausflur bzw. Treppenhaus wird so viel Parfüm der Marke «Je reviens» versprüht, dass über einen längeren Zeitraum der Duft in der Luft wahrnehmbar bleibt. Die Arbeit steht als Bild für das sicherlich bekannte Phänomen, dass man ein Treppenhaus betritt, durch das gerade eine frisch parfümierte Person gegangen ist. Das im Katalog von 1989 publizierte Foto zeigt ein Treppenhaus, in dem die Arbeit ausgeführt wurde.

42. **Kerze,** 1984
Höhe 80 cm, Durchmesser 3 cm
2 Ausführungen:
a) Polyesterabguss, Bestandteil von «Acht Tische mit acht Gegenständen» (Kat. 48)
b) Wachs, Bestandteil von «Kerzenständer» (Kat. 54)

This work is a plain, thirty-one-and-a-half-inch high candle in hard white wax with an upright wick. The rod-shaped candle has clear upper and lower edges and is still unused.

Eine schlichte, 80 cm hohe Kerze aus hartweissem Wachs mit aufgerichtetem Docht. Der obere und untere Abschluss der stabförmigen Kerze weist eine klare Kante auf. Die Kerze ist noch unbenutzt.

43. **Oval Cardboard Box,** 1984
cardboard
23 ⁵/₈ x 31 ¹/₂ x 47 ¹/₄ in.
component of *Acht Tische mit acht Gegenständen* (cat. 48)

43. **Ovaler Pappkarton,** 1984
Graupappe
60 x 80 x 120 cm
Bestandteil von «Acht Tische mit acht Gegenständen» (Kat. 48)

A large oval box of matte gray cardboard is topped by a shallow lid. The box is constructed in such a way that a scant hairline is all that is visible at the edges of the lid and the bottom, as well as on the side joints. The height of the box represents half the length and three quarters of the width of the oval. The work was considerably enlarged in relation to its prototype, a plain cardboard box.

Eine grosse, ovale Schachtel aus mattem, grauem Karton, die mit einem flachen Deckel verschlossen ist. Die Schachtel ist so gearbeitet, dass an den Kanten des Deckels und des Bodens nur eine kaum sichtbare Haarfuge entsteht, ebenso an der seitlichen Kante. Die Höhe der Kiste beträgt die Hälfte der Länge sowie 3/4 der Breite des Ovales. Die Arbeit wurde im Vergleich zu dem Vorbild – eine schlichte Pappschachtel – erheblich vergrössert.

44. **Key Ring,** 1984
metal, paint
diameter 11 ¹³/₁₆ in.
component of *Acht Tische mit acht Gegenständen* (cat. 48)

44. **Schlüsselring,** 1984
Metall, Farbe
Durchmesser 30 cm
Bestandteil von «Acht Tische mit acht Gegenständen» (Kat. 48)

Eight identical keys are attached to a ring that may be opened or closed. They are spread out at equidistant intervals, rather like the sails of a windmill, always with two facing each other. Each key has a flat oval handle, a long rounded shaft, and a flat bit with four notches. The key ring and the keys are also lacquered with alu-bronze.

An einem Metallring, der an einer Stelle geöffnet werden kann, sind acht identische Schlüssel befestigt. Sie sind ähnlich den Flügeln einer Windmühle in gleichem Abstand zueinander ausgebreitet, jeweils zwei befinden sich auf einer Linie einander gegenüber. Die Schlüssel haben einen ovalen, flachen Henkel, einen langen, runden Schaft und einen flachen, mit vier Einkerbungen versehenen Bart. Nachträglich wurden der Schlüsselring und die Schlüssel mit Alubronze lackiert.

44.

45. **Bowl,** 1984
Plexiglas, paint
height 18 ⁷/₈ in., diameter 39 ³/₈ in.
component of Acht *Tische mit acht Gegenständen* (cat. 48)

45. **Schüssel,** 1984
Plexiglas, Farbe
Höhe 48 cm, Durchmesser 100 cm
Bestandteil von «Acht Tische mit acht Gegenständen» (Kat. 48)

The work consists of a large, two toned hemisphere that is somewhat flattened at the base. The outer bowl is azure painted Plexiglas, the inner of white painted Plexiglas, with a fine hairline marking the union of the two.

Die Arbeit besteht aus einer grossen, zweifarbigen, am Boden etwas abgeflachten Halbkugel. Die Aussenseite ist aus azurblauem, die Innenseite aus weisslackiertem Plexiglas gefertigt. Eine feine Naht bezeichnet die Trennlinie zwischen der Innen- und Aussenseite.

The work was modeled on plastic bowls from the 1950s, where the inside was a different color from the outside.

Vorbild für die Schüssel waren Kunststoffschüsseln aus den fünfziger Jahren, bei denen die Innenseite eine andere Farbigkeit als die Aussenseite aufwies.

46. **Plate with Marine Animals,** 1984
metal, lacquer, silicone
diameter 11 ¹³/₁₆ in.
component of Acht *Tische mit acht Gegenständen* (cat. 48)

46. **Teller mit Meerestieren,** 1984
Metall, Lack, Silikon
Durchmesser 30 cm
Bestandteil von «Acht Tische mit acht Gegenständen» (Kat. 48)

Eight orange silicone squids are arranged close together in a circle on a large white plate. The squids' eight arms are curled slightly inward toward the body, and are of different sizes. The point of contact between the creatures is at the largest tentacle, immediately below the head. The surface of the figures is marked by slight bulges and shallow indentations. The eyes in the heads and the suckers on the tentacles protrude. The harsh white plate on which the creatures lie has a broad, slightly raised edge and matte coloring. Both the plate and the squids were specially made for this work. The plate is made of lacquered metal, and the squids from casted silicone that was subsequently lacquered.

Acht orangerote Tintenfische aus Silikon liegen im Kreis angeordnet dicht nebeneinander auf einem grossen, weissen Teller. Die Köpfe der Tiere zeigen zur Innenseite des Kreises. Die acht Arme der Tintenfische sind zum Körper leicht eingerollt und von unterschiedlicher Grösse. Der Berührungspunkt der Tiere liegt bei den grössten, direkt unterhalb des Kopfes liegenden Armen. Die Oberfläche der Figuren ist unregelmässig und weist leichte Beulen und flache Vertiefungen auf. Die Augen an den Köpfen und die Saugnäpfe an den Armen zeichnen sich ab. Der hartweisse Teller auf dem die Fische liegen, besitzt einen leicht erhöhten, breiteren Rand und eine matte Farbigkeit. Sowohl der Teller als auch die Tintenfische wurden hierfür hergestellt. Der Teller ist aus lackiertem Metall, die Tiere aus Silikon gegossen und anschliessend lackiert.

46.

47. **Black Vase,** 1984
polystyrene, paint
height 16 ⁹/₁₆ in., diameter 7 ⁷/₈ in.
component of Acht *Tische mit acht Gegen-*
ständen (cat. 48)

The vase, made of polystyrene and sprayed with matte black lacquer, features a fat, olive-shaped belly that tapers to about one-third of its diameter at the neck and then widens again at the rim of the neck. The oval shape flattens somewhat at the bottom so that the vase can stand upright. The balance of the design is underscored by the proportions: the diameter of the vase represents about half the height at the widest point.

48. **Eight Tables with Eight Objects,** 1984 (pl. 3)
MDF board, steel
objects dating from 1981-1984:
Käse (cat. 21), *Töpfe* (cat. 22), *Kerze*
(cat. 42), *Ovaler Pappkarton* (cat. 43), *Schlüs-*
selring (cat. 44), *Schüssel* (cat. 45), *Teller mit*
Meerestieren (cat. 46), *Schwarze Vase* (cat. 47)
eight tables each: 29 ¹/₂ x 78 ³/₄ (outside) -
13 ³/₄ (inside) x 78 ³/₄ in.
assembled table: diameter 189 in.
Emanuel Hoffmann-Stiftung, on permanent
loan to the Museum für Gegenwartskunst,
Basel

Eight identical trapezium-shaped tables are assembled to form a single large octagonal table with a space in the center. Each table is made of an MDF board spray-painted gray-green and three rectangular tubes lacquered matte black. The three table legs are fitted in such a way that two are about 7 ³/₄ inches from the front edge and one about 7 ³/₄ inches from the inside edge.
In the middle of each of the table is one of the following ordinary-looking objects: a large yellow block of cheese; a tall white candle; a huge gray cardboard box; a key ring; a blue-and-white bowl; a plate with squid; two aluminum pans; and a black vase. Viewed from above, the rhythmic arrangement of the objects can be discerned. Large forms that appear firmly closed, for example the cardboard box, alternate with small, seemingly open forms, such as the key-ring. The small and large objects are always arranged crosswise in pairs.

All the objects arranged on the table are listed as individual works in the catalogue. The arrangement on the large octagonal table represents a possible way of displaying goods.

49. **Key Ring,** 1985
ink on transparent paper
11 ¹³/₁₆ x 11 ¹³/₁₆ in.
Dr. Peter Littmann, Metzingen

This precisely executed schematic drawing of the *Schlüsselring* (cat. 44) is neither a sketch nor a design drawing but a graphic work in its own right.

50. **Plate with Marine Animals,** 1985
ink on transparent paper
11 ¹³/₁₆ x 11 ¹³/₁₆ in.
Dr. Peter Littmann, Metzingen

Like the previous catalogue entry, this is a schematic drawing illustrating the work *Teller mit Meerestieren* (cat. 46). Unlike the realized sculpture, the squids are represented by small ovals and not represented in greater detail. The plate is indicated by two circles of different sizes.

47. **Schwarze Vase,** 1984
Polystyrol, Farbe
Höhe 42 cm, Durchmesser 20 cm
Bestandteil von «Acht Tische mit acht Gegen-
ständen» (Kat. 48)

Die mit einem matten schwarzen Lack gespritze, aus Polystyrol hergestellte Vase besitzt einen dicken, olivenförmigen Bauch, der sich zum Hals auf etwa ¹/₃ seines Durchmessers verjüngt, um sich dann zur Oberkante des Halses wieder zu weiten. An der Unterseite ist die Ovalform etwas abgeflacht, um der Vase eine Standfläche zu geben. Die Ausgewogenheit der Gestaltung wird durch die Proportionen – der Durchmesser der Vase beträgt an der dicksten Stelle ungefähr die Hälfte der Höhe – unterstrichen.

48. **Acht Tische mit acht Gegenständen,** 1984
(Taf. 3)
MDF-Platte, Stahl
Objekte von 1981-1984:
«Käse» (Kat. 21), «Töpfe» (Kat. 22), «Kerze» (Kat.
42), «Ovaler Pappkarton» (Kat. 43), «Schlüssel-
ring» (Kat. 44), «Schüssel» (Kat. 45), «Teller mit
Meerestieren» (Kat. 46), «Schwarze Vase» (Kat. 47)
Acht Tische je: 75 x 200 (aussen) - 35 (innen) x
200 cm
zusammengefügter Tisch: Durchmesser 480 cm
Emanuel Hoffmann-Stiftung, Depositum im
Museum für Gegenwartskunst, Basel

Acht gleiche, trapezförmige Tische wurden zu einem grossen achteckigen Tisch mit ausgespartem Zentrum zusammengesetzt. Jeder Tisch wurde aus einer grau-grün gespritzten MDF-Platte und drei matt schwarz lackierten Vierkant-Stahlrohren gefertigt. Die drei Tischbeine sind so angebracht, dass zwei etwa 20 cm von der Vorderkante und eines etwa 20 cm von der Innenkante entfernt ist. In der Mitte eines jeden Tisches liegen bzw. stehen folgende, alltäglich wirkende Gegenstände: ein grosser, gelber Käse, eine hohe, weisse Kerze, ein riesiger, grauer Pappkarton, ein Schlüsselring, eine blauweisse Schüssel, ein Teller mit Tintenfischen, zwei Aluminiumtöpfe und eine schwarze Vase. Blickt man von einem erhöhten Standpunkt auf den grossen Tisch, so erkennt man eine rhythmische Anordnung der Objekte. Grosse, fest geschlossen wirkende Formen, wie z.B. die Pappschachtel, und kleine, offen scheinende Formen, wie z.B. der Schlüsselbund, lösen sich ab. Die grossen bzw. kleinen Objekte sind sich immer über Kreuz paarweise zugeordnet.

Alle auf dem Tisch angeordneten Gegenstände sind als einzelne Arbeiten im Werkverzeichnis aufgeführt. Die Zusammenstellung auf dem grossen, achteckigen Tisch stellt eine Möglichkeit der Präsentation von Waren dar.

49. **Schlüsselring,** 1985
Tusche auf Transparentpapier
30 x 30 cm
Dr. Peter Littmann, Metzingen

Eine präzise ausgeführte, schematisierte Zeichnung des «Schlüsselrings» (Kat. 44). Es handelt sich hierbei aber nicht um eine Skizze oder Entwurfszeichnung, sondern um eine eigenständige grafische Arbeit.

50. **Teller mit Meerestieren,** 1985
Tusche auf Transparentpapier
30 x 30 cm
Dr. Peter Littmann, Metzingen

Vergleichbar mit Kat. 49 handelt es sich um eine schematisierte Zeichnung, die Arbeit «Teller mit Meerestieren» (Kat. 46) zeigt. Im Gegensatz zu der ausgeführten Skulptur sind die Tintenfische mit kleinen Ovalen wiedergegeben und nicht weiter spezifiziert. Der Teller ist durch zwei unterschiedlich grosse Kreise angedeutet.

47.

51.

51. **Table Ware,** 1985
polystyrene, paint
prototype

Geschirr features white place setting printed in black
and consisting of a plate, cup, and saucer. The image in
the middle of the plate and the cup shows two similar-
looking men sitting opposite each other at a laid table
with four chairs. The plate, cup and saucer are in fact
made of plastic, with a painted pattern.

52.

52. **Black Table with Table Ware,** 1985
wood, paint, plastic
table: height 29 ¹/₂ in., 39 ³/₈ in.
with chairs: height 35 ⁷/₁₆ in., diameter 59 ¹/₁₆ in.
The Werner and Elaine Dannheisser Collection,
on long term loan to The Museum of Modern
Art, New York

The sculpture consists of a round black table accompa-
nied by four chairs and four place settings on it. The
table and chairs are made of black lacquered wood.
The table's round legs slope slightly outward and are
rounded off at the bottom. Each chair has a seat that
curves at the back, but is otherwise rectangular; round
legs sloping lightly outward; and a rectangular back-
rest. On the table is a white place setting with a black
pattern for each chair (cat. 51).

53. **Black Table with Identical Twins,** 1985 (pl. 6)
Herr Wiegmann and Herr Wiegmann, wood,
paint, plastic
height 59 ¹/₁₆ in., diameter 59 ¹/₆ in.
exhibition version

Two identical-looking men are sitting facing each other
at the *Schwarzer Tisch mit Geschirr* (cat. 52). Their
posture seems relaxed. Their legs are bent at right
angles at the knees and are together. Their feet are
parallel to each other and almost touching at the tips.
The torso is erect: arms, bent at right angles, are held
closely to the body and rest on the table just above the

51. **Geschirr,** 1985
Polystyrol, Farbe
Prototyp

Ein weisses Gedeck mit schwarzem Aufdruck, beste-
hend aus Teller, Unterteller und Tasse. Das Bild, das
sich in der Mitte des Tellers und auf der Tasse befindet,
zeigt zwei sich ähnelnde Männer, die sich an einem
gedeckten Tisch mit vier Stühlen gegenübersitzen.
Gefertigt wurde das Geschirr aus Kunststoff, das Muster ist aufgemalt.

52. **Schwarzer Tisch mit Geschirr,** 1985
Holz, Farbe, Kunststoff
Tisch: Höhe 75 cm, Durchmesser 100 cm
mit Stühlen: Höhe 90 cm, Durchmesser 150 cm
Sammlung Werner und Elaine Dannheisser,
Dauerleihgabe im Museum of Modern Art,
New York

Die Skulptur besteht aus einem runden, schwarzen Tisch,
an dem vier Stühle stehen und auf dem sich vier Gedecke
befinden. Der Tisch und die vier Stühle sind aus matt
schwarz lackiertem Holz gefertigt. Die runden Beine des
Tisches sind leicht nach aussen gestellt und unten abge-
rundet. Die Stühle besitzen eine am Rücken runde, sonst
rechteckige Sitzfläche, runde, leicht nach aussen gestell-
te Beine und eine schwach gebogene Lehne aus vier
Stäben und einem rechteckigen Querbalken. Auf dem
Tisch befindet sich jedem Stuhl zugeordnet je ein weisses Gedeck mit schwarzem Aufdruck (Kat. 51).

53. **Schwarzer Tisch mit eineiigen Zwillingen,**
1985 (Taf. 6)
Herr Wiegmann und Herr Wiegmann, Holz,
Farbe, Kunststoff
Höhe 150 cm, Durchmesser 150 cm
Ausstellungsversion

An dem «Schwarzen Tisch mit Geschirr» (Kat. 52) sitzen
sich zwei identisch aussehende Männer gegenüber. Sie
verharren in einer entspannt erscheinenden Haltung.
Ihre Beine sind in den Gelenken jeweils rechtwinklig
geknickt und geschlossen. Die Füsse stehen parallel
nebeneinander und berühren sich an den Fussspitzen

wrists. The hands are lightly closed in a fist. Their heads are held upright, and they are looking straight ahead so that they can look each other in the eye. Their dark hair is parted on the right, and both wear short moustaches. They are both dressed in the same way: black shoes, socks, and trousers, and a white short-sleeved shirt. Both are wearing watches with black straps on their wrists; the watches have silver cases and white faces.

Katharina Fritsch presented this version of *Schwarzer Tisch mit Geschirr* at an exhibition opening at the Galerie Johnen & Schöttle, Cologne. She used identical twins Ulrich and Lothar Wiegmann as "living sculptures." The photograph taken at the opening illustrates this version.

54. **Candle Stand,** 1985 (pl. 7)
steel, wax
4 candle stands, each: 31 $^{1}/_{2}$ x 23 $^{5}/_{8}$ x 3 $^{9}/_{16}$ in.
80 candles, each: height 31 $^{1}/_{2}$ in., diameter 1 $^{13}/_{16}$ in.
with burning candles: 63 x 47 $^{1}/_{4}$ x 47 $^{1}/_{4}$ in.
burnt down: 47 $^{1}/_{4}$ x 47 $^{1}/_{4}$ x 47 $^{1}/_{4}$ in.; candles each: height 15 $^{3}/_{4}$ in., diameter 1 $^{13}/_{16}$ in.
Dakis Joannou Collection, Athens

Four identical grid stands lacquered black and white are arranged in an open square. The outer edges of the square measure twice the length of one stand. The twenty steel tubes comprising each stand are grouped in two rows of ten tubes and fastened to each other at the top with metal bands laid crosswise. On each stand are twenty candles, corresponding to the work *Kerze* (cat. 42), in a double row. This makes each candle look like a white continuation of the black steel tube.

The work was first exhibited with burning candles. After the candles had burned down to half their height they were blown out and the work remains in this form.

55. **Green Bottle,** 1985
Plexiglas, sheet metal, paint
15 $^{3}/_{4}$ x 2 $^{3}/_{8}$ x 2 $^{3}/_{8}$ in.
component of *Beistelltisch mit Engel und Flasche* (cat. 57)

The slender yet hard-edged body of the dark green Plexiglas bottle rises from a square bottom and concludes in a pyramid shape topped by the neck. A dark sheet-metal capsule is pulled over the neck of the bottle to close it. All the edges are cut and glued precisely, and the joints are visible only as thin seams. The bottle was sprayed with clear, dark green varnish upon completion, and the sheet metal capsule was painted black.

56. **Angel,** 1985
sheet tin
height 7 $^{7}/_{8}$ in.
component of *Beistelltisch mit Engel und Flasche* (cat. 57)

The body of the small, bulky angel consists of a funnel-shaped undergarment and a semicircular cloak, both made of folded sheet tin. The angel's head emerges from the opening in the middle of the cloak and is characterized by child-like features and short, lightly wavy hair. The angel's eyes seem to be closed, yet the small mouth is open, ready to sing. Small, slightly rounded

117

fast. Der Oberkörper ist aufgerichtet, die am Körper anliegenden, rechtwinklig abgeknickten Arme liegen etwas oberhalb der Handgelenke auf dem Tisch auf, die Hände sind locker zur Faust geschlossen. Der Kopf ist aufgerichtet, der Blick geht starr geradeaus, so dass sie sich genau in die Augen sehen können. Das dunkle Haar ist auf der rechten Seite gescheitelt, beide tragen einen kurzen Oberlippenbart. Beide sind gleich gekleidet: Schuhe, Strümpfe und Hose in Schwarz, das kurzärmlige Hemd ist weiss. Beide tragen am linken Handgelenk eine Uhr mit schwarzem Uhrband und silbernem Uhrgehäuse mit weissem Zifferblatt.

In dieser Form präsentierte Katharina Fritsch die Arbeit «Schwarzer Tisch mit Geschirr» während der Ausstellungseröffnung in der Galerie Johnen & Schöttle, Köln. Als «Lebende Skulptur» dienten ihr das eineiige Zwillingspaar, Ulrich und Lothar Wiegmann. Die bei der Eröffnung angefertigte Fotografie gibt die Version wieder.

54. **Kerzenständer,** 1985 (Taf. 7)
Stahl, Wachs
4 Kerzenständer je: 80 x 60 x 9 cm
80 Kerzen je: Höhe 80 cm, Durchmesser 3 cm, mit brennenden Kerzen: 160 x 120 x 120 cm abgebrannt: 120 x 120 x 120 cm; Kerzen je: Höhe 40 cm, Durchmesser 3 cm
Sammlung Dakis Joannou, Athen

Vier identische, matt-schwarz lackierte Gittergestelle, die aus je zwanzig parallel laufenden Stahlrohren gefertigt wurden, sind zu einem offenen Quadrat angeordnet. Die Aussenkanten des Quadrates entsprechen der doppelten Länge eines Gestells. Die zwanzig Stahlrohre eines jeden Ständers sind in zwei Reihen à 10 Rohre gruppiert und an der Oberseite mit über Kreuz gelegten Metallbändern miteinander befestigt. Auf ihnen sind je zwanzig Kerzen, die der «Kerze» (Kat. 42) entsprechen, in einer Doppelreihe angebracht. Jede Kerze erscheint dadurch wie eine weisse Weiterführung des schwarzen Stahlrohres.

Die Arbeit wurde das erste Mal mit brennenden Kerzen gezeigt. Nachdem die Kerzen auf die Hälfte abgebrannt waren, wurden sie ausgeblasen und die Arbeit in der Form belassen.

54.

55. **Grüne Flasche,** 1985
Plexiglas, Blech, Farbe
40 x 6 x 6 cm
Bestandteil von «Beistelltisch mit Engel und Flasche» (Kat. 57)

Eine schlanke, rechteckige Flasche aus dunkelgrünem Plexiglas. Über dem quadratischen Boden der Flasche erhebt sich der mit harten Kanten geformte Körper, dessen oberer Abschluss in einer pyramidenartigen Form mit sich anschliessendem Flaschenhals endet. Über den Flaschenhals wurde eine dunkle Blechhülse als Verschluss gestülpt. Alle Kanten sind präzise geschnitten und verklebt, die Fugen nur als dünne Nähte erkennbar. Die Flasche wurde nach der Herstellung mit einem dunkelgrünen Klarlack gespritzt, die Blechhülse schwarz gestrichen.

56. **Engel,** 1985
Zinnblech
Höhe 20 cm
Bestandteil von «Beistelltisch mit Engel und Flasche» (Kat. 57)

Der Körper des kleinen, voluminösen Engels setzt sich aus einem trichterförmigen Untergewand und einem halbkreisförmigen Umhang, beide aus in Falten gelegtem Zinnblech, zusammen. Aus der Öffnung in der Mitte des Umhangs erhebt sich der Kopf des Engels, der mit kindlichen Zügen und kurzen, leicht gewellten Haaren gekennzeichnet ist. Seine Augen scheinen ge-

hands at the end of outspread arms appear at the upper edge of the cloak. Two wings are attached to the angel's back, each of which has two upward-curving tips. Like the body, the wings were cut out of thin sheet tin, while the head and the two hands were cast in molds.

In form, material, and color the angel is similar to figures that are fastened at the top of Christmas trees as ornaments.

57. Side Table with Angel and Bottle, 1985 (pl. 9)
wood, paint, Plexiglas, sheet tin
19 ¹¹/₁₆ x 31 ¹/₂ x 15 ³/₄ in.
Dr. Peter Littmann, Metzingen

The angel (cat. 56), made of folded and molded sheet tin, and the green angular Plexiglas bottle (cat. 55) stand on a low, small light grey-spraypainted wooden table. A lattice of intersecting wooden slats set diagonally at right angles to each other is fixed between the legs and edges of the table. The table feet have small casters. The two objects, the angel and the bottle, are placed at a precisely determined distance from each other and from the edges of the table. The angel faces the narrow edge of the table.

58. Trade Fair Stand with Four Figures, 1985/86
(pl. 8)
wood, gypseous alabaster paint, plaster of Paris
110 ¹/₄ x 78 ³/₄ x 78 ³/₄ in.
edition: 2
Dr. Peter Littmann, Metzingen
Collection Reinhard Onnasch, Berlin

A rectangular white block stands approximately 110 inches high and 79 inches wide on a square base. A small rectangular niche – whose height corresponds with its distance from the upper edge – is cut into each side surface, roughly twelve inches below the upper edge. A statuette of Saint Nicholas is placed in each of the empty spaces. Both the block and the four figures are painted with matte white gypseous alabaster paint.

59. Bookcase, 1986
wood, paint, plastic, cardboard, paper
94 ¹/₂ x 39 ³/₈ x 11 ¹³/₁₆ in.
Kaiser Wilhelm Museum, Krefeld

Twenty-five books with red cardboard binding and white pages are placed without gaps on each of the eight shelves of a rectangular black bookcase. The distance between the top edge of the books and the next shelf leaves a small gap, so that it is possible to look down at the top of the books and see the white pages. The books themselves, which are similar to linen-bound editions, are identical in thickness, height, size, and binding. Nothing is printed on the spines of the books that might indicate their contents. The bookcase is suspended about 15 ³/₄ inches from the floor.

60. Man Out for a Walk with Dog, 1986 (pl. 4)
Herr Reimers, Arnheim, with English bulldog Rose
exhibition version

On the opening day of the *Sonsbeek '86* exhibition in Arnheim, Herr Reimers, one of the attendants, walked his dog Rose through the park in which the exhibition was held. Both Herr Reimer's clothes and the dog's collar were specified precisely. Herr Reimers – an elderly, white-haired man with receding hair – wore a plain, light-gray single-breasted suit; a white shirt; a tie with

schlossen, der kleine Mund ist zum Gesang geöffnet. An der Oberkante des Umhangs kommen die kleinen, leicht gerundeten Hände der weit ausgebreiteten Arme zum Vorschein. Auf dem Rücken des Engels sind zwei Flügel befestigt, die je vier nach oben geschwungene Spitzen haben. Die Flügel sind wie der Körper aus dünnen Zinnblech geschnitten, der Kopf und die beiden Hände sind in Formen gegossen.

In Form, Material und Farbigkeit ähnelt der Engel Figuren, die an den Spitzen von Christbäumen als Weihnachtsdekoration befestigt wurden.

57. Beistelltisch mit Engel und Flasche, 1985 (Taf. 9)
Holz, Farbe, Plexiglas, Zinnblech
50 x 80 x 40 cm
Dr. Peter Littmann, Metzingen

Der aus Zinnblech gefaltete und geformte Engel (Kat. 56) und die grüne, eckige Flasche aus Plexiglas (Kat. 55) stehen auf einem niedrigen, hellgrau gespritzten Tischchen aus Holz. Zwischen den Tischbeinen und den Tischkanten spannt sich ein Gitter aus rechtwinklig übereinander gelegten, sich kreuzenden Holzleisten. An den Füssen des Tischchens sind kleine Rollen angebracht. Die beiden Objekte, der Engel und die Flasche, sind in einem genau festgelegten Abstand zueinander und zu den Tischkanten aufgestellt. Der Engel ist mit dem Gesicht zu der Schmalseite des Tisches gedreht.

58. Messekoje mit vier Figuren, 1985/86 (Taf. 8)
Holz, Alabastergipsfarbe, Gips
280 x 200 x 200 cm
Auflage 2
Dr. Peter Littmann, Metzingen
Sammlung Reinhard Onnasch, Berlin

Ein fast drei Meter hoher und zwei Meter breiter, rechteckiger, weisser Block über einer quadratischen Grundfläche. Ungefähr dreissig Zentimeter unterhalb seiner Oberkante wurden in jede Ecke eine kleine, rechteckige Nische eingeschnitten, deren Höhe dem Abstand zur Oberkante entspricht. In die Aussparungen wurden je eine weiss angestrichene Statuette des hl. Nikolaus gestellt. Sowohl der Block als auch die vier Figuren sind mit einer mattweissen Alabastergipsfarbe angestrichen.

59. Bücherregal, 1986
Holz, Farbe, Kunststoff, Pappe, Papier
240 x 100 x 30 cm
Kaiser Wilhelm Museum, Krefeld

In ein hochrechteckiges, schwarzes Regal mit acht Unterteilungen sind lückenlos je 25 in rote Pappe gebundene Bücher mit weissen Seiten eingestellt. Der Abstand zwischen der Oberkante der Bücher und des nächsten Regalbrettes lässt einen kleinen Spalt, so dass man auf die Oberseite der Bücher blicken und die weissen Seiten sehen kann. Die Bücher selbst, die von der Form her leinengebundenen Ausgaben ähneln, sind identisch in Stärke, Höhe, Grösse und Einband. Auf den Buchrücken befinden sich keinerlei Aufdrucke, die auf den Inhalt schliessen liessen. Das Regal ist im Abstand von etwa 40 cm zum Boden aufgehängt.

60. Spaziergänger mit Hund, 1986 (Taf. 4)
Herr Reimers, Arnheim, mit englischer Bulldogge «Rose»
Ausstellungsversion

Am Eröffnungstag der Ausstellung «Sonsbeek '86» in Arnheim spazierte Herr Reimers, eine der Aufsichten, mit dem Hund «Rose» durch den Park, in dem die Ausstellung stattfand. Sowohl die Kleidung Herrn Reimers als auch das Halsband des Hundes waren genau festgelegt. Herr Reimers – ein älterer, weisshaariger Mann mit Halbglatze – trug einen schlichten, hellgrauen, einreihigen

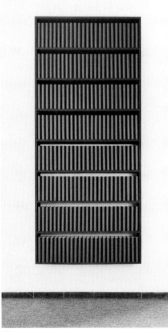

59.

blue-and-white diagonal block stripes; black shoes; and a plain watch, wedding band, and signet ring. Rose, a white, English bulldog, wore a wide red collar with large silver five-pointed stars and a loop onto which a leash could be fastened. The original plan called for Herr Reimers to walk the dog through the park on every day of the exhibition, but this proved impossible.

The work was documented in a photograph. In it Herr Reimers is standing upright, with his legs slightly apart, on a gravel path. His hand is placed over his stomach in such a way that the left hand is holding the right. The bulldog is sitting at his feet to the right, turned away from him, with his head in the air and wearing a fixed expression.

Subsequent pictures, documenting the same situation but with another dog, were taken but not authorized by the artist.

61. **Chimney-sweep Sticker,** 1986
self-adhesive black foil
height: each 1 3/4 in.
unlimited multiple

A stylized figure of a chimney-sweep in self-adhesive black foil is captured at the furthest extent of his stride. His body curves slightly inward, down from the head through the back to the rear leg. One hand seems to be in his trouser pocket, while the other is holding the short ladder that he carries on his shoulder. His head is thrust slightly forward, and he is wearing a top hat.

The sticker is reminiscent of chimney-sweep figures that are used to bring luck (on birthdays or New Year's Eve).

61.

62. **Showcase with Chimney-sweep Stickers,** 1986
glass, self-adhesive black foil, wood
Barbara Gladstone, New York

Several staggered rows of the chimney-sweep figure (cat. 61) are applied to the inside of the glass panes of a simple, rectangular wooden showcase. There are two versions: one with two staggered rows of four–five–four figures and the other with five rows, starting with three chimney-sweeps.

63. **Rain,** 1987
long-playing vinyl record
Edition Katharina Fritsch, Düsseldorf and
Walther König, Cologne

A pale, yellow greenish sleeve labeled *Regen* (Rain) in the center contains a long-playing record. In the middle of the record is a round label, also yellow-green, bearing details about copyright, the recording, and the record company, and the instruction "Bitte leise abspielen" ("Please play softly"). The recording reproduces the endlessly repeated noise of raindrops on the leaves of a rhododendron bush.

62.

64. **Elephant,** 1987 (pl. 12)
polyester, wood, paint
149 5/8 x 165 3/8 x 63 in.
Katharina Fritsch, Düsseldorf

The life-size model of a female elephant stands on a tall, light gray oval plinth. The elephant is reproduced in a very calm, almost static pose. The forelegs are set parallel to each other, but the hind legs look as though they are just starting to take a step. The head is held

Anzug, ein weisses Hemd, eine Krawatte mit blau-weissen, schrägen Blockstreifen und schwarze Schuhe, sowie eine schlichte Uhr, einen Ehe- und einen goldenen Siegelring. Der Hund – eine weisse, englische Bulldogge – trug ein breites, rotes Halsband mit grossen, silbernen, fünfzackigen Sternen und einer Schlaufe, an der eine Hundeleine befestigt werden könnte. Ursprünglich war geplant, Herrn Reimers mit dem Hund während der Dauer der Ausstellung täglich durch den Park spazieren zu lassen; dies liess sich aber nicht verwirklichen.

Dokumentiert wurde die Arbeit mit einem Foto. Auf diesem steht Herr Reimers aufrecht, die Beine leicht auseinandergestellt, auf einem Kiesweg. Er hat seine Hände über dem Bauch so übereinandergelegt, dass die Linke die Rechte hält. Rechts zu seinen Füssen sitzt von ihm abgewandt die Dogge, den Kopf nach oben erhoben, mit starrem Blick.

Andere Abbildungen, die die gleiche Situation, nur mit einem anderen Hund, zeigen, sind nachträglich angefertigt und von der Künstlerin nicht autorisiert.

61. **Schornsteinfeger-Aufkleber,** 1986
selbstklebende schwarze Folie
Höhe je 4,5 cm
unlimitiertes Multiple

Die stilisierte Figur eines Schornsteinfegers aus selbstklebender schwarzer Folie. Sie ist in einer weit ausholenden Schrittstellung wiedergegeben. Der Körper wölbt sich in einer leichten Rundung vom Kopf über den Rücken zum hinteren Bein. Die eine Hand ist scheinbar in die Hosentasche gesteckt, die andere hält die über die Schulter gelegte kurze Leiter. Auf dem etwas vorgestreckten Kopf befindet sich ein Zylinder.

Der Aufkleber erinnert an Schornsteinfegerfiguren, die als Glücksbringer (an Geburtstagen oder Silvester) benutzt werden.

62. **Vitrine mit Schornsteinfeger-Aufklebern,** 1986
Glas, selbstklebende schwarze Folie, Holz
Barbara Gladstone, New York

Auf die Innenseiten der Glasscheiben einer einfachen, rechteckigen Holzvitrine wurde in mehreren Reihen versetzt die Figur des Schornsteinfegers (Kat. 61) geklebt. Es existieren zwei Versionen: einmal mit drei versetzten Reihen mit vier – fünf – vier Figuren, das andere Mal mit fünf Reihen, beginnend mit drei Schornsteinfegern.

63. **Regen,** 1987
Langspielplatte
Edition Katharina Fritsch, Düsseldorf und
Walther König, Köln

In einem gelbgrünen Cover mit der in schwarzen Buchstaben mittig gesetzten Aufschrift «Regen» befindet sich eine Langspielplatte. In deren Mitte ist ein runder, ebenfalls gelbgrüner Aufkleber, auf dem neben den Angaben zum Copyright, zur Aufnahme und zum Verleger die Anweisung «Bitte leise abspielen» zu lesen ist. Die Aufnahme gibt die sich permanent wiederholenden Geräusche von Regentropfen auf den Blättern eines Rhododendronbusches wieder.

63.

64. **Elefant,** 1987 (Taf. 12)
Polyester, Holz, Farbe
380 x 420 x 160 cm
Katharina Fritsch, Düsseldorf

Auf einem ovalen, hohen, hellgrauen Sockel steht die lebensgrosse Nachbildung eines weiblichen Elefanten. Die Elefantenkuh ist in einer sehr ruhigen, fast statisch wirkenden Haltung wiedergegeben. Während die Vorderbeine parallel aufgestellt sind, befinden sich die

high, the large ears lean slightly forward, and the small eyes are open. Both the tail and the trunk hang straight down. Only the tip of the trunk turns inward, pointing toward the body. The large tusks, which start at the beginning of the trunk, are posed slightly outward. Both the physical proportions of the animal and the surface structure of the skin replicate those of a living creature: the skin has a large number of folds and cracks. The color, a deep, dark bluegreen, however, is by no means based on reality: it is more reminiscent of the green of the jungle, the elephant's home.

A stuffed African cow elephant from the Alexander Koenig Museum in Bonn was used as a model for the mold.

Hinterbeine in einer leichten Schrittstellung. Der Kopf ist aufgerichtet, die grossen Ohren sind leicht nach vorne aufgestellt, die kleinen Augen sind geöffnet. Sowohl der Schwanz als auch der Rüssel hängen gerade herunter. Nur die Rüsselspitze ist nach innen gebogen und weist zum Körper hin. Die grossen Stosszähne, die am Rüsselansatz beginnen, sind leicht nach aussen gerichtet. Nicht nur die Körperproportionen, sondern auch die Oberflächenstruktur der Haut sind der eines lebenden Tieres nachgebildet, sie weist viele Falten und Schrunden auf. Entspricht die Skulptur in Grösse und Ausformung einem lebendigen Tier, ist ihre Farbe – ein sattes, dunkles Blaugrün – keineswegs der Natur nachempfunden. Die Farbe erinnert eher an das Grün des Urwalds, der Heimat des Elefanten.

Als Modell für den Abguss wurde eine ausgestopfte, afrikanische Elefantenkuh aus dem Museum Alexander Koenig in Bonn benutzt.

65.

65.	**Lawn with Eighty Trees,** 1987
	model
	wood, PU-foam, paint
	6 $^{11}/_{16}$ x 31 $^1/_2$ x 31 $^1/_2$ in.
	owner: Katharina Fritsch, Düsseldorf
	location: Westfälisches Landesmuseum für
	Kunst und Kulturgeschichte, Münster

This model for the *Rasenplatz mit achtzig Bäumen* project (cat. 38) comprises eighty small trees made of PU-foam glued onto an oval corresponding with the drawing. The lawn area is sprayed light green, and the trees are painted green.

The project was to have been executed in a central square of a 1920s or 1960s/1970s housing estate for the *Skulptur Projekte* (Sculpture Projects) exhibition in Münster 1987. Neither of the suggested sites could be used because of restrictions imposed by the historic monuments office, in the first case, and the sites' owners in the second case.

65.	**Rasenplatz mit achtzig Bäumen,** 1987
	Modell
	Holz, PU-Schaum, Farbe
	17 x 80 x 80 cm
	Besitzer: Katharina Fritsch, Düsseldorf
	Standort: Westfälisches Landesmuseum für
	Kunst und Kulturgeschichte, Münster

Das Modell des Projektes «Rasenplatz mit achtzig Bäumen» (Kat. 38). Auf einer quadratischen Grundplatte aus MDF sind achtzig kleine Modellbäume aus PU-Schaum entsprechend der Zeichnung in einem Oval aufgeklebt. Der Rasenplatz ist hellgrün gespritzt, die Bäume mit grüner Farbe angestrichen.

Für die Ausstellung «Skulptur Projekte in Münster 1987» sollte zunächst das Projekt an einem zentralen Platz einer Wohnsiedlung der zwanziger bzw. der sechziger/siebziger Jahre ausgeführt werden. Beide vorgeschlagenen Standorte scheiterten an den Auflagen des Denkmalsamtes bzw. an den Grundstücksbesitzern.

66.	**Tennis Court,** 1987
	model
	wood, wire
	10 $^1/_4$ x 59 $^1/_{16}$ x 49 $^3/_{16}$ in.
	owner: Katharina Fritsch, Düsseldorf
	location: Westfälisches Landesmuseum für
	Kunst und Kulturgeschichte, Münster

An architectural model of a modern housing estate, with a large tennis court in the center, is built on a rectangular MDF board. The tennis court is surrounded by a 172-foot-high wire netting fence.

This work was also proposed for the *Skulptur Projekte* (Sculpture Projects) exhibition in Münster 1987, but was not realized.

66.	**Tennisplatz,** 1987
	Modell
	Holz, Draht
	26 x 150 x 125 cm
	Besitzer: Katharina Fritsch, Düsseldorf
	Standort: Westfälisches Landesmuseum für
	Kunst und Kulturgeschichte, Münster

Auf einer rechteckigen MDF-Platte ist das Architekturmodell einer modernen Wohnsiedlung aufgestellt, in deren Zentrum ein grosser Tennisplatz errichtet wurde. Der Tennisplatz ist von einem 22 Meter hohen Maschendrahtzaun eingegrenzt.

Auch diese Arbeit war ein Vorschlag für die Ausstellung «Skulptur Projekt in Münster 1987», der nicht realisiert wurde.

66.

67. **Madonna Figure,** 1987 (pl. 13)
epoxy resin, paint
66 $^{15}/_{16}$ x 15 $^{3}/_{4}$ x 13 $^{3}/_{8}$ in.
edition: 2
Ydessa Hendles Art Foundation, Toronto
CAPC, Musée d'art Moderne, Bordeaux

This sculpture is a life-size replica of the unlimited multiple *Madonnenfigur* (cat. 31). It corresponds with the multiple both in formal design and color. It was made as a contribution to the *Skulptur Projekte* (Sculpture Projects) exhibition in Münster 1987, originally in painted epoxy resin. However, it was damaged by vandals and had to be remade, this time as a stone casting. After the stone casting had also been destroyed, Katharina Fritsch restored the version in epoxy resin and made the second version from the same material. In Münster it was installed in the middle of a shopping street between a department store and a church, and in Toronto it was on display in a shopping center.

68. **Vase with Ship,** 1987-1988
plastic, silk-screen print
height 11 $^{13}/_{16}$ in., diameter 4 $^{15}/_{16}$ in.
component of *Warengestell mit Vasen* (cat. 69)
unlimited multiple

A white plastic vase is created by combining spherical and cubic shapes. The round shape is roughly the same as that of the *Schwarze Vase* (cat. 47), but more slender. A picture of an ocean liner is printed on each of the four curved sides. The print, which is reminiscent of transfers, shows a large, black-and-white ocean liner with red trim on the funnels and upper edges of the ship. The sea is represented by a half of a blue oval.

69. **Display Stand with Vases,** 1987/89 (pl. 11)
plastic, silk-screen print, aluminum
106 $^{5}/_{16}$ x 44 $^{5}/_{16}$ - 4 $^{15}/_{16}$ x 44 $^{5}/_{16}$ - 4 $^{15}/_{16}$ in.
edition: 3 + artist's proof
Katharina Fritsch, Düsseldorf
Collection Jörg Johnen, Cologne
Private Collection, Boston
Collection of Ruth and Jacob Bloom, New York

The artist stacked 145 copies of the unlimited multiple *Vase mit Schiff* (cat. 68) into a steep, tall pyramid, set nine square aluminum sheets as supporters. There are nine vases per side on the bottom sheet, and this number is reduced by one at each higher level. Touching at their widest point, the vases are placed on the outer edge of the sheet, which rests on the inner third of the necks of the vases below.
This shelving method is vaguely reminiscent of the way goods are presented in supermarkets.

70. **Display Stand with Madonnas,** 1987/89 (pl. 10)
aluminum, plaster of Paris, paint
height 106 $^{5}/_{16}$ in., diameter 32 $^{5}/_{16}$ in.
edition: 3 + artist's proof
Collection Anette und Udo Brandhorst, Cologne
La Caixa de Pensions, Barcelona
Private Collection, Boston
Staatsgalerie, Stuttgart

Thirty-two small yellow Madonna figures – copies of the unlimited multiple *Madonnenfigur* (cat. 31) – are placed closely together, facing outward, on each of nine round aluminum disks. The lower edges of the Madonna figures align precisely with the edge of the metal sheets, and the figures touch only slightly at their widest point. Each layer forms a solid, dense circle that supports the next layer. The individual sheets with the figures are lay-

67. **Madonnenfigur,** 1987 (Taf. 13)
Epoxidharz, Farbe
170 x 40 x 34 cm
Auflage 2
Ydessa Hendles Art Foundation, Toronto
CAPC, Musée d'art Moderne, Bordeaux

Die Skulptur ist die lebensgrosse Nachbildung des unlimitierten Multiples «Madonnenfigur» (Kat. 31). Sowohl in der formalen Gestaltung als auch in der Farbigkeit entspricht sie dem Multiple. Sie wurde als Beitrag für die Ausstellung «Skulptur Projekte in Münster 1987» zuerst aus bemaltem Epoxidharz hergestellt, musste aber, nachdem sie von Randalierern beschädigt worden war, erneut – diesmal als Steinguss – gefertigt werden. Nachdem auch der Steinguss in Münster zerstört worden war, restaurierte Katharina Fritsch die Version aus Epoxidharz und stellte aus dem gleichen Material die zweite Auflage her. In Münster war sie mitten auf einer Einkaufsstrasse zwischen einem Kaufhaus und einer Kirche aufgestellt, in Toronto war sie eine Zeit lang in einem Einkaufszentrum zu sehen.

68. **Vase mit Schiff,** 1987-1988
Kunststoff, Siebdruck
Höhe 30 cm, Durchmesser 12,5 cm
Bestandteil von «Warengestell mit Vasen» (Kat. 69)
unlimitiertes Multiple

Eine weisse, durch das Ineinanderschieben von Kugel- und Kubusformen konstruierte Vase aus Kunststoff. Die runde Form entspricht ungefähr der «Schwarzen Vase» (Kat. 47), ist aber etwas schlanker. Auf den vier gewölbten Seiten der Vase ist jeweils das Bild eines Ozeandampfers aufgedruckt. Der Aufdruck, der an Abziehbildchen erinnert, zeigt einen grossen schwarz-weissen Ozeandampfer mit roter Dekoration an Schornsteinen und Schiffoberkanten. Das Meer ist als halbes Oval in Blau wiedergegeben.

69. **Warengestell mit Vasen,** 1987/89 (Taf. 11)
Kunststoff, Siebdruck, Aluminium
270 x 112,5 - 12,5 x 112,5 - 12,5 cm
Auflage 3 + AP
Katharina Fritsch, Düsseldorf
Sammlung Jörg Johnen, Köln
Privatsammlung, Boston
Sammlung Ruth und Jacob Bloom, New York

145 Exemplare des unlimitierten Multiples «Vase mit Schiff» (Kat. 68) wurden mit Hilfe von neun quadratischen Aluminiumplatten zu einer hohen, steilen Pyramide aufgestapelt. Sind auf der untersten Platte noch pro Seite neun Vasen zu sehen, so nimmt ihre Anzahl nach oben pro Stufe stetig auf jeder Seite um eine ab. Die Vasen stehen jeweils an der Aussenkante einer Platte, die auf dem inneren Drittel des Vasenhalses aufliegt, und sie berühren sich an ihrer dicksten Stelle.
Das Warengestell erinnert vage an die Präsentation von Waren in einem Supermarkt.

70. **Warengestell mit Madonnen,** 1987/89 (Taf. 10)
Aluminium, Gips, Farbe
Höhe 270 cm, Durchmesser 82 cm
Auflage 3 + AP
Sammlung Anette und Udo Brandhorst, Köln
La Caixa de Pensions, Barcelona
Privatsammlung, Boston
Staatsgalerie Stuttgart

Je 32 kleine gelbe Madonnenfiguren – Exemplare des unlimitierten Multiples «Madonnenfigur» (Kat. 31) – wurden mit den Gesichtern nach aussen am Rand von neun runden Aluminiumscheiben eng aneinandergestellt. Die Unterkanten der Madonnenfiguren schliessen genau an der Kante der Platten ab, die Figuren berühren sich gegenseitig nur leicht an ihrer dicksten Stelle. Jede Lage bildet ein festes, dichtes Rund, das die nächste Lage

68.

121

ered in such a way that the Madonnas stand precisely above one another. The hands folded in prayer or the tips of the figures' noses form a clear line to the top. The clear, glowing lemon-yellow serves to counter the density of the figures to a degree and creates an enormous luminosity.

trägt. Die einzelnen Platten mit den Figuren sind so übereinandergestellt, dass sich die Madonnen exakt übereinanderbefinden. Die zum Gebet gefalteten Händen oder die Nasenspitzen der Figuren bilden eine klare Linie nach oben. Das klare, leuchtende Zitronengelb scheint die Dichte der Figuren etwas aufzuheben und erzeugt eine ungeheure Leuchtkraft.

71.

71. **Bargain Counter,** 1987/89
sheet iron, printed silk scarfs
31 1/2 x 35 7/16 x 35 7/16 in.
edition: 3 + artist's proof
Institut für Auslandsbeziehungen, Stuttgart
Collection Siebenstern, Munich
Jeffrey Winter, New York

71. **Wühltisch,** 1987/89
Eisenblech, bedruckte Seidentücher
80 x 90 x 90 cm
Auflage 3 + AP
Institut für Auslandsbeziehungen, Stuttgart
Sammlung Siebenstern, München
Jeffrey Winter, New York

Fifty-five folded and starched multiples *Grünes Seidentuch* (cat. 27) are carefully piled up to form a pyramid on a matte black lacquered bargain counter. The lowest of the five layers of squares protrudes only slightly above the upper edge of the counter. The division between the layers is not marked by a clear line.
The work is strongly reminiscent of bargain counters on which mountains of garments are piled for summer or winter end-of-season sales.

In einem matt-schwarz lackierten, quadratischen Wühltisch sind sorgfältig 55 gefaltete und gestärkte Multiples «Grünes Seidentuch» (Kat. 27) zu einer Pyramide aufgestapelt. Von den fünf Lagen, in denen die Tücher angeordnet sind, reicht die unterste nur etwas über die Oberkante des Wühltisches hinaus. Die Trennung zwischen den Lagen ist nicht durch eine klare Linie gekennzeichnet.
Die Arbeit erinnert stark an Wühltische, auf denen beim Sommer- bzw. Winterschlussverkauf Berge von Kleidungsstücken gehäuft werden.

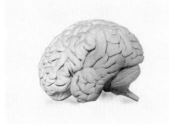

72.

72. **Brain,** 1987/89
plaster of Paris, paint
4 1/2 x 5 7/8 x 5 1/8 in.
unlimited multiple

72. **Gehirn,** 1987/89
Gips, Farbe
11,5 x 15 x 13 cm
unlimitiertes Multiple

A life-size human brain in plaster of Paris is represented in every detail – from the cerebrum via the diencephalon and mesencephalon to the brain-stem and the point of connection with the spinal cord. The form was created by casting the two congruent hemispheres of the brain and carefully fitting them together. It was then painted a uniform matte white.
The mold was made from a brain model typically used for teaching in schools.

Ein lebensgrosses, menschliches Gehirn aus Gips, das in allen Details – vom Grosshirn über das Zwischen- und Mittelhirn bis zum Hirnstamm und dem Rückenmarkanschluss – dargestellt ist. Die Form wurde in den beiden kongruenten Hemisphären, aus denen das Gehirn besteht, gegossen und sorgfältig zusammen gefügt. Anschliessend erhielt sie eine einheitlich mattweisse Farbigkeit.
Für den Abguss wurde ein Gehirnmodell benutzt, das üblicherweise im Schulunterricht verwendet wird.

73.

73. **Money,** 1988
aluminum, anodized
diameter 1 3/8 in.
unlimited multiple
component of *Geldkisten* (cat. 74)

73. **Geld,** 1988
Aluminium, eloxiert
Durchmesser 3,5 cm
unlimitiertes Multiple
Bestandteil von «Geldkisten» (Kat. 74)

This unlimited multiple consists of one hundred aluminum disks with a hole punched in each center. The disks are somewhat larger than a five-mark piece and anodized silver in color. They are presented either stacked in a column or mixed up in a small transparent plastic bag.

Das unlimitierte Multiple besteht aus 100 Aluminiumscheiben mit einem eingestanzten Loch in der Mitte. Die Scheiben sind etwas grösser als ein Fünfmarkstück und silbern eloxiert. Präsentiert werden sie entweder zu einer Säule gestapelt oder durcheinander in einem durchsichtigen Plastiktütchen.

74.

74. **Money Chests,** 1988
aluminum, steel, paint
49 3/16 x 37 x 37 in.
edition: 2 + artist's proof
Collection Anette und Udo Brandhorst, Cologne
Katharina Fritsch, Düsseldorf
Ydessa Hendeles Foundation, Toronto

74. **Geldkisten,** 1988
Aluminium, Stahl, Farbe
125 x 94 x 94 cm
Auflage 2 + AP
Sammlung Anette und Udo Brandhorst, Köln
Katharina Fritsch, Düsseldorf
Ydessa Hendeles Foundation, Toronto

122

Four half-open small golden chests on thin steel stands are arranged in a cruciform pattern. An empty space is created in the center, where the back edges of the open lids touch each other. The lids and bodies of the chests are made of gold-anodized, mitered aluminum sheets that are fitted precisely together as in a box. The rear section of the body of the chests and the lids are made of one piece. The small, rectangular chests are filled to the top with artificial coins from the multiple *Geld* (cat. 73) arranged in sixty tidy piles – ten broad and six deep – of eighty-four coins each.

Vier halb geöffnete, goldene Kästchen sind auf dünnen, mattschwarz lackierten Stahlgestellen in Kreuzform aufgestellt. In der Mitte sparen sie ein quadratisches Zentrum aus, da die hinteren Ecken der geöffneten Deckel sich zu berühren scheinen. Die Deckel und die Körper der Kästchen sind aus golden eloxierten, auf Gehrung geschnittenen Aluminiumplatten, die wie bei einer Schachtel präzise zusammengefügt sind. Der hintere Teil der Kistenkörper und der Deckel sind aus einem Stück gearbeitet. Die kleinen, rechteckigen Kästchen sind bis zum Rand mit den künstlichen Münzen des Multiple «Geld» (Kat. 73) gefüllt. Sie sind in sechzig ordentlichen Stapeln – zehn in der Breite, sechs in der Tiefe – à 84 Münzen angeordnet.

75. **Company at Table,** 1988 (pl. 17)
polyester, wood, cotton, paint
55 1/8 x 629 15/16 x 68 7/8 in.
Permanent loan from the Dresdner Bank,
Frankfurt am Main, to the Museum für Moderne Kunst, Frankfurt am Main

Sixteen identical, life-size, slender young men are sitting opposite each other at a long table with a patterned tablecloth. The distance between them is determined by the legs of the long table and the two benches: the spaces between two table legs, which are aligned with the legs of the benches, are alternately occupied by a man's legs or left open. The tablecloth has a constantly repeated geometrical pattern suggestive of flowers.

All the men have the same slightly leaning body and head posture. They are sitting with their backs curved, lower arms and hands laid flat on the table, and legs stretched out parallel to each other. Each of their heads is leaning slightly forward and is lowered toward the table. Their arms stick out diagonally from the torso, bend at right angles at the elbow, and point toward an imaginary object on the tablecloth. This point is always precisely at the same place in the repeating pattern on the cloth. The legs and feet of the individual figures are close together and bend at right angles at the knees and ankles. The men are wearing plain trousers, a simple man's shirt, and laced shoes.

The uniform posture and the regularity of the figures is reinforced by the fact that the shirts are buttoned to the neck and by their motionless faces. The heads of the figures show the face of a male with a strong, slightly angular chin, a broad mouth, high cheekbones, a large nose, and a high forehead. The hair, which is slightly receding, is combed back tightly and cut straight at the neckline in the back. The men's individual expressions show no sign of emotion. Their eyes, which are only slightly open, are directed at the table and appear to consider the hands or the geometrical pattern of the tablecloth. None of the men takes notice of his opposite; each appears deep in thought.

The arrangement of the figures, which are placed at the same distance between and across from each other, produces an almost infinite perspective when seen from the narrow end of the table. The figures move closer and closer together, and individual details like faces blend into a uniform, stereotyped composition. The work is defined by the colors black, white, and red. The men's faces and necks are matte white and thus form a stark contrast to the matte black of the hair and clothing. The white tablecloth has a geometrically symmetrical red pattern, and the table and the two benches are painted light gray. The figures were cast in polyester reinforced with fiberglass and the tablecloth was made of bleached printed cotton. The tables and benches were assembled from simple MDF sheets.

Frank Fenstermacher, an acquaintance of Katharina Fritsch, was the model for the figure of the young man. He was chosen because of his height, large head, and large hands; his looks are striking, and he is very much a "type". He also had the ability to sustain the desired gestures and facial expression during the long casting process. The pattern on the tablecloth is re-created from a tablecloth that the artist saw while traveling through Switzerland. The arrangement of the men in rows was inspired by pictures of rows of figures on church façades or Indian temples.

123

75. **Tischgesellschaft,** 1988 (Taf. 17)
Polyester, Holz, Baumwolle, Farbe
140 x 1600 x 175 cm
Dauerleihgabe der Dresdner Bank, Frankfurt am Main, an das Museum für Moderne Kunst, Frankfurt am Main

An einem langen Tisch mit einer gemusterten Tischdecke sitzen sich jeweils 16 identische lebensgrosse, schlanke, junge Männer im gleichen Abstand gegenüber. Die Entfernung der Figuren zueinander wird durch die Beine des langen Tisches und der beiden Bänke bestimmt. Abwechselnd sind die Freiräume zwischen zwei Tischbeinen, die auf einer Linie mit den Beinen der Bänke liegen, mit den Beinen eines Mannes besetzt oder sie sind freigelassen. Die auf dem Tisch liegende Decke zeigt ein geometrisches, floral anmutendes Muster, das sich beständig wiederholt.
Alle Männer weisen die gleiche, leicht gesenkte Körper- und Kopfhaltung auf. Sie sitzen mit gekrümmtem Rücken, flach auf den Tisch gelegten Unterarmen und Händen und parallel ausgerichteten Beinen bewegungslos nebeneinander. Der Kopf ist etwas nach vorne gebeugt und zum Tisch gesenkt. Die Arme, die vom Oberkörper schräg nach aussen laufen, knicken im Ellbogen rechtwinklig ab und laufen auf einen imaginären Punkt auf der Tischdecke zu. Dieser liegt immer genau an der selben Stelle auf dem Rapportmuster der Decke und zwischen den Fingerspitzen der sehr grossen, leicht gespreizten Hände. Die Beine und Füsse der einzelnen Figuren liegen eng aneinander und sind rechtwinklig in den Knie- bzw. Fussgelenken abgeknickt. Bekleidet sind die Männer mit einer schlichten Hose, einem einfachen Herrenhemd und geschnürten Halbschuhen.
Die Geschlossenheit der Haltung und die Regelmässigkeit der Figuren wird durch die hochgeschlossenen, bis zum Hals zugeknöpften Hemden und die regungslosen Gesichter verstärkt. Die grossen Köpfe geben ein männliches Gesicht wieder mit ausgeprägtem, leicht kantigem Kinn, breitem Mund, hohen Wangenknochen, grosser Nase und hoher Stirn. Das Haar, bei dem der Ansatz zu Geheimratsecken angedeutet ist, ist straff nach hinten gekämmt, an den Ohren kurz und am Hinterkopf beim Halsansatz gerade abgeschnitten. Der Gesichtsausdruck der einzelnen Männer weist auf keinerlei Gefühlsregung hin. Der Blick der nur schwach geöffneten Augen ist auf den Tisch gerichtet und scheint die Hände oder das geometrische Muster der Tischdecke zu betrachten. Keiner der Männer bemerkt sein Gegenüber, jeder ist in sich oder in seine Gedanken versunken.
Die Anordnung der Figuren im gleichen Abstand voneinander und zueinander ergibt von der Schmalseite des Tisches gesehen eine fast unendliche Perspektive. Die Figuren rücken immer enger zusammen, differenzierbare Einzelformen, wie die Gesichter, verschmelzen zu einer einheitlichen, schablonenhaften Form.
Die Arbeit wird von den Farben Schwarz, Weiss und Rot bestimmt. Die Gesichter, Hälse und Hände der Männer sind in einem matten Weiss gehalten und bilden so einen starken Kontrast zu dem matten Schwarz der Haare und der Kleidung. Die auf den langen Tisch gelegte weisse Tischdecke zeigt ein geometrisch-symmetrisches, rotes Muster, der Tisch und die beiden Bänke sind in einem hellen Grau gestrichen. Die Figuren wurden aus mit Fiberglas verstärktem Polyester gegossen, die Tischdecke aus gebleichtem, bedrucktem Baumwollstoff gefertigt. Die Tische und Bänke wurden aus einfachen MDF-Platten zusammen geschraubt.

Als Modell für die Figur des jungen Mannes diente ein Bekannter Fritschs, Frank Fenstermacher. Die Wahl fiel auf ihn, da er sehr gross ist, einen grossen Kopf und grosse Hände besitzt und von der Erscheinung her bildhaft, typhaft wirkt. Auch ist er fähig, während der langwierigen Prozedur des Abgiessens die gewünschte Mimik und Gestik zu halten. Das Muster der Tischdecke ist einer Tischdecke nachempfunden, die die Künstlerin bei einer Reise durch die Schweiz gesehen hatte. Die Reihung der Männer wurde durch Bilder von Figurenreihen an Kirchenfassaden oder indischen Tempeln angeregt.

76. **Ghost and Pool of Blood,** 1988 (pl. 18)
     ghost:
     polyester, paint
     78 ³/₄ x 23 ⁵/₈ in.
     pool of blood:
     Plexiglas, lacquer
     20 ¹⁵/₁₆ x 82 ⁷/₁₆ in.
     edition: 3 + artist's proof
     Bowes Collection, Santa Monica
     Ydessa Hendeles Art Foundation, Toronto
     Private Collection

The slender figure of a white ghost is turned toward a long, red pool some distance away on the floor.
The ghost is an erect human figure with a sheet placed over it. The sheet fits relatively tightly over the head and shoulders, but falls in loose, straight folds of different depths over the figure's face, back of head, and body. Details like face, arms or legs cannot be distinguished. The edge of the sheet is draped precisely so that it ends evenly at the floor. The figure is cast in polyester and painted in matte white paint.

The pool of blood is long and shallow in form, with irregular edges. It is made of red-painted Plexiglas.
For the ghost a large cloth was placed over a mannequin; the folds were left as they fell, and a plaster of Paris impression was subsequently made of the figure. To determine the shape of the pool of blood, Katharina Fritsch laid down on the floor and had liquid poured around her. The puddle produced provided an outline for the pool.

77. **Display Stand with Brains,** 1989
     Plexiglas, plastic, paint
     height 78 ³/₄ in., diameter 47 ¹/₄ in.
     destroyed, is being produced again

Two hundred and sixty copies of the multiple *Gehirn* (cat. 72) are arranged into two 39 ³/₈-inch-high double cones, one inverted over the other and placed tip to tip, like an hour-glass, using transparent Plexiglas disks. The brains are placed with their front – the cerebrum – precisely aligned with the edge of the individual disks, and the center of the shelves, which is scarcely visible, remains empty. In contrast with the other two sets of display stand in which multiples are shown (cat. 69, cat. 70), the multiples here are staggered slightly to the right or left in relation to the layer below, suggesting a spindle. The two tips of the cones meet at two layers that each consists of four brains; there are twenty-four brains on the top and bottom layers.

The brains were made of synthetic material especially for this arrangement, as plaster of Paris would have been too heavy and would have considerably impaired stability. When the work was installed in the Portikus in 1989 it became clear that the shape would not stand permanently without internal support. The work was produced again with a different internal structure and glass shelves (instead of Plexiglas). It is documented in a photograph that appears in several catalogs and articles.

78. **Mill,** 1990 (pl. 14)
     concrete, wood, motor
     height 275 ⁹/₁₆ in.
     Römerbrücke heat and power plant, Saarbrücken municipal services department

An enlarged and simplified version of the *Graue Mühle* (cat. 5) was set up on the bank of a lake near Saarbrücken. In executing the 275-inch-high structure, all decorative details, like the masonry or sections adjacent to the building, were omitted. The large mill-wheel with eight spokes is placed on the side facing the lake and

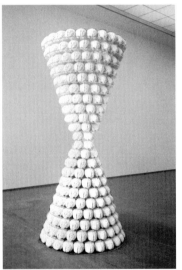

77.

78.

76. **Gespenst und Blutlache,** 1988 (Taf. 18)
     Gespenst:
     Polyester, Farbe
     200 x 60 cm
     Blutlache:
     Plexiglas, Lack
     53,2 x 209, 4 cm
     Auflage 3 + AP
     Sammlung Bowes, Santa Monica, USA
     Ydessa Hendeles Art Foundation, Toronto
     Privatsammlung

Die schlanke Figur eines weissen Gespenstes ist einer länglichen, roten Lache zugewandt, die in einiger Entfernung auf dem Boden liegt.
Das Gespenst besteht aus einer hochaufgerichteten menschlichen Figur, über die ein Laken gelegt wurde. Liegt das Laken auf dem Kopf und den Schultern noch relativ straff auf, so fällt es in lockeren, unterschiedlich tiefen, geradlinigen Falten über Gesicht, Hinterkopf und Körper der Figur. Einzelheiten, wie Gesicht, Arme oder Beine zeichnen sich nicht ab. Die Kanten des Lakens schliessen exakt mit dem Boden ab. Die Figur aus Polyesterguss ist mit einer mattweissen Farbe gestrichen.

Eine längliche, flache Form mit unregelmässigen Aussenkanten bestimmt die Blutlache. Sie ist aus rot lackiertem Plexiglas gefertigt.
Für das Gespenst wurde ein grosses Tuch über eine Schaufensterpuppe gelegt, die Falten so belassen wie sie fielen und anschliessend von der Figur ein Gipsabdruck genommen. Um den Umriss der Blutlache festzulegen, hat Katharina Fritsch sich auf den Boden gelegt und eine Flüssigkeit um sich herum giessen lassen. Die dadurch entstandene Pfütze ergab den Umriss der Lache.

77. **Warengestell mit Gehirnen,** 1989
     Plexiglas, Kunststoff, Farbe
     Höhe 250 cm, Durchmesser 120 cm
     zerstört, wird neu hergestellt

260 Exemplare des Multiple «Gehirn» (Kat. 72) wurden mit Hilfe von durchsichtigen Plexiglasscheiben zu einem zweieinhalb Meter hohen, auf den Spitzen stehenden Doppelkegel, vergleichbar mit einer Sanduhr, gestapelt. Sie sind mit ihrer Vorderseite – dem Grosshirn – genau an den Aussenkanten der einzelnen Scheiben plaziert, die kaum sichtbare Mitte des Gestells bleibt leer. Im Gegensatz zu den anderen beiden Warengestellen, bei denen Multiples gezeigt werden (Kat. 69, Kat. 70), sind hier die Multiples im Vergleich zur darunterliegenden Lage leicht nach links bzw. rechts verschoben. Dadurch entsteht eine angedeutete Spindelform. Die beiden aufeinandertreffenden Spitzen der Kegel sind jeweils aus vier Gehirnen zusammengestellt, auf der untersten und der obersten Lage liegen jeweils 24 Gehirne.

Für das Gestell wurden die Gehirne aus Kunststoff speziell hergestellt, da Gips zu schwer gewesen wäre und die Stabilität stark beeinträchtigt hätte. Bei der Aufstellung im Portikus 1989 zeigte sich, dass die Form ohne innere Stütze nicht dauerhaft stehen würde. Die Arbeit wird mit einer veränderten Innenkonstruktion und mit Glasscheiben (anstatt Plexiglas) nochmals hergestellt. Dokumentiert ist sie mit einem Photo, das in mehreren Katalogen und Artikeln abgebildet ist.

78. **Mühle,** 1990 (Taf. 14)
     Beton, Holz, Motor
     Höhe 700 cm
     Heizkraftwerk Römerbrücke, Stadtwerke Saarbrücken

Am Ufer eines Sees in der Nähe von Saarbrücken wurde die vergrösserte und vereinfachte Version der «Grauen Mühle» (Kat. 5) aufgestellt. Bei der Ausführung des sieben Meter hohen Gebäudes verzichtete man auf alle schmückenden Details, wie das Mauerwerk oder die an das Gebäude anschliessenden Teile. Das grosse Mühl-

can be turned by a motor inside. Like the small mill, this version too is sprayed with a matte gray.

The work *Mühle* was originally intended for the Krefeld municipal services department, but was not realized there. When Katharina Fritsch was invited to take part in the *Kunstprojekt Heizkraftwerk Römerbrücke* (Römerbrücke Heat and Power Plant Art Project) in Saarbrücken, she decided to realize the work planned for Krefeld there. The design for Krefeld is documented by photomontages.

79. **Ambulance,** 1990
45-inch vinyl record
Edition *Parkett* 25, with *Unken* (cat. 32) and *Mühle* (cat. 80)

A single record in a matte white sleeve is labeled in the center with the word *Krankenwagen* (Ambulance) in black letters. In the middle of the record is a round label, also white, on which is printed, alongside the details about copyright, the recording, and the record company, the instruction "Bitte leise abspielen" ("Please play softly"). The recording reproduces a constantly repeated ambulance siren.

Krankenwagen was produced by *Parkett* in 1990 as a special edition with two other 45-inch records.

80. **Mill,** 1990
45-inch vinyl record
Edition *Parkett* 25, with *Unken* (cat. 32) and *Krankenwagen* (cat. 79)

A single record in a matte white sleeve is labeled in the center with the word *Mühle* (Mill) in black letters. In the middle of the record is a round label, also white, on which is printed, alongside the details about copyright, the recording, and the record company, the instruction "Bitte leise abspielen" ("Please play softly"). The recording reproduces the constantly repeated sound of a mill-wheel.

Mühle was produced by *Parkett* in 1990 as a special edition with two other 45-inch records.

81. **Table with Cheese,** 1981/90
MDF board, steel, silicone, paint
29 ¹/₂ x 47 ¹/₄ x 47 ¹/₄ in.
edition: 5
Collection Garnatz, Cologne
Goldberg Collection, New York
Jablonka Galerie, Cologne
Collection Jedermann, N.A.
Collection Lehmann, Lausanne

A copy of the object *Käse* (cat. 21) rests on a table consisting of a square MDF sheet lacquered in matte white and four angular steel legs lacquered in matte black.

125

82. **Red Painting,** 1990-1991
wood, foil, lacquer, untreated cotton cloth, paint
55 ¹/₈ x 39 ³/₈ x 3 ³/₈ in.
edition: 2 + artist's proof
Eric Decelle Collection, Brussels
Matthew Marks Gallery, New York
Private Collection, Zürich

The monochrome, rectangular *Rotes Bild* is mounted in a plain, broad gold frame with edges angled inward. Thin joints between the frame and the surface of the picture and on the edges and corners of the frame are visible as dark lines. The picture itself consists of an even, crimson area of color, with no composition at all.

rad mit acht Speichen, das an der dem See zugewandten Seite liegt, kann durch einen Motor im Inneren bewegt werden. Wie die kleine Mühle ist auch diese Version mit grauer Aussenwandfarbe gespritzt.

Die Arbeit «Mühle» war zunächst für die Stadtwerke Krefeld vorgesehen, wurde dort aber nicht realisiert. Als Fritsch zu dem «Kunstprojekt Heizkraftwerk Römerbrücke» in Saarbrücken eingeladen wurde, beschloss sie, die für Krefeld geplante Arbeit dort auszuführen. Der Entwurf für Krefeld ist mit Fotomontagen dokumentiert.

79. **Krankenwagen,** 1990
Single
Edition Parkett 25 zusammen mit «Unken» (Kat. 32) und «Mühle» (Kat. 80)

In einem mattweissem Cover mit der in schwarzen Buchstaben mittig gesetzten Aufschrift «Krankenwagen» befindet sich eine Single-Schallplatte. In deren Mitte ist ein runder, ebenfalls weisser Aufkleber, auf dem neben den Angaben zum Copyright, zur Aufnahme und zum Verleger die Anweisung «Bitte leise abspielen» zu lesen ist. Die Aufnahme gibt die sich ständig wiederholende Sirene eines Krankenwagens wieder.

1990 wurde die Single als Vorzugsausgabe mit zwei weiteren Singles von der Zeitschrift «Parkett» verlegt.

80. **Mühle,** 1990
Single
Edition Parkett 25 zusammen mit «Unken» (Kat. 32) und «Krankenwagen» (Kat. 79)

In einem hellgrauen Cover mit der in schwarzen Buchstaben mittig gesetzten Aufschrift «Mühle» befindet sich eine Single-Schallplatte. In deren Mitte ist ein runder, ebenfalls grauer Aufkleber befestigt, auf dem die Angaben zum Copyright, zur Aufnahme und zum Verleger angegeben sind. Die Aufnahme gibt die sich ständig wiederholenden Geräusche eines Mühlrads wieder.

1990 wurde die Single als Vorzugsausgabe mit zwei weiteren Singles von der Zeitschrift «Parkett» verlegt.

81. **Tisch mit Käse,** 1981/90
MDF-Platte, Stahl, Silikon, Farbe
75 x 120 x 120 cm
Auflage 5
Sammlung Garnatz, Köln
Sammlung Goldberg, New York
Jablonka Galerie, Köln
Sammlung Jedermann, N.A.
Sammlung Lehmann, Lausanne

Im Zentrum eines kleinen Tisches liegt ein Exemplar des Objektes «Käse» (Kat. 21). Der Tisch besteht aus einer mattweiss lackierten, quadratischen MDF-Platte und vier mattschwarz lackierten, kantigen Stahlbeinen. Diese sind etwa 20 cm von der Tischkante nach innen gerückt festgeschraubt.

82. **Rotes Bild,** 1990-1991
Holz, Folie, Lack, Nessel, Farbe
140 x 100 x 8,5 cm
Auflage 2 + AP
Eric Decelle Collection, Brüssel
Matthew Marks Gallery, New York
Privatsammlung, Zürich

Die monochrome, rechteckige Farbfläche des «Roten Bildes» wird von einem schlichten, breiten Goldrahmen, mit nach innen abgeschrägten Leisten, gerahmt. Zwischen Rahmen und Bildfläche sowie an den Kanten und Ecken des Rahmens ziehen sich dünne Fugen, die als dunkle Striche sichtbar sind. Das Bild selbst weist

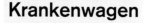

Krankenwagen

79.

Mühle

80.

81.

The unadorned wooden frame was constructed from strips of wood 7 7/8 inches wide and 3 3/8 inches deep, angled at the ends at forty-five degrees. It was then covered in mirrored foil and sprayed with yellow transparent varnish. For the picture untreated cotton cloth was stretched over a wooden support and sprayed evenly with paint.

eine monochrome, gleichmässige, purpurrote Farbfläche auf, die keinerlei Struktur besitzt.

Der schmucklose Holzrahmen wurde aus nach innen abgeschrägten, 20 cm breiten und 8,5 cm tiefen Holzleisten, die an den Enden im 45°-Winkel abgeschrägt wurden, gefertigt. Er wurde dann mit Spiegelfolie bezogen und mit gelbem Lasurlack gespritzt. Für das Bild wurde Nessel über einen Holzkern gezogen und sehr gleichmässig mit Farbe gespritzt.

83. **Blue Painting,** 1990-1991
wood, foil, lacquer, untreated cotton cloth, paint
55 1/8 x 39 3/8 x 3 3/8 in.
edition: 2 + artist's proof
Galerie Ghislaine Hussenot, Paris
Thomas Ruff, Düsseldorf
Shiraishi Contemporary Art, Tokyo

83. **Blaues Bild,** 1990-1991
Holz, Folie, Lack, Nessel, Farbe
140 x 100 x 8,5 cm
Auflage 2 + AP
Galerie Ghislaine Hussenot, Paris
Thomas Ruff, Düsseldorf
Shiraishi Contemporary Art, Tokio

Formally, *Blaues Bild* corresponds with cat. 82, except that the canvas was spray-painted a glowing ultramarine.

In der formalen Ausführung entspricht die Arbeit Kat. 82, nur wurde die Leinwand in einem leuchtenden Ultramarinblau gespritzt.

84. **Green Painting,** 1990-1991
wood, foil, lacquer, untreated cotton cloth, paint
55 1/8 x 39 3/8 x 3 3/8 in.
edition: 2 + artist's proof
None realized to date.

84. **Grünes Bild,** 1990-1991
Holz, Folie, Lack, Nessel, Farbe
140 x 100 x 8,5 cm
Auflage 2 + AP
Bisher ist keines ausgeführt worden.

Formally *Grünes Bild* corresponds with cat. 82, except that the canvas is to be spray-painted an intense chromium oxide green.

In der formalen Ausführung entspricht die Arbeit Kat. 82, nur wird die Leinwand in einem intensiven Chromoxidgrün gespritzt.

85. **Black Painting,** 1990-1991
wood, foil, lacquer, untreated cotton cloth, paint
55 3/8 x 39 3/8 x 3 3/8 in.
edition: 2 + artist's proof
Katharina Fritsch, Düsseldorf
Museum Haus Koekkoek, Kleve
Matthew Marks Gallery, New York

85. **Schwarzes Bild,** 1990-1991
Holz, Folie, Lack, Nessel, Farbe
140 x 100 x 8,5 cm
Auflage 2 + AP
Katharina Fritsch, Düsseldorf
Museum Haus Koekkoek, Kleve
Matthew Marks Gallery, New York

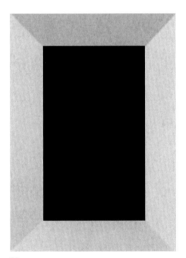

85.

Formally, this work corresponds with cat. 82, except that the canvas was sprayed with matte black paint.

In der formalen Ausführung entspricht die Arbeit Kat. 82, nur wurde die Leinwand in einem matten Schwarz gespritzt.

86. **White Painting,** 1990-1991
wood, foil, lacquer, untreated cotton cloth, paint
55 1/8 x 39 3/8 x 3 3/8 in.
edition: 2 + artist's proof
Matthew Marks Gallery, New York
Only one realized to date.

86. **Weisses Bild,** 1990-1991
Holz, Folie, Lack, Nessel, Farbe
140 x 100 x 8,5 cm
Auflage 2 + AP
Matthew Marks Gallery, New York
Bisher ist nur eines ausgeführt worden.

Formally, this work corresponds with cat. 82, except that the canvas was sprayed with pure white paint.

In der formalen Ausführung entspricht die Arbeit Kat. 82, nur wurde die Leinwand in einem reinen Weiss gespritzt.

87. **Yellow Painting,** 1990-1991
wood, foil, lacquer, untreated cotton cloth, paint
55 1/8 x 39 3/8 x 3 3/8 in.
edition: 2 + artist's proof
Collection Jedermann, N.A.
Klagsbrun Collection, Belgium
AP not realized to date.

87. **Gelbes Bild,** 1990-1991
Holz, Folie, Lack, Nessel, Farbe
140 x 100 x 8,5 cm
Auflage 2 + AP
Sammlung Jedermann, N.A.
Klagsbrun Collection, Belgium
AP ist bisher nicht ausgeführt worden.

Formally, this work corresponds with cat. 82, except that the canvas was spray-painted a glowing lemon yellow.

In der formalen Ausführung entspricht die Arbeit Kat. 82, nur wurde die Leinwand in einem leuchtenden Zitronengelb gespritzt.

88. **Light Green Painting,** 1990-1991
wood, foil, lacquer, untreated cotton cloth, paint
55 1/8 x 39 3/8 x 3 3/8 in.
edition: 2 + artist's proof
Hokin Collection, Chicago
Rossi Collection, Turin
AP not realized to date.

88. **Hellgrünes Bild,** 1990-1991
Holz, Folie, Lack, Nessel, Farbe
140 x 100 x 8,5 cm
Auflage 2 + AP
Hokin Collection, Chicago
Sammlung Rossi, Turin
AP ist bisher nicht ausgeführt worden.

Formally, this work corresponds with cat. 82, except that the canvas was sprayed a light yellow-green paint.

In der formalen Ausführung entspricht die Arbeit Kat. 82, nur wurde die Leinwand in einem hellen Gelbgrün gespritzt.

89. **Orange Painting,** 1990-1991
     wood, foil, lacquer, untreated cotton cloth, paint
     55 ^{1}/$_8$ x 39 ^{3}/$_8$ x 3 ^{3}/$_8$ in.
     edition: 2 + artist's proof
     Collection Palodetto, Milan
     Only one realized to date.

89. **Oranges Bild,** 1990-1991
     Holz, Folie, Lack, Nessel, Farbe
     140 x 100 x 8,5 cm
     Auflage 2 + AP
     Sammlung Palodetto, Mailand
     Bisher ist nur eines ausgeführt worden.

Formally, this work corresponds with cat. 82, except that the canvas was spray-painted cadmium orange.

In der formalen Ausführung entspricht die Arbeit Kat. 82, nur wurde die Leinwand in einem Cadmium-Orange gespritzt.

90. **Red Painting, Blue Painting, Green Painting,** 1990-1991
     each: wood, foil, lacquer, untreated cotton cloth, paint
     each: 55 ^{1}/$_8$ x 39 ^{3}/$_8$ x 3 ^{3}/$_8$ in., total: 55 ^{1}/$_8$ x 196 ^{7}/$_8$ x 3 ^{3}/$_8$ in.
     edition: 2 + artist's proof
     Goldberg Collection, New York
     Only one set realized to date.

90. **Rotes Bild, Blaues Bild, Grünes Bild,** 1990-1991
     je: Holz, Folie, Lack, Nessel, Farbe
     je: 140 x 100 x 8,5 cm; insgesamt: 140 x 500 x 8,5 cm
     Auflage 2 + AP
     Sammlung Goldberg, New York
     Bisher ist nur ein Set ausgeführt worden.

The work consists of three paintings in red, blue, and green that correspond to catalogue entries 82, 83, and 84, both formally and in color. The paintings are hung in a row at a distance of 39 ^{3}/$_8$ inches both from each other and from the floor in the following order: red, blue, green.

Die Arbeit besteht aus drei Bildern in den Farben Rot, Blau und Grün, die den Nummern Kat. 82, Kat. 83 und Kat. 84 sowohl formal als auch in ihrer Farbigkeit entsprechen. Die Bilder sind in einer Reihe mit einem Abstand von einem Meter zueinander und zum Boden in der folgenden Ordnung von links aufgehängt: Rot, Blau, Grün.

91. **Black Painting, White Painting, Yellow Painting,** 1990-1991
     each: wood, foil, lacquer, untreated cotton cloth, paint
     each: 55 ^{1}/$_8$ x 39 ^{3}/$_8$ x 3 ^{3}/$_8$ in.; total: 55 ^{3}/$_8$ x 196 ^{7}/$_8$ x 3 ^{3}/$_8$ in.
     edition: 2 + artist's proof
     FRAC Aquitaine
     Collection Garnatz, Cologne
     Jason Rubell Collection

91. **Schwarzes Bild, Weisses Bild, Gelbes Bild,** 1990-1991
     je: Holz, Folie, Lack, Nessel, Farbe
     je: 140 x 100 x 8,5 cm; insgesamt: 140 x 500 x 8,5 cm
     Auflage 2 + AP
     FRAC Aquitaine
     Sammlung Garnatz, Köln
     Sammlung Jason Rubell

The work consists of three paintings in black, white, and yellow that correspond to catalogue entries 85, 86, and 87, both formally and in color. The paintings are hung in a row at a distance of 39 ^{3}/$_8$ inches both from each other and from the floor in the following order: black, white, yellow.

Die Arbeit besteht aus drei Bildern in den Farben Schwarz, Weiss und Gelb, die den Nummern Kat. 85, Kat. 86 und Kat. 87 sowohl formal als auch in der Farbigkeit entsprechen. Die Bilder sind in einer Reihe mit einem Abstand von einem Meter zueinander und zum Boden in der folgenden Ordnung von links aufgehängt: Schwarz, Weiss, Gelb.

92. **Light Green Painting, Orange Painting,** 1990-1991
     each: wood, foil, lacquer, untreated cotton cloth, paint
     each: 55 ^{1}/$_8$ x 39 ^{3}/$_8$ x 3 ^{3}/$_8$ in., total: 55 ^{1}/$_8$ x 118 x 3 ^{3}/$_8$ in.
     edition: 2 + artist's proof
     Collection Dapillo, Genoa
     Only one set realized to date.

92. **Hellgünes Bild, Oranges Bild,** 1990-1991
     je: Holz, Folie, Lack, Nessel, Farbe
     je: 140 x 100 x 8,5 cm; insgesamt: 140 x 300 x 8,5 cm
     Auflage 2 + AP
     Sammlung Dapillo, Genua
     Bisher ist nur ein Set ausgeführt worden

The work consists of two paintings in light green and orange that correspond to catalogue entries 88 and 89, both formally and in color. The paintings are hung next to each other – light green on the left and orange on the right – at a distance of 39 ^{3}/$_8$ inches both from each other and from the floor.

Die Arbeit besteht aus zwei Bildern in den Farben Hellgrün und Orange, die den Nummern Kat. 88 und Kat. 89 sowohl formal als auch in der Farbigkeit entsprechen. Die Bilder werden nebeneinander – links das hellgrüne, rechts das orange – mit einem Abstand von einem Meter zueinander und zum Boden aufgehängt.

93. **Eight Paintings in Eight Colors: Red Painting, Blue Painting, Green Painting, Black Painting, White Painting, Yellow Painting, Light Green Painting, Orange Painting,** 1990-1991 (pl. 15)
     each: wood, foil, lacquer, untreated cotton cloth, paint
     each: 55 ^{1}/$_8$ x 39 ^{3}/$_8$ x 3 ^{3}/$_8$ in.; total: 55 ^{1}/$_8$ x 590 ^{5}/$_8$ x 3 ^{3}/$_8$ in.
     edition: 2 + artist's proof
     Collection Simone Ackermans, Xanten
     Only one set realized to date.

93. **Acht Bilder in acht Farben: Rotes Bild, Blaues Bild, Grünes Bild, Schwarzes Bild, Weisses Bild, Gelbes Bild, Hellgrünes Bild, Oranges Bild,** 1990-1991 (Taf. 15)
     je: Holz, Folie, Lack, Nessel, Farbe
     je: 140 x 100 x 8,5 cm; insgesamt: 140 x 1500 x 8,5 cm
     Auflage 2 + AP
     Sammlung Simone Ackermans, Xanten
     Bisher ist nur ein Set ausgeführt worden

The work consists of all eight individual paintings listed in catalogue entries 82 through 89. Like the other three sets (cat. 90 - cat. 92), they are hung at a distance of 39 3/8 inches from each other and from the floor. The sequence of colors seen from the left corresponds with the sequence in the title. When the paintings are hung in this sequence, it is clear that the work is divided into two parts that are symmetrical in mirror image: a dark half, containing from the left the colors red, blue, green, and black, and a light half, with the colors white, yellow, light green, and orange, also from the left. The intensity of the dark and light colors also increases from outside to inside. The two central paintings, the black and the white, are the darkest and lightest respectively; working from them outward, the colors become lighter to the left and darker to the right.

These paintings represent a compilation of all the colors used in Katharina Fritsch's work to date. At the same time they are reminiscent of the paintboxes that one had as a child, but also – as she once articulated – a sculptor's comment on painting.

94. **Red Room with Chimney Noise,** 1991 (pl. 16)
     paint, tape recorder
     Katharina Fritsch, Düsseldorf

The mirror-smooth polished walls of an empty room are sprayed evenly with a mixture of cadmium red. No composition or color-layering can be made out on the surface of the walls; the room is dominated by a uniformly matte crimson color. In addition, the monotonous, circling noise of wind howling through a chimney can be heard playing on an endless loop from a tape recorder.

Katharina Fritsch realized this work as a contribution to the *Metropolis* exhibition in the Martin-Gropius-Bau in Berlin. She chose one of the rooms from which one can view the rubble site of the "topography of horror," toward the buildings of the former Reich Air Ministry and the Axel Springer Press.

95. **Silver Painting,** 1991-1992
     wood, foil, lacquer, untreated cotton cloth,
     paint
     55 1/8 x 39 3/8 x 3 3/8 in.
     edition: 5 + artist's proof
     Katharina Fritsch, Düsseldorf
     Dr. Stefan Motzer, Xanten
     Lia Rumma, Naples
     Shiraishi Contemporary Art, Tokyo (destroyed)

Formally, *Silbernes Bild* corresponds with the various colored versions of the paintings (cat. 82 - cat. 89). The difference is that a shimmering, evenly matte silver canvas is placed in the golden frame.

96. **Man and Mouse,** 1991-1992 (pl. 19)
     polyester, paint
     94 1/2 x 51 3/16 x 88 9/16 in.
     edition: 2 + artist's proof
     Collection Simone Ackermans, Xanten
     Bagley and Virginia Wright Collection, Seattle
     AP not realized to date.

The upright, gigantic black mouse sits enthroned on a simple white bed in which a male figure is lying flat on his back under a blanket. The sleeping man does not seem to notice the animal, which is sitting on him. He has drawn the blanket over his body, right up to his chin. His narrow head, which is facing upward, is pressed lightly into the large, plump pillow. His eyes are closed and his features seem very relaxed. The monster mouse is sitting on its hind legs with its front

Die Arbeit besteht aus allen acht Einzelbildern, die in Kat. 82 bis Kat. 89 aufgeführt sind. Sie werden entsprechend der anderen drei Sets (Kat. 90 - Kat. 92) in einem Abstand von 1 Meter zueinander und zum Boden aufgehängt. Die Reihenfolge der Farben von links gesehen entspricht der im Titel angegebenen. Bei der symmetrischen und gleichmässig wirkenden Reihung der Bilder fällt auf, dass die Arbeit in zwei spiegelsymmetrische Seiten geteilt ist: eine dunkle, mit den Farben Rot, Blau, Grün und Schwarz und eine helle in den Farben Weiss, Gelb, Hellgrün und Orange; jeweils von links gesehen. Des weiteren ergibt sich eine Steigerung in der Farbintensität hell bzw. dunkel von aussen nach innen. Die beiden mittleren Bilder, das schwarze und das weisse sind die dunkelsten bzw. hellsten, von ihnen aus nach links gehend werden die Farben heller, nach rechts dunkler.

Die Bilder stellen eine Zusammenstellung aller Farben dar, die bisher im Werk von Katharina Fritsch benutzt wurden. Sie sind gleichzeitig eine Erinnerung an die Farbkästen, die man als Kinder besass, aber auch – wie sie einmal formulierte – der Kommentar eines Bildhauers zur Malerei.

94. **Roter Raum mit Kamingeräusch,** 1991 (Taf. 16)
     Farbe, Tonband
     Katharina Fritsch, Düsseldorf

Die spiegelglatt geschliffenen Wände eines leeren Raumes sind gleichmässig mit einer Kadmiumrot-Mischung gespritzt. Es ist keinerlei Struktur oder Farbschichtung auf der Oberfläche der Wände erkennbar, der Raum wird von der einheitlich matten, purpurroten Farbe beherrscht. Dazu erklingt das monotone, kreisende Geräusch von heulendem Wind in einem Kamin, das von einem Endlosband eines versteckten Tonbandes abgespielt wird.

Katharina Fritsch hat diese Arbeit als Beitrag zur Ausstellung «Metropolis» im Martin-Gropius-Baus in Berlin ausgeführt. Sie wählte dafür einen der Räume aus, von denen man über das Trümmergelände, in dem sich die «Topographie des Grauens» befindet, auf das Gebäude des ehemaligen Reichsluftfahrt-Ministerium und des Axel-Springer-Verlages blicken kann.

95. **Silbernes Bild,** 1991-1992
     Holz, Folie, Lack, Nessel, Farbe
     140 x 100 x 8,5 cm
     Auflage 5 + AP
     Katharina Fritsch, Düsseldorf
     Dr. Stefan Motzer, Xanten
     Lia Rumma, Neapel
     Shiraishi Contemporary Art, Tokio (zerstört)

In der formalen Ausführung entspricht das «Silberne Bild» den farbigen Versionen der Bilder (Kat. 82 - Kat. 89). Im Unterschied zu ihnen ist in den goldenen Rahmen eine matt silbern schimmernde, gleichmässige Farbfläche eingesetzt.

96. **Mann und Maus,** 1991-1992 (Taf. 19)
     Polyester, Farbe
     240 x 130 x 225 cm
     Auflage 2 + AP
     Sammlung Simone Ackermans, Xanten
     Sammlung Bagley und Virginia Wright, Seattle
     AP ist bisher nicht ausgeführt worden.

Auf einem einfachen, weissen Bett, in dem eine männliche Gestalt unter einer Bettdecke flach ausgestreckt auf dem Rücken liegt, thront eine aufgerichtete, riesige, schwarze Maus. Der schlafende Mann scheint das schwer auf ihm lastende Tier nicht zu bemerken. Er hat die Bettdecke über seinen Körper, seine Arme und Beine bis ans Kinn gezogen. Sein schmaler Kopf, der nach oben ausgerichtet ist, drückt sich leicht in das dicke, grosse Kissen. Seine Augen sind geschlossen, die Ge-

paws slightly drawn in, roughly at the level of his thorax. Its body is turned toward the man, and its head, with closed mouth, open eyes, and small ears, is staring straight ahead. Its long tail curls like a question mark over the end of the duvet, which hangs slightly over the edge of the bed. Both the man's head and the mouse are reproduced faithfully. The man's head is depicted in every detail: hair structure, eyebrows, eyelid fold etc. On the mouse the muscles of the limbs can be seen clearly and the structure of its fur and tail is precisely detailed, as are the paws with their pointed claws. The work is rigidly divided into black and white. The bed, with pillow and blanket, and the man's head are matte white, while the mouse is a dull pitch black.

The work, which can be dismantled into two parts – bed with man, and mouse with mouse-tail – is made of cast polyester and painted with several coats of paint. The same model was available for the man's head as for *Tischgesellschaft* (cat. 75). A plaster cast was taken and then used for the mold. The mouse was based on a small stuffed mouse that had been treated in the desired pose.

97. **Rat-King,** 1991-1993 (pl. 20)
polyester, paint
height 110 1/4 in., diameter 511 13/16 in.
Katharina Fritsch, Düsseldorf

Sixteen larger-than-life-size black rats in the work *Rattenkönig* form a tightly closed circle, side by side, crouching upright on their hind paws and facing outward. The animals' solid bodies, with front paws drawn inward and claws pointing down, are leaning forward. The rounded backs blend straight in with the small, angular heads, which are thrusting rigidly forward. The heads have pointed snouts, delicate-looking ears pulled slightly back, and small, close-set, almond-shaped eyes. The mouths are tightly shut, with the upper jaw slightly overlapping the lower jaw. The short forepaws are held symmetrically parallel beneath the heads, and precisely above the large hind paws with their enormous claws. The thick, straight tails on the rats' backs point inward like the spokes of a cartwheel, and end in a large, carefully tied knot in the center of the circle formed by the animals. The ball-like knot is made up of eight curved segments in each of which eight tail sections lie parallel with each other. The segments are always staggered at right angles to each other, so that the ends of the tails always disappear under the one that is diagonal to them. This artfully tied knot means that the sixteen animals are inextricably fastened together and held in a crown-like circle. They, too, like the *Elefant* (cat. 64) or *Mann und Maus* (cat. 96) are realistically reproduced. The shaggy fur, the grooves on the tails, and the notches on the claws are clearly formed, and the whiskers on the noses delicately suggested. These details are not apparent at first glance, as the work is bathed in a matte dark black that renders them difficult to discern.

Although the animals seem frightening at first – it is possible to walk under their forepaws – one soon notices that the aggression that they emanate is controlled and harmless. As the artful knot cannot be undone, they form a vicious circle from which there is no escape.

Katharina Fritsch got the idea for this work from images and associations while visiting the exhibition galleries at the Dia Center for the Arts in New York. She felt that a work with demonic qualities – half human, half animal – would fit into this place. The image

129

sichtszüge wirken sehr entspannt. Ungefähr auf Höhe seines Brustkorbes sitzt die monströse Maus in Hab-Acht-Stellung auf ihren Hinterbeinen, die Vorderpfoten leicht angezogen. Sie ist mit ihrem Körper dem Mann zugewandt, ihr Kopf mit geschlossenem Maul, geöffneten Augen und kleinen Ohren blickt starr nach vorne. Ihr langer Schwanz ringelt sich in Form eines Fragezeichens auf der hinteren Hälfte des Federbetts, das etwas über die Bettkante übersteht. Sowohl der Kopf des Mannes als auch die Maus sind naturgetreu wiedergegeben. Der Kopf des Mannes ist in allen Einzelheiten wie Haarstruktur, Augenbrauen, Lidfalte usw. abgebildet; bei der Maus zeichnen sich die Muskeln der Gliedmassen klar ab und die Struktur des Felles und des Schwanzes ist, ebenso wie die Pfoten mit ihren spitzen Krallen, präzise ausgearbeitet. Die Arbeit ist streng in Schwarz und Weiss geschieden. Das Bett, mit Kissen und Bettdecke sowie dem Kopf des Mannes ist in mattem Weiss gehalten, die Maus in glanzlosem Pechschwarz.

Die Arbeit, die in zwei Teile (Bett mit Mann und Mäuseschwanz bzw. Maus) zerlegbar ist, besteht aus gegossenem Polyester und ist nachträglich mit mehreren Schichten Farbe einheitlich bemalt worden. Für den Kopf des Mannes stand das gleiche Modell wie bei der «Tischgesellschaft» (Kat. 75) zur Verfügung. Von ihm wurde ein Gipsabdruck genommen, der dann für die Gussform benutzt wurde. Die Maus wurde nach einer kleinen, ausgestopften Maus geformt, die in der gewünschten Haltung präpariert worden war.

97. **Rattenkönig,** 1991-1993 (Taf. 20)
Polyester, Farbe
Höhe 280 cm, Durchmesser 1300 cm
Katharina Fritsch, Düsseldorf

Dicht an dicht, aufrecht auf den Hinterpfoten hockend und nach aussen blickend, bilden die sechzehn überlebensgrossen, schwarzen Ratten des «Rattenkönigs» einen fest geschlossenen Kreis. Die massiven Körper der Tiere, deren Vorderpfoten angezogen sind und mit den Krallen nach unten zeigen, lehnen sich weit nach vorne. Die gerundeten Rücken gehen direkt über in die starr vorgestreckten, kleinen, kantigen Köpfe. Diese besitzen spitz zulaufende Schnauzen, zierlich wirkende, leicht angelegte Ohren und kleine, eng aneinanderliegende, mandelförmige Augen. Die Mäuler sind fest verschlossen, der Oberkiefer überlappt etwas den Unterkiefer. Unter den Köpfen sind die kurzen Vorderpfoten, die genau über den grossen Hinterpfoten mit ihren enormen Krallen liegen, symmetrisch parallel ausgestreckt. Am Rücken der Ratten sind die dicken, geraden Schwänze ähnlich den Speichen eines Wagenrades nach innen gerichtet und enden in einem grossen, ordentlich geknüpften Knoten, der sich im Zentrum des von den Tieren gebildeten Kreises befindet. Der ballartige Knoten setzt sich aus acht gewölbten Segmenten zusammen, in denen jeweils acht Schwanzabschnitte parallel nebeneinander geführt werden. Die Segmente sind immer rechtwinklig zueinander versetzt, so dass jeweils die Enden der Schwänze unter den quer dazu liegenden Knoten verschwinden. Durch diesen kunstvoll geknüpften Knoten sind die sechzehn Tiere unentrinnbar miteinander verflochten und in eine kronenartige Kreisform gebannt. Auch sie sind, wie der «Elefant» (Kat. 64) oder «Mann und Maus» (Kat. 96) naturalistisch dargestellt. Das struppige Fell, die Rillen an den Schwänzen und die Kerben an den Krallen sind deutlich ausgearbeitet, die Barthaare an den Nasen zart angedeutet. Auf den ersten Blick fallen diese Details nicht auf, da die Arbeit in ein mattes, dunkles Schwarz getaucht ist, das alle Einzelheiten optisch verschwinden lässt.

Obwohl die Tiere, unter deren Vorderpfoten man bequem durchgehen kann, auf den ersten Blick erschreckend wirken, merkt man doch bald, dass die Aggression, die von ihnen ausgeht, gebremst und verharmlost ist. Der kunstvolle Knoten lässt sie nicht auseinander, sie bilden einen Teufelskreis, aus dem es kein Entrinnen gibt.

that emerged was then confirmed by stories about the *Rattenkönig* motif that constantly recurs in German folk tales in particular. This motif refers to an extremely rare natural phenomenon in which up to thirty young rats in a nest are indissolubly stuck or joined together by their tails.

The huge animals were based on a small stuffed rat that had been treated in the desired pose. A mold was cast from a large rat prepared in plaster of Paris. The tails and the knot were made separately; the knot was made to precise instructions given by the artist.

Angeregt zu dieser Arbeit wurde Katharina Fritsch durch Bilder und Assoziationen, die während der Besichtigung der Ausstellungsräume des Dia Center for the Arts in New York vor ihrem inneren Auge entstanden. Sie hatte das Gefühl, dass in diese Räume eine Arbeit gehöre, die – halb Mensch, halb Tier – an einen Dämon erinnert. Das entstandene Bild wurde dann durch Erzählungen von dem Motiv des «Rattenkönigs», das vorwiegend in deutschen Volkssagen immer wieder auftaucht, bestätigt. Bei diesem Motiv handelt sich um einen äusserst selten Vorgang aus der Natur, bei dem bis zu 30 junge Ratten im Nest mit den Schwänzen sich unlösbar miteinander verkleben oder verschlingen.

Als Vorbild für die riesigen Tiere diente eine kleine, ausgestopfte Ratte, die in der gewünschten Haltung präpariert worden war. Von der aus Gips hergestellten grossen Ratte wurde eine Gussform abgenommen. Die Schwänze und der Knoten wurden separat hergestellt; der Knoten ist nach genauen Angaben der Künstlerin gefertigt.

98. **Knot,** 1992/93
      plaster of Paris, paint
      diameter 55 ¹/₈ in.
      The Philadelphia Museum of Art, purchased
      with funds from the gift (by exchange) of Mr.
      and Mrs. Sturgis Ingersoll

98. **Knoten,** 1992/93
      Gips, Farbe
      Durchmesser 140 cm
      The Philadelphia Museum of Art, erworben
      mit Mitteln aus der Schenkung Mr. und Mrs.
      Sturgis Ingersoll

The artful knot formed from the sixteen rats' tails was detached as an individual item. Its underside showed the severed stands of the tails as a circle. On this stands the ball that they form. Like *Rattenkönig*, the *Knoten* is also steeped in matte black.

Der kunstvolle Knoten, der aus den Schwänzen der 16 Ratten gebildet wurde, ist als Einzelstück herausgelöst worden. An seiner Unterseite zeigen sich die abgeschnittenen Stränge der Schwänze als Kranz. Auf diesem sitzt das Knäuel, das sie bilden. Wie der «Rattenkönig» so ist auch der «Knoten» in ein mattes Schwarz getaucht.

99. **Panthers and Shelves with Eight Figures,** 1994/95
polyester, paint, wood, plaster of Paris
panther: height 35 $^7/_{16}$ in., diameter 63 in.
shelves with eight figures: 94 $^1/_2$ x 39 $^3/_8$ x 39 $^3/_8$ in.
Institut für Auslandsbeziehungen, Stuttgart

Eight identical black panthers and a set of eight shelves with eight figures on the top shelf are placed side by side at a distance of 63 inches. The panthers are crouching in a circle, relatively close together and with their backs to the viewer, snarling at an empty center. They are rendered in realistic detail, with the muscles in their bodies and their curled tails clearly visible. The relatively small heads are also very precise in detail. The same is true of the folds produced by their wide-open mouths.

Four high sets of shelves with seven intermediate boards seem to have been pushed inside each other to produce an octagonal center with coupled outer sections that describe a circle with their edges. A small, triangular gap is left between the individual edges of the sets of shelves, which makes it possible to look into or through the center of the shelves. On the top shelf of each set is a small white figure, a replica of a devotional statue. The panthers seem to be poised at the moment of rebellion, but one has the impression that the figure of Saint Katharina is circling around the space enclosed by the shelves, rather like figures on a roundabout.

The panthers are modeled on a small porcelain ornament, made in Italy and sold in furniture shops. The small plaster figures on the shelves were cast from a statue of Saint Katharina of Sienna with lily and rosary, acquired from a devotional shop.

A preliminary version of the shelves with two figures was shown in the *Doubletake* exhibition in the Hayward Gallery, London, in 1992, together with six paintings in the colors red, blue, green, black, white, and yellow, and the recording *Unken* (cat. 32) played on a tape. This version is illustrated in the exhibition catalog.

100. **Museum, Model 1:10,** 1995 (pl. 21)
wood, aluminum, Plexiglas, foil, paint
129 $^{15}/_{16}$ x 409 $^7/_{16}$ x 409 $^7/_{16}$ in.
Katharina Fritsch, Düsseldorf

A model of an octagonal, two-story building stands in the middle of an octagonal plinth 63 inches high, and painted a harsh white on the outer edges and grass-green on the top. It is surrounded by a dense cocoon of two hundred stylized aluminum trees, with trunks precisely as long as their crowns. The trees are reminiscent of the brush trees used in architects' models, but they are made more precisely and clearly. Eight slender rods, staggered from row to row, were arranged above each other in twenty-one rows to form the crowns. Their ends touch precisely to the millimeter, so that a clear line between the trunks is produced. If the work is viewed from above, the tips are seen to be arranged in triangles, each with twenty-five trees, and each of the tips of these triangles points toward a corner of the building. In this way they create a space in the shape of a star in the green surface, in the center of the octagonal building's location. The building itself consists of two distinct levels. The lower story has glazed outer walls with glazed double wing doors in the middle and white interior walls forming narrow corridors with a gray floor. The corridors lead to a stairwell that rises in a cone shape to an inner courtyard halfway up and from there in a funnel shape to the upper story. The upper story has gilded exterior walls, white interior walls, and colored glazed walls on the inner courtyard. These are lacquered in red, blue, green, black, white, yellow, light green, and orange and have narrow corri-

99. **Panther und Regal mit acht Figuren,** 1994/95
Polyester, Farbe, Holz, Gips
Panther: Höhe 90 cm, Durchmesser 160 cm
Regal mit acht Figuren: 240 x 100 x 100 cm
Institut für Auslandsbeziehungen, Stuttgart

Acht identische, schwarze Panther und ein achtflügliges weisses Regal mit acht Figuren auf dem obersten Brett sind in einem Abstand von 1,60 m nebeneinander gestellt. Die Panther hocken relativ dicht aneinander im Kreis, kehren dem Betrachter den Rücken zu und fauchen ein leeres Zentrum an. Sie sind realistisch durchgearbeitet, die Muskeln ihres Körpers und die angelegten Schwänze zeichnen sich deutlich ab. Die relativ kleinen Köpfe besitzen eine grosse Detailgenauigkeit. So sind die Falten, die sich durch das weite Aufreissen des Maules ergeben, präzise geformt.
Für das Regal wurden scheinbar vier hohe Regale mit sieben Zwischenbrettern so ineinander geschoben, dass ein achteckiges Zentrum mit angehängten Aussenteilen entsteht, die mit ihren Kanten einen Kreis beschreiben. Zwischen den einzelnen Regalaussenkanten bleibt eine schmale, dreieckige Lücke, die es erlaubt, in das Zentrum des Regals bzw. durch es hindurch zu blikken. Auf dem jeweilig obersten Brett der Regalflügel befindet sich immer die gleiche kleine weisse Figur, eine Replik einer Devotionalienfigur. Erscheinen die Panther fast im Moment des Aufbegehrens gegenüber der Leere erstarrt, so meint man, dass sich die Figur der hl. Katharina um das geschlossene Zentrum des Regals dreht, beinah wie Figuren eines Karussells.

Vorbild für die Panther aus Polyester ist eine Nippesfigur aus Porzellan, die in Italien gefertigt und in Einrichtungshäusern verkauft wird. Die kleinen Gipsfiguren auf dem Regal wurden von einer Figur der hl. Katharina von Siena mit Lilie und Rosenkranz aus dem Devotionalienhandel abgegossen.

Eine Vorläuferversion des Regals mit zwei Figuren wurde gemeinsam mit sechs Bildern in den Farben Rot, Blau, Grün, Schwarz, Weiss und Gelb sowie der vom Band abgespielten Aufnahme «Unken» (Kat. 32) 1992 in der Ausstellung «Doubletake», Hayward Gallery, London gezeigt. Im Katalog zu der Ausstellung ist diese Version abgebildet.

100. **Museum, Modell 1:10,** 1995 (Taf. 21)
Holz, Aluminium, Plexiglas, Folie, Farbe
330 x 1040 x 1040 cm
Katharina Fritsch, Düsseldorf

In der Mitte eines 1,60 m hohen, achteckigen, an den Aussenkanten hartweiss, auf der Oberfläche grasgrün gestrichenen Sockels steht ein achteckiges, zweigeschossiges Gebäudemodell. Umgeben wird es von einem dichten Gespinst aus 200 stilisierten, schwarzen Aluminiumbäumen, deren Stämme genauso lang sind wie die Astzonen. Die Bäume erinnern an Bürstenbäume, die für Architekturmodelle benutzt werden, sind aber klarer und präziser gearbeitet. Für die Astzone wurden in 21 Reihen übereinander jeweils acht dünne Stäbe von Reihe zu Reihe versetzt angeordnet. Sie berühren sich millimetergenau an ihren Enden, so dass eine klare Linie zwischen den Stämmen entsteht. Blickt man von oben auf die Arbeit, so erkennt man, dass die Bäume in Dreiecken zu je 25 Bäumen angeordnet sind und dass deren Spitzen jeweils auf eine Ecke des Gebäudes zulaufen. Dadurch sparen sie auf dem Grün die Form eines Sternes aus, in dessen Zentrum sich das achteckige Gebäude befindet. Das Gebäude selbst besteht aus zwei unterschiedlichen Geschossen. Das untere besitzt gläserne Aussenwände mit ebensolchen Flügeltüren in der Mitte sowie weisse Wände im Inneren, in die schmale Durchgänge ausgespart sind, und einen grauen Fussboden. Die Durchgänge führen zu einem Treppenhaus, das bis auf halbe Höhe kegelförmig zu einem Innenhof ansteigt und von dort trichterförmig zum Obergeschoss ansteigt. Das obere Geschoss hat vergoldete Aussenwände, weisse Innenwän-

99.

dors – leading to the stairwell – corresponding with the lower story. The building has a silver roof.

Katharina Fritsch sees this work as a model for a museum that is to be built with a diameter of 26 ¼ yards and a height of 17 ½ yards. But this building is not – as is usually the case with museums – to house a permanent collection, but should offer artists a forum for exhibitions lasting one to two years. The two stories are to be used differently. The lower, glazed story is intended for sculpture, with paintings in the upper level. The planned wood surrounding the building will consist of tall deciduous trees: they will form a green environment for the museum in summer and a black one in winter. These trees are to be accessible to all, so that this part of the exhibition can be seen independent of museum hours.

de und ist zum Innenhof hin mit farbigen Glaswänden versehen. Diese sind in den Farben Rot, Blau, Grün, Schwarz, Weiss, Gelb, Hellgrün und Orange lackiert und besitzen – zum Treppenhaus hin – schmale Durchgänge entsprechend dem Untergeschoss. Auf dem Gebäude befindet sich ein silbernes Dach.

Katharina Fritsch sieht diese Arbeit als ein Modell für ein zu bauendes Museum mit einem Durchmesser von 24 Metern und einer Höhe von 16 Metern. Dieses Gebäude soll aber nicht – wie bei Museen üblich – für eine ständige Sammlung zur Verfügung stehen, sondern Künstlern ein Forum für Ausstellungen bieten. Als Dauer ist jeweils ein Zeitraum von ein bis zwei Jahren vorgesehen. Die beiden Stockwerke sollen dabei unterschiedlich benutzt werden. Im unteren, verglasten Geschoss sollen Skulpturen ihren Platz finden, im oberen Malerei. Der um das Gebäude gepflanzte Wald soll aus hohen Laubbäumen bestehen, damit im Sommer ein grüner, im Winter ein schwarzen Kranz um das Museum gebildet wird. Das Gelände soll jedermann zugänglich sein, so dass auch unabhängig von den Öffnungszeiten des Museums ein Teil der Ausstellung zu besichtigen wäre.

101.

101. **Poodle**, 1995
plaster of Paris, paint
15 ¾ x 16 ¹⁵/₁₆ x 6 ¹¹/₁₆ in.
edition: 64
signed, dated, and numbered

This multiple is identical in shape and color to the poodles in the work *Kind mit Pudeln* (cat. 102). It bears the following inscription on its left hind paw: *Auflagennummer/64 K. Fritsch 96* (Edition number/64 K. Fritsch 96).

101. **Pudel,** 1995
Gips, Farbe
40 x 43 x 17 cm
Auflage 64
signiert, datiert und numeriert

Das Multiple ist in Form und Farbe identisch mit den Pudeln der Arbeit «Kind mit Pudeln» (Kat. 102). Er ist auf der linken, hinteren Pfote mit Tinte wie folgt beschriftet: *Auflagennummer/64 K. Fritsch 96.*

102. **Child with Poodles**, 1995-1996 (pl. 22)
plaster of Paris, foil, polyurethane, paint
height 15 ¾ in., diameter 201 ⁹/₁₆ in.
edition: 2 + artist's proof
Emanuel Hoffmann-Stiftung, on permanent loan to the Museum für Gegenwartskunst, Basel
Katharina Fritsch, Düsseldorf

A small, white plaster of Paris baby is lying on its back with its hand and feet raised to the ceiling on an octagonal golden star of lacquered mirrored foil. It is circled by 224 black poodles made out of synthetic material placed in four rows, with their muzzles pointing toward the inside of the circle. The star, which is flat on the floor, corresponds with the multiple *Stern* (cat. 34) in form and color. The baby is of indeterminable sex; it has a large head and a powerful body with baby fat on the stomach, arms, and legs. Both the child's hands are closed into fists with thumbs protruding, and the toes are somewhat drawn up. The little poodles stand around the child lying on the star in four closed circles. They are standing so close together that the fur on their legs touch. The individual poodles are slightly stylized versions of miniature poodles, with their coats trimmed in typical poodle style. The hair is left relatively long on the legs and body, which is indicated by a roughened surface, and cut to a cap on the head. The long ears are reduced to an oval shape, and the upright tail ends in an elongated sphere. The delicate head is made up of pointed muzzle without hair, with indentations for mouth and nose worked into it, the hood trimmed in a round shape, and long ears hanging straight down. The legs are bulky and end in little feet with clearly defined claws.

A so-called teaching baby was used as model for the child. The poodles were shaped freely in plaster of Paris on the basis of examples in books and cast in synthetic material.

In the *Zeichen und Wunder* (Signs and Wonders) exhibition, which took place in 1995 in the Kunsthaus in Zürich and the Centro Galego de Arte Contemporánea in Santiago de Compostela, the work was

102. **Kind mit Pudeln,** 1995-1996 (Taf. 22)
Gips, Folie, Polyurethan, Farbe
Höhe: 40cm, Durchmesser 512 cm
Auflage 2 + AP
Emanuel Hoffmann-Stiftung, Depositum im Museum für Gegenwartskunst, Basel
Katharina Fritsch, Düsseldorf

Auf einem achteckigen, goldenen Stern aus lackierter Spiegelfolie liegt ein kleines weisses Baby aus Gips auf dem Rücken, die Hände und Füsse zur Decke erhoben. Umzingelt ist es von 224 in vier Reihen plazierten schwarzen Kunststoffpudeln, die mit den Schnauzen dem Kreisinneren zugewandt sind. Der Stern, der flach auf dem Boden aufliegt, entspricht in seiner Form und der Farbigkeit dem Multiple «Stern» (Kat. 34). Das Baby, das keinem Geschlecht eindeutig zugeordnet werden kann, besitzt einen grossen Kopf und einen kräftigen Körper, der am Bauch, den Armen und Beinen Babyspeck aufweist. Die beiden Hände des Kindes sind zu einer Faust geschlossen, nur die Daumen sind vorgestreckt, die Zehen der Füsse etwas angezogen. Die kleinen Pudel umstehen das auf dem Stern liegende Kind in vier fest geschlossenen Kreisen. Sie stehen so dicht aneinander, dass sich ihr Fell an den Beinen berührt. Die einzelnen Pudel sind leicht stilisiert wiedergegebene Zwergpudel, deren Fell in einer pudeltypischen Art getrimmt wurde. An den Beinen und am Körper relativ lang belassen, ist das Fell, das durch eine aufgeraute Oberfläche angedeutet ist, am Kopf zu einer Haube geschnitten. Die länglichen Ohren sind in eine Ovalform gebracht, der aufgerichtete Schwanz endet in einer länglichen Kugel. Der zierliche Kopf setzt sich aus einer felllosen spitzen Schnauze, bei der die Vertiefungen für Mund und Nase ausgearbeitet sind, der rund geschnittenen Haube und langen, gerade herabhängenden Ohren zusammen. Die voluminös erscheinenden Beine enden in kleinen Füsschen mit ausgearbeiteten Krallen.

Als Modell für das Kind wurde ein sogenanntes Lehrbaby benutzt. Der Pudel wurde nach Vorlagen aus Pudelbüchern aus Gips frei geformt und in Kunststoff abgegossen.

132

shown with only thirty-two poodles in four rows. The poodles were placed at even intervals and formed a star on the floor.

In der Ausstellung «Zeichen und Wunder», die 1995 im Kunsthaus Zürich und im Centro Galego de Arte Contemporánea in Santiago de Compostela stattfand, wurde die Arbeit nur mit 32 Pudeln in vier Reihen gezeigt. Die Pudel standen in einem regelmässigen Abstand zueinander und bildeten einen imaginären Stern auf dem Boden ab.

103. **Money,** 1996
aluminum, anodized, paint
diameter of coins: 1 $^3/_8$ in.
pool : 1794 sq. yd.
competition suggestion
Katharina Fritsch, Düsseldorf

103. **Geld,** 1996
Aluminium, eloxiert, Farbe
Durchmesser der Münzen: 3,5 cm
Becken: 1500 m²
Wettbewerbsvorschag
Katharina Fritsch, Düsseldorf

Geld was conceived as an entry for the *Art on Building Project* by the Landesgirokasse Stuttgart for a new building by Peter Behnisch. A pool of about 1794 square yards, intended as an area of water in the inner courtyard of the building, was to be filled with five million coins of the multiple *Geld* (cat. 73) to produce a shining silver surface. The pool itself was less than an inch deep and painted light gray inside.

Als Wettbewerbsbeitrag für das «Kunst am Bau-Projekt» der Landesgirokasse Stuttgart (für den Neubau durch Peter Behnisch) entwickelt. Ein ca. 1500 m² grosses Becken, das als Wasserfläche im Innenhof des Gebäudes vorgesehen ist, sollte mit ca. fünf Millionen Münzen des Multiples «Geld» (Kat. 73) angefüllt werden, sodass eine silbrig glänzende Oberfläche entsteht. Das Becken selbst sollte eine Höhe von 10-20 mm besitzen und innen hellgrau angestrichen sein.

The design was submitted as a portfolio containing the following sheets: an outline drawing of the pool of water, a description of the project, a photographic collage showing the coins in the pool, two detailed photographs of the coins (top and side view), a list of the anticipated production costs and timing, and a Mickey Mouse scene showing Dagobert Duck in a money-bath.

Der Entwurf wurde in Form einer Mappe eingereicht, in der sich folgende Blätter befinden: eine Umrisszeichnung des Wasserbassins, eine Beschreibung des Projekts, eine Fotocollage, die die Münzen in dem Bassin zeigt, zwei Detailfotos der Münzen (Ansicht von oben und von der Seite), eine Auflistung der voraussichtlichen Produktionskosten und -dauer sowie eine Szene aus Mickey Mouse, die Dagobert Duck beim Geldbad zeigt.

104. **Lexicon Drawing Bremer Stadtmusikanten,** 1996
silkscreen print, paper, wood, foil
40 x 21 $^1/_4$ in.
Ed. 40
Katharina Fritsch, Düsseldorf
Kunstmuseum Bremen

104. **Lexikonzeichnung Bremer Stadtmusikanten,** 1996
Siebdruck, Papier, Holz, Folie
104 x 54 cm
Ed. 40
Katharina Fritsch, Düsseldorf
Kunstmuseum Bremen

104.

This line drawing presents the *Bremer Stadtmusikanten* (Bremen Town Musicians: donkey, dog, cat, and cock) in a plain portrait mounted in a wooden frame with silver semicircular beading. The drawing occupies the full area of the picture. The four animals stand on top of each other and are shown from behind, in front of an open window.

In einem schlichten, hochrechteckigen Holzrahmen mit silbernen, halbrunden Leisten, befindet sich eine Strichzeichnung mit der Darstellung der Bremer Stadtmusikanten (Esel, Hund, Katze und Hahn). Die Zeichnung füllt die gesamte Bildfläche aus. Dargestellt sind die vier übereinander stehenden Tiere von hinten vor einem geöffneten Fenster.

For the silkscreen print Katharina Fritsch enlarged the drawing of the *Bremer Stadtmusikanten* from the *Bildwörterduden* (Duden Pictorial Lexicon). A specific area of the original was selected and extraneous details, for example the numbers on the picture in the lexicon, were removed.

Als Vorlage für den Siebdruck vergrösserte Katharina Fritsch die Zeichnung «Bremer Stadtmusikanten», die sich in der Auflage des Bildwörterdudens befand. Von der Vorlage wurde ein bestimmter Ausschnitt gewählt und die störenden Details entfernt, wie z.B. die zur Darstellung im Bildwörterdudens gehörenden Nummern.

105. **First Series Fairy Tales,** 1996
7 framed silkscreen prints
each: silkscreen print, paper, wood, foil
Lexicon drawing Sleeping Beauty
21 $^1/_4$ x 21 $^1/_4$ in.
Lexicon drawing Baron Münchhausen
21 $^1/_4$ x 21 $^1/_4$ in.
Lexicon drawing Pied Piper of Hamelin
21 $^1/_4$ x 21 $^1/_4$ in.
Lexicon drawing Seven League Boots
21 $^1/_4$ x 40 $^{13}/_{16}$ in.
Lexicon drawing Siegfried
21 $^1/_4$ x 21 $^1/_4$ in.
Lexicon drawing Erl King
21 $^1/_4$ x 21 $^1/_4$ in.
Lexicon drawing Kaiser Barbarossa
21 $^1/_4$ x 21 $^1/_4$ in.
Ed. 3 + 2 artist's proofs
Katharina Fritsch, Düsseldorf

105. **1. Serie Märchen,** 1996
7 gerahmte Siebdrucke
je: Siebdruck, Papier, Holz, Folie
Lexikonzeichnung Dornröschen
54 x 54 cm
Lexikonzeichnung Münchhausen
54 x 54 cm
Lexikonzeichnung Rattenfänger von Hameln
54 x 54 cm
Lexikonzeichnung Siebenmeilenstiefel
54 x 103,6 cm
Lexikonzeichnung Siegfried
54 x 54 cm
Lexikonzeichnung Erlkönig
54 x 54 cm
Lexikonzeichnung Barbarossa
54 x 54 cm
Ed. 3 + 2 AP
Katharina Fritsch, Düsseldorf

The work consists of one landscape and six square prints, produced and framed like the *Bremer Stadt-*

Die Arbeit besteht aus einem querrechteckigen und sechs quadratischen Drucken, die wie die «Bremer

musikanten (cat. 104). All seven depict scenes from German fairy tales or legends (from left to right):
1. Sleeping Beauty with her court in a building surrounded by creepers, and the rescuing prince
2. Baron Münchhausen flying on a cannonball
3. The Pied Piper of Hamelin with the procession of rats leaving a medieval town
4. Six children flying over a landscape with the owner of the Seven League Boots
5. Siegfried and the dragon in a forest
6. The Erl King and one of his daughters threatening a rider with a small child in his arms
7. Emperor Barbarossa sleeping in the mountain

The model and the production method for the silkscreen prints were the same as for cat. 104.

106. **Second Series Fairy Tales,** 1996
    7 framed silkscreen prints
    each: silkscreen print, paper, wood, foil
    Lexicon drawing Snow White (pl. 23)
    21 ¼ x 21 ¼ in.
    Lexicon drawing Little Red Riding Hood
    21 ¼ x 21 ¼ in.
    Lexicon drawing Cinderella
    21 ¼ x 21 ¼ in.
    Lexicon drawing Frau Holle
    40 ¹³/₁₆ x 21 ¼ in.
    Lexicon drawing Gudrun on the Sea Shore
    21 ¼ x 21 ¼ in.
    Lexicon drawing Lorelei
    21 ¼ x 21 ¼ in.
    Lexicon drawing Rübezahl
    21 ¼ x 21 ¼ in.
    Ed. 3 + 2 artist's proofs
    Nancy and Bob Magoon Collection, Aspen
    Katharina Fritsch, Düsseldorf

The work consists of one portrait format and six square prints, produced and framed like the *Bremer Stadtmusikanten* (cat. 104). All seven depict scenes from German fairy tales or legends (from left to right):
1. Snow White lying in a glass coffin with the mourning dwarfs
2. Red Riding Hood meeting the wolf in the forest for the first time
3. Cinderella and the doves sorting lentils
4. Frau Holle shaking an eiderdown over a landscape to make it snow
5. Gudrun kneeling on the beach with her wash and looking into the distance
6. The Rhine with a boatman and the Lorelei on her rock
7. Angry Rübezahl on a rock

The model and the production method for the silkscreen prints were the same as for cat. 104.

107. **Third Series Fairy Tales,** 1996
    3 framed silkscreen prints
    each: silkscreen print, paper, wood, foil
    Lexicon drawing Schlaraffenland
    21 ¼ x 21 ¼ in.
    Lexicon drawing Seven Swabians
    21 ¼ x 40 ¹³/₁₆ in.
    Lexicon drawing Hansel and Gretel
    21 ¼ x 21 ¼ in.
    Ed. 3 + 2 artist's proofs
    Katharina Fritsch, Düsseldorf

The work consists of one landscape format and two square prints, produced and framed like the *Bremer Stadtmusikanten* (cat. 104). All three illustrate scenes from German fairy tales or legends (from left to right):

Stadtmusikanten» (Kat. 104) gefertigt und gerahmt sind. Alle sieben stellen Szenen aus deutschen Märchen bzw. Sagen dar: von links nach rechts:
1.das schlafende Dornröschen mit ihrem Hofstaat in einem von Ranken umgebenen Gebäude und dem rettenden Prinzen
2. Münchhausen auf einer Kanonkugel fliegend
3. Der Rattenfänger von Hameln mit dem Zug der Ratten beim Verlassen einer mittelalterlichen Stadt
4. Sechs Kinder, die gemeinsam mit dem Besitzer der Siebenmeilenstiefel über eine Landschaft fliegen
5. Siegfried und der Drache im Wald
6. Der Erlkönig bedroht gemeinsam mit seiner Tochter einen Reiter mit kleinem Kind im Arm
7. Kaiser Barbarossa schlafend im Berg

Die Vorlage und die Art der Herstellung der Siebdrucke entspricht Kat. 104.

106. **2. Serie Märchen,** 1996
    7 gerahmte Siebdrucke
    je: Siebdruck, Papier, Holz, Folie
    Lexikonzeichnung Schneewittchen (Taf. 23)
    54 x 54 cm
    Lexikonzeichnung Rotkäppchen
    54 x 54 cm
    Lexikonzeichnung Aschenbrödel
    54 x 54 cm
    Lexikonzeichnung Frau Holle
    103,6 x 54 cm
    Lexikonzeichnung Gudrun am Meeresstrand
    54 x 54 cm
    Lexikonzeichnung Lorelei
    54 x 54 cm
    Lexikonzeichnung Rübezahl
    54 x 54 cm
    Ed. 3 + 2 AP
    Sammlung Nancy and Bob Magoon, Aspen
    Katharina Fritsch, Düsseldorf

Die Arbeit besteht aus einem hochrechteckigen und sechs quadratischen Drucken, die wie die «Bremer Stadtmusikanten» (Kat. 104) gefertigt und gerahmt sind. Alle sieben stellen Szenen aus deutschen Märchen bzw. Sagen dar: von links nach rechts:
1.Schneewittchen im gläsernen Sarg liegend mit den trauernden Zwergen
2. Rotkäppchen bei der ersten Begegnung mit dem Wolf im Wald
3. Aschenbrödel sortiert gemeinsam mit den Tauben Linsen
4. Frau Holle schüttelt ein Federbett über einer Landschaft aus, so dass es schneit
5. Gudrun kniet mit Wäsche am Meeresstrand und blickt in die Ferne
6. Der Rhein mit einem Schiffer und der Lorelei auf dem Felsen
7. Der erzürnte Rübezahl auf einem Felsen

Die Vorlage und die Art der Herstellung der Siebdrucke entspricht Kat. 104.

107. **3. Serie Märchen,** 1996
    3 gerahmte Siebdrucke
    je: Siebdruck, Papier, Holz, Folie
    Lexikonzeichnung Schlaraffenland
    54 x 54 cm
    Lexikonzeichnung Sieben Schwaben
    54 x 103,6 cm
    Lexikonzeichnung Hänsel und Gretel
    54 x 54 cm
    Ed. 3 + 2 AP
    Katharina Fritsch, Düsseldorf

Die Arbeit besteht aus einem querrechteckigen und zwei quadratischen Drucken, die wie die «Bremer Stadtmusikanten» (Kat. 104) gefertigt und gerahmt sind. Alle drei stellen Szenen aus deutschen Märchen bzw. Sagen dar: von links nach rechts:

107.

1. A man lying under a tree in the land of plenty (Schlaraffenland), which is identified by gingerbread houses, roast pigs and chickens, boiled fish, and other things
2. The Seven Swabians attempting to fight a hare with a lance
3. Hansel and Gretel outside the witch's gingerbread house

The model and the production method for the silkscreen prints were the same as for cat. 104.

108. **Fourth Series Superstition,** 1996
4 framed silkscreen prints
each: silkscreen print, paper, wood, foil
Lexicon drawing Necromancy
29 $^1/_8$ x 20 $^1/_2$ in.
Lexicon drawing Flagellants
29 $^1/_8$ x 20 $^1/_2$ in.
Lexicon drawing Witch-dance
29 $^1/_8$ x 20 $^1/_2$ in.
Lexicon drawing Fortune teller
29 $^1/_8$ x 20 $^1/_2$ in.
Ed. 3 + 2 artist's proofs
Katharina Fritsch, Düsseldorf

The work consists of four portrait format prints, produced and framed like the *Bremer Stadtmusikanten* (cat. 104). All four show scenes of superstition (from left to right):
1. A young man standing in a zodiac circle with a book and a staff is exorcizing a spirit that is hovering above him.
2. A procession with standard-bearers, a cross-bearer and flagellants. All are wearing medieval costume.
3. A group of naked young women and clothed men dancing round a flute-playing devil. A witch is flying over them on a broomstick.
4. A woman is sitting with a fortune-teller and having her palm read. The room in which the two women are sitting has a fortune-teller's attributes: they include a skull, Tarot cards, a black cat, a ghost, and an hourglass.

The model and the production method for the silkscreen prints were the same as for cat. 104.

109. **Fifth Series Church,** 1996
5 framed silkscreen prints
each: silkscreen print, paper, wood, foil
Lexicon drawing Communion
21 $^1/_4$ x 21 $^1/_4$ in.
Lexicon drawing Baptism
21 $^1/_4$ x 21 $^1/_4$ in.
Lexicon drawing Burial
21 $^1/_4$ x 40 $^{13}/_{16}$ in.
Lexicon drawing Wedding
21 $^1/_4$ x 21 $^1/_4$ in.
Lexicon drawing Confirmation
21 $^1/_4$ x 21 $^1/_4$ in.
Ed. 3 + 2 artist's proofs
Katharina Fritsch, Düsseldorf

1. Einen Mann unter einem Baum liegend im Schlaraffenland, das mit Lebkuchenhäusern, gebratenen Schweinen und Hähnchen, gekochten Fischen und anderen Dingen gekennzeichnet ist
2. Die Sieben Schwaben versuchen mit einer Lanze einen Hasen zu bekämpfen
3. Hänsel und Gretel vor dem Hexenhaus aus Lebkuchen

Die Vorlage und die Art der Herstellung der Siebdrucke entspricht Kat. 104.

108. **4. Serie Aberglaube,** 1996
4 gerahmte Siebdrucke
je: Siebdruck, Papier, Holz, Folie
Lexikonzeichnung Geisterbeschwörung
74 x 52 cm
Lexikonzeichnung Geisselerzug
74 x 52 cm
Lexikonzeichnung Hexentanz
74 x 52 cm
Lexikonzeichnung Wahrsagerin
74 x 52 cm
Ed. 3 + 2 AP
Katharina Fritsch, Düsseldorf

Die Arbeit besteht aus vier rechteckigen Drucken, die wie die «Bremer Stadtmusikanten» (Kat. 104) gefertigt und gerahmt sind. Alle vier stellen Szenen des Aberglaubens dar (von links nach rechts):
1. Ein junger Mann, der in einem Tierkreis steht, beschwört mit einem Buch und einem Stab einen über ihm schwebenden Geist.
2. Eine Prozession mit Fahnenträgern, einem Kreuz-Träger und sich geisselnden Personen. Alle tragen mittelalterliche Kleidung.
3. Eine Gruppe von nackten jungen Frauen und bekleideten Männern tanzen um einen Flöte spielenden Teufel. Über ihnen fliegt eine Hexe auf einem Besen.
4. Eine Frau sitzt bei einer Wahrsagerin und lässt sich aus der Hand lesen. In dem Raum, in dem sich die beiden Frauen befinden, sind Attribute einer Wahrsagerin versammelt: unter anderem ein Totenkopf, Tarot-Karten, eine schwarze Katze, eine Geisterfigur und eine Sanduhr.

Die Vorlage und die Art der Herstellung der Siebdrucke entspricht Kat. 104.

109. **5. Serie Kirche,** 1996
5 gerahmte Siebdrucke
je: Siebdruck, Papier, Holz, Folie
Lexikonzeichnung Kommunion
54 x 54 cm
Lexikonzeichnung Taufe
54 x 54 cm
Lexikonzeichnung Beerdigung
54 x 103,6 cm
Lexikonzeichnung Trauung
54 x 54 cm
Lexikonzeichnung Konfirmation
54 x 54 cm
Ed. 3 + 2 AP
Katharina Fritsch, Düsseldorf

The work consists of one landscape format and four square prints, produced and framed like the *Bremer Stadtmusikanten* (cat. 104). All five depict church scenes (from left to right):
1. Two priests serving communion to members of a congregation
2. Baptism of a baby, with parents and godparents
3. Solemn procession to the cemetery with decorated coffin and mourners
4. A bridal couple kneeling before a priest to have their marriage blessed.
5. Two kneeling confirmants are blessed by a pastor.

The model and the production method for the silkscreen prints were the same as for cat. 104.

Die Arbeit besteht aus einem rechteckigen und vier quadratischen Drucken, die wie die «Bremer Stadtmusikanten» (Kat. 104) gefertigt und gerahmt sind. Alle fünf stellen Szenen des religiösen Brauchtums dar, von links nach rechts:
1. Die Austeilung der Kommunion an Gemeindemitglieder durch zwei Priester
2. Die Taufe eines Babys mit Eltern und Paten
3. Die feierliche Prozession zum Friedhof mit dem geschmückten Sarg und der Trauergemeinde
4. Die Erteilung des Hochzeitssegens an ein vor dem Priester kniendes Brautpaar
5. Die Segnung zweier kniender Konfirmanden durch einen Pastor.

Die Vorlage und die Art der Herstellung der Siebdrucke entspricht Kat. 104.

110. **Sixth Series Public Festivals**, 1996
    4 framed silkscreen prints
    each: silkscreen print, paper, wood, foil
    Lexicon drawing May Day
    25 ³/₁₆ x 29 ¹⁵/₁₆ in.
    Lexicon drawing Summer solstice
    25 ³/₁₆ x 29 ¹⁵/₁₆ in.
    Lexicon drawing Thanksgiving
    25 ³/₁₆ x 29 ¹⁵/₁₆ in.
    Lexicon drawing Shooting match
    25 ³/₁₆ x 29 ¹⁵/₁₆ in.
    Ed. 3 + 2 artist's proofs
    Collection Landesgirokasse, Stuttgart
    Katharina Fritsch, Düsseldorf

110. **6. Serie Volksfeste**, 1996
    4 gerahmte Siebdrucke
    je: Siebdruck, Papier, Holz, Folie
    Lexikonzeichnung Maifest
    64 x 76 cm
    Lexikonzeichnung Sonnwendfeier
    64 x 76 cm
    Lexikonzeichnung Erntedankfest
    64 x 76 cm
    Lexikonzeichnung Schützenfest
    64 x 76 cm
    Ed. 3 + 2 AP
    Sammlung Landesgirokasse, Stuttgart
    Katharina Fritsch, Düsseldorf

The work consists of four landscape format prints, produced and framed like the *Bremer Stadtmusikanten* (cat. 104). All four show traditional German scenes (from left to right):
1. Dancing around a maypole
2. Jumping over Saint John's fire
3. Harvest thanksgiving in a barn
4. The procession at the beginning of the shooting festival

The model and the production method for the silkscreen prints were the same as for cat. 104.

Die Arbeit besteht aus vier rechteckigen Drucken, die wie die «Bremer Stadtmusikanten» (Kat. 104) gefertigt und gerahmt sind. Alle vier stellen Szenen des deutschen Brauchtums dar (von links nach rechts):
1. Den Tanz um den Maibaum
2. Den Sprung über das Johannisfeuer
3. Das Erntedankfest in einer Scheune
4. Der Umzug, mit dem das Schützenfest eingeleitet wird

Die Vorlage und die Art der Herstellung der Siebdrucke entspricht Kat. 104.

111. **Seventh Series Family Celebrations**, 1996
    4 framed silkscreen prints
    each: silkscreen print, paper, wood, foil
    Lexicon drawing Birthday
    21 ¹/₄ x 24 in.
    Lexicon drawing St. Nicholas' Day
    21 ¹/₄ x 24 in.
    Lexicon drawing New Year's Eve
    21 ¹/₄ x 24 in.
    Lexicon drawing Prenuptial celebration
    21 ¹/₄ x 24 in.
    Ed. 3 + 2 artist's proofs
    Katharina Fritsch, Düsseldorf

111. **7. Serie Familienfeste**, 1996
    4 gerahmte Siebdrucke
    je: Siebdruck, Papier, Holz, Folie
    Lexikonzeichnung Geburtstagsfeier
    54 x 61 cm
    Lexikonzeichnung Nikolausabend
    54 x 61 cm
    Lexikonzeichnung Silvester
    54 x 61 cm
    Lexikonzeichnung Polterabend
    54 x 61 cm
    Ed. 3 + 2 AP
    Katharina Fritsch, Düsseldorf

The work consists of four landscape format prints, produced and framed like the *Bremer Stadtmusikanten* (cat. 104). All four illustrate scenes of family celebrations (from left to right):
1. Children and grandchildren giving an elderly woman birthday presents.
2. St. Nicholas bringing presents for a little girl and boy.
3. The New Year's Eve punch being distributed.
4. Crockery being smashed outside a young couple's front door on the night before their wedding

The model and the production method for the silkscreen prints were the same as for cat. 104.

Die Arbeit besteht aus vier rechteckigen Drucken, die wie die «Bremer Stadtmusikanten» (Kat. 104) gefertigt und gerahmt sind. Alle vier stellen Szenen von Feiern im Familienkreis dar: von links nach rechts:
1. Einer älteren Frau werden von den Kinder und Enkelkindern Geschenke zum Geburtstag überreicht.
2. Nikolaus bringt einem Mädchen und einem kleinen Jungen Geschenke.
3. Die Silvesterbowle wird ausgeteilt.
4. Vor der Haustür eines jungen Paares wird am Abend vor der Hochzeit Geschirr zerschlagen.

Die Vorlage und die Art der Herstellung der Siebdrucke entspricht Kat. 104.

112. **Lexicon Drawing Christmas,** 1996
silkscreen print, paper, wood, foil
25 ³/₁₆ x 33 in.
Ed. 3 + 2 artist's proofs
Katharina Fritsch, Düsseldorf

The work consists of a landscape silkscreen print, produced and framed like the *Bremer Stadtmusikanten*
(cat. 104). It shows a view of the festively decorated
living room of a family on Christmas morning. The
mother is sitting at the piano, while the father is leaning on it. Two children are playing with their presents;
these include a rocking-horse, a train set, a doll's
house, and a doll's pram. By the decorated Christmas
tree, which is on the table, is a small crib. An advent
wreath hangs from the ceiling.

The model and the production method for the silkscreen prints were the same as for cat. 104.

112. **Lexikonzeichnung Weihnachten,** 1996
Siebdruck, Papier, Holz, Folie
64 x 84 cm
Ed. 3 + 2 AP
Katharina Fritsch, Düsseldorf

Die Arbeit besteht aus einem rechteckigen Siebdruck,
der wie die «Bremer Stadtmusikanten» (Kat. 104) gefertigt und gerahmt ist. Der Druck zeigt einen Blick in das
festlich geschmückte Wohnzimmer einer Familie mit
zwei Kindern am Weihnachtsmorgen. Die Mutter sitzt
an einem Klavier, der Vater hat sich an das Klavier gelehnt. Die Kinder spielen mit ihren Geschenken: unter
anderem einem Schaukelpferd, einer Eisenbahn, einem
Puppenhaus und einem Puppenwagen. Neben dem
geschmückten Weihnachtsbaum, der auf dem Tisch
steht, befindet sich eine kleine Krippe. Von der Decke
hängt ein Adventskranz.

Die Vorlage und die Art der Herstellung des Siebdrucks
entspricht Kat. 104.

112.

Katharina Fritsch

1956 geboren in Essen

1977 - 1981 Studium an der Kunstakademie
Düsseldorf bei Fritz Schwegler,
Meisterschülerin
lebt und arbeitet in Düsseldorf

1956 born in Essen

1977 - 1981 studied at the Düsseldorf
Kunstakademie under
Fritz Schwegler, master-class student
lives and works in in Düsseldorf

EINZELAUSSTELLUNGEN / INDIVIDUAL EXHIBITIONS

1984 Galerie Rüdiger Schöttle, München (mit Thomas Ruff)

1985 Galerie Johnen & Schöttle, Köln

1987 Kaiser Wilhelm Museum, Krefeld

1988 Kunsthalle Basel
Institute of Contemporary Art (ICA), London

1989 Westfälischer Kunstverein, Münster
Portikus, Frankfurt/Main

1993 Dia Center for the Arts, New York

1994 Galerie Ghislaine Hussenot, Paris

1995 Biennale Venedig, Deutscher Pavillon (mit Martin Honert und
Thomas Ruff)

1996 Matthew Marks Gallery, New York
San Francisco Museum of Modern Art
Ludwigforum, Aachen

GRUPPENAUSSTELLUNGEN / GROUP EXHIBITIONS

1982 «Möbel perdu», Museum für Kunst und Gewerbe, Hamburg

1984 «von hier aus», Messegelände (Halle 13), Düsseldorf

1985 Galerie Schneider, Konstanz

1986 «von Raum zu Raum», Kunstverein Hamburg
«Sonsbeek '86», Arnheim
«Aus den Anfängen», Kunstfonds Bonn
«Europa/Amerika», Museum Ludwig, Köln
«Junge Rheinische Kunst», Galerie Schipka, Sofia
«A distanced view», The New Museum of Contemporary Art, New York

1987 «Anderer Leute Kunst», Museum Haus Lange, Krefeld
«Skulptur Projekte Münster», Münster
«Bestiarium», Galerie Rüdiger Schöttle, München
«Multiples», Galerie Daniel Buchholz, Köln
The Ydessa Gallery, Toronto

1988 «Cultural Geometry», Deste Foundation for Contemporary Art, House
of Cyprus, Athen
«Collections pour une région», Musée d'Art Contemporain, Bordeaux
Galerie Johnen & Schöttle, Köln
Biennale Sydney, Sydney
«BiNationale, Deutsche Kunst der späten 80er Jahre», Boston
«Carnegie International 1988», Carnegie Institute, Pittsburgh

1989 Stichting De Appel, Amsterdam
«What is Contemporary Art?», Rooseum, Malmö
«Mondi Possibili», Galerie Monika Sprüth, Köln
Galerie Ghislaine Hussenot, Paris

1990 «New Work: A New Generation», San Francisco Museum of Modern
Art, San Francisco
«Culture and Commentary: an Eighties Perspective», Hirshhorn Museum
and Sculpture Garden, Smithsonian Institute, Washington D.C.
«Weitersehen 1980-1990», Museum Haus Esters/Haus Lange, Krefeld
«Hanne Darboven, Walter Dahn, Katharina Fritsch, Reinhard Mucha,
Rosemarie Trockel», Barbara Gladstone Gallery, New York
«OBJECTives: The New Sculpture», Newport Harbor Museum, Newport
Beach
«Semi-Objects», John Good Gallery, New York
«Color and/or Monochrome», National Museum of Modern Art, Tokyo

1991 «Metropolis», Martin-Gropius-Bau, Berlin
«Carnegie International 1991», Carnegie Institute, Pittsburgh
«In anderen Räumen», Museum Haus Esters/Haus Lange, Krefeld
«Standpunkt der Moderne. Von Picasso bis Clemente: Werke aus der
Emanuel Hoffmann-Stiftung Basel», Deichtorhallen, Hamburg
Luhring Augustine Gallery, New York

Galerie Locus Solus, Genua
«Contemporary Art from the Collection of Jason Rubell», Duke University Museum of Art, Durham, North Carolina
«L' espai i la idea. Selecció d'obres de la collecció d'art contemporani Fundació La Caixa», Barcelona (Wanderausstellung von 1989-1993)

1992 «Doubletake: Collective Memory & Current Art», Hayward Gallery, London
«Der Teppich des Lebens», Museum Haus Koekkoek, Kleve
«7: Thomas Bernstein, Günther Förg, Katharina Fritsch, Isa Genzken, Hubert Kiecol, Wilhelm Mundt», Galeria Zacheta, Warschau
«Oh! Cet écho!», Centre Culturel Suisse, Paris
«Ars Pro Domo: Zeitgenössische Kunst aus Kölner Privatbesitz», Museum Ludwig, Köln
«Tropismes: Collección Fundació la Caixa», Centre Cultural de la Fundació Caixa de Pensions, Barcelona

1993 «Doubletake: Kollektives Gedächtnis & Heutige Kunst», Kunsthalle Wien
«Lieux de la vie moderne», Centre d'Art Contemporain de Quimper

1994 «Power Works», Museum of New Zealand, Wellington
«Meme si c'est la nuit», capc Musée d'art contemporain, Bordeaux
«Zimmer in denen die Zeit nicht zählt». Die Sammlung Udo und Anette Brandhorst», Museum für Gegenwartskunst, Basel
«Das Jahrhundert des Multiple», Deichtorhallen, Hamburg
«Aura», Wiener Secession, Wien
«Arca de Noè/Noah's Ark, works from the collections of the capc Musée of Bordeaux and the frac Aquitaine», Fundacao de Serralves, Porto
«Junge deutsche Kunst der 90er Jahre», Sonje Museum of Contemporary Art, Kyongju, Korea (Wanderausstellung Hong-Kong, Peking, Taipei, Osaka, u.a.O. bis 1996)

1995 «Leiblicher Logos», Institut für Auslandsbeziehungen, Staatsgalerie Stuttgart, Altes Museum Berlin u.a.O.
«Zeichen & Wunder», Kunsthaus Zürich
«Segnos & Milagros», Centro Galego de Arte Contemporánea, Santiago de Compostela
«Sleeper», Museum of Contemporary Art, San Diego

1996 «Private View», The Bowes Museum, Barnard Castle, County Durham

AUSGEWÄHLTE BIBLIOGRAPHIE / SELECTED BIBLIOGRAPHY

1981 **Fritsch, Katharina**, Werbeblatt 1, Düsseldorf

1983 **Fritsch, Katharina**, «Friedhöfe», in: Kunstforum International, Nr. 65, Sept. 1983, S. 74-75

1984 **Hecht, Axel**, «von hier aus», in: Art, Nr. 11, Nov. 1984, S. 58-61
Kraft, Monika, «Katharina Fritsch», in: von hier aus, Ausst.kat. Messegelände Halle 13, Düsseldorf, S. 280-283

1986 **Europa/Amerika**, Ausst.kat. Museum Ludwig, Köln
Bos, Saskia und Jan Brand, «Katharina Fritsch», in: Ausst.kat. Sonsbeek '86, Arnhem 1986, S. 186-187
Dank, Ralf, «Sonsbeek '86», in: Kunstforum, Sept./Okt. 1986
Javault, Patrick, «Sonsbeek '86», in: Art Press, Sept. 1986
Jochimsen, M., «Alles hat seine Vorgeschichte», in: Junge Rheinische Kunst, Ausst.kat. Galerie Schipka, Sofia, S. 13-23
Locker, Ludwig, «Architektonische Aspekte in der Düsseldorfer Gegenwartskunst», in: Artefaktum
Messler, Norbert, «Raum und Bildwelt», in: Von Raum zu Raum, Ausst.kat. Hamburger Kunstverein, S. 23

1987 **Cameron, Dan**, «The Critic's Way», in: Artforum, Bd. 26, Nr. 1, Sept.1987, S. 119
Cooke, Lynne, «A Distanced View at the New Museum», in: Artscribe International, Nr. 61, Jan./Feb. 1987, S. 68-70
Galloway, David, «Report from Germany», in: Art in America, Bd. 75, Nr. 12, Dez. 1987, S. 21
Heartney, Eleanor, «Sighted in Münster», in: Art in America, Bd. 75, Nr. 9, Sept. 1987, S. 140-143
Hermes, Manfred, «Katharina Fritsch. Kaiser Wilhelm Museum, Krefeld», in: Flash Art Nr. 137, Nov./Dez. 1987, S. 112/113
Heynen, Julian, Katharina Fritsch. Elefant, Ausst.kat. Kaiser Wilhelm Museum, Krefeld

ders., Anderer Leute Kunst, Ausst.kat. Museum Haus Lange, Krefeld
Koether, Jutta, «Katharina Fritsch. Kaiser Wilhelm Museum Krefeld», in: Artscribe, Mai 1987, S. 84
dies., «Elephant», in: Parkett, Nr. 13, S. 90-92
Ponti, L.L., «Il progetto scultura a Münster», in: Domus, Nr. 686, Sept. 1987, S. 110-111
Puvogel, Renate, «Katharina Fritsch - Elefant», in: Kunstforum International, Nr. 89
Schmidt-Wulffen, Stephan, «Enzyklopädie der Skulptur», in: Kunstforum International, Nr. 89
Tazzi, Pier Luigi, «Skulptur Projekte Münster», in: Wolkenkratzer, Nr. 5, Sept./Okt. 1987
Wilms, Ulrich, «Madonna», in: Skulptur Projekte Münster, Ausst.kat. Westfälisches Landesmuseum für Kunst und Kulturgeschichte, Köln 1987, S. 89-92

1988 **Ammann, Jean-Christophe**, Katharina Fritsch, Ausst.kat. Kunsthalle Basel/ICA London
Archer, Michael, «Rosemarie Trockel and Katharina Fritsch», in: Art monthly, Nov. 1988
Beyer, Lucie und Karen Marta, «Report from Germany: Why Cologne?», in: Art in America, Bd. 76, Nr. 12, Dez. 1988, S. 45-52
Christov-Bakargiev, Carolyn, «Something Nowhere. A Mute Statement of recent sculpture attempts», in: Flash Art, Nr. 140, Mai/Juni 1988
Godfrey, Tony, «Report from Germany: A Tale of Four Cities», in: Art in America, Bd. 76, Nr. 11, Nov. 1988, S. 33-41
Koether, Jutta, «A report from the field», in: Flash Art, Nr. 141, Sommer 1988
Krebs, Edith, Katharina Fritsch/Rosemarie Trockel, in: Noema, Nr. 20, S. 79
Puvogel, Renate, «Katharina Fritsch, Rosemarie Trockel, Anna Winteler», in: Kunstforum International, Nr. 97, S. 313-317
Salvioni, Daniela, «Trockel and Fritsch», in: Flash Art, Nr. 142, Okt. 1988, S. 110
Schenker, Christophe, «Interview mit Jean-Christophe Ammann, Kunsthalle Basel», in: Flash Art News 2, Supplement zu Flash Art Nr. 141, Sommer 1988, o.S.
Syring, Marie Luise und Christiane Vielhaber, «Interview mit Katharina Fritsch», in: BiNationale, Deutsche Kunst der späten achtziger Jahre, Ausst.kat. Kunsthalle Düsseldorf/Kunstverein für Rheinland und Westfalen/Kunstsammlung NRW, Köln, S. 116/117

1989 **Beyer, Lucie**, «Katharina Fritsch: Kunstverein Münster/Portikus Frankfurt», in: Arena, Nr. 4
Blase, Christoph, «Die Kunst mit den reproduzierenden Medien», in: Artis, Sept. 1989, S. 54-57
Bos, Saskia, «Topics on Atopy», in: De Appel, Nr. 2, 1989/1990
Cameron, Dan, «How We Have Changed, Revisited», in: Arena, Nr. 1, S. 70
Cottingham, Laura, «The Feminine De-Mystique», in: Flash Art, Nr. 147, S. 91-95
Gniffke, Franz, «Madonna, Himmel und Granit. Philosophische Reflexionen zu drei Skulpturen einer Ausstellung in Münster, 1987», in: Weite des Herzens. Weite des Lebens. Beiträge zum Christsein in Moderner Gesellschaft. Festschrift für Abt Odilo Lechner, hrsg. v. Michael Langer und Anselm Bilgri, Regensburg, S. 343-362
Graw, Isabella, «Carnegie International», in: Galeries Magazine, Dez./Jan. 1989
Heynen, Julian, Katharina Fritsch 1979-1989, Ausst.kat. Westfälischer Kunstverein, Münster/Portikus, Frankfurt, Köln
Heymer, Kay, «Katharina Fritsch. Alles gleichzeitig», in: Bremer Kunstpreis, Ausst.kat. Kunsthalle Bremen, S. 29/30
Koether, Jutta, «Katharina Fritsch: Kunstverein Münster/Portikus Frankfurt», in: Artscribe, Nr. 78, Nov./Dez. 1989, S. 85-86
Magnani, Gregorio, «This Is Not Conceptual», in: Flash Art, Nr. 145, S. 84-87
Messler, Norbert, «Ordnungstrieb und Präzision», in: Wolkenkratzer, Nr. 5, S. 80/81
ders., «Katharina Fritsch at Kunstverein Münster», in: Artforum, Bd. 28, Nr. 2, S. 189
Reust, Hans-Rudolf, «Rosemarie Trockel - Katharina Fritsch», in: Artscribe, Bd. 73, S. 88/89
Smolik, Noemi, «Katharina Fritsch, Portikus Frankfurt», in: Noema, Nr. 27, S. 97
dies., «Kunstpreis Glockengasse», in: Kunst in Köln, Nr. 1
Spector, Nancy, «Carnegie International», in: Contemporanea, Nr. 5, Feb. 1989, S. 104/105
Strecker, Raimund, «Über junge Düsseldorfer Künstler», in: Das Kunstwerk, 4-5 XLI, Jan. 1989, S. 129-147
Suermann, Marie-Theres, «Katharina Fritsch», in: Contemporanea, Nr. 9, Dez. 1989

1990   **New Work: A New Generation**, Ausst.kat. San Francisco Museum of
Modern Art
Weitersehen 1980-1990, Ausst.kat. Museum Haus Esters/Haus Lange,
Krefeld, S. 67-74
Bruyn, Gerd de, «Braucht der öffentliche Raum Kunst? Ein Gespräch
mit Kasper König», in: Baukultur, Nr.6, o.S.
Cameron, Dan, «Massstäbe setzen», in: Parkett, Nr. 25, S. 68-73
Garrels, Gary, «Disarming Perception», in: Parkett, Nr. 25, S. 36-43
Halbreich, Kathy, «Katharina Fritsch», in: Culture and Commentary: An
Eighties Perspective, Ausst.kat. Hirshhorn Museum and Sculpture
Garden, Smithsonian Institution, Washington, S. 56-61
Heynen, Julian, «Spekulationen über Lastwagen, Friedhöfe, Füchse und
andere Bilder», in: Parkett, Nr. 25, S. 44-51
Kuoni, Carin, «Kultur und Kommentar, ein Ansatz der achtziger Jahre»,
in: Das Kunst-Bulletin, Nr. 7/8, Juli/Aug. 1990, S. 28-35
Schloss, C., «Katharina Fritsch», in: Juliet, April 1990, S. 30
Schmidt-Wulffen, Stephan, «Katharina Fritsch. Mechanisms of Epipha-
ny», in: Objectives: The New Sculpture, Ausst.kat. Newport Harbor Art
Museum, S. 48-52

1991   **Metropolis**, Ausst.kat. Martin-Gropius-Bau, Berlin, S. 130-132
Contemporary Art from the Collection of Jason Rubell, Ausst.kat. Duke
University Museum of Art, Durham, S. 28/29
Cooke, Lynne, «Katharina Fritsch», in: Carnegie International 1991,
Ausst.kat. Carnegie Institute, Pittsburgh, S. 74/75
Fritsch, Katharina, in: Der öffentliche Blick, Jahresring 38, München
1991, S. 161-169
Giesbergen, Drieke van, «De energie van de Kunst», in: Archis, Nr. 6
Knight, Christopher, «Carnegie International Strikes a One-Note The-
me», in: Los Angeles Times, 26.10.1991
Vischer, Theodora, «Katharina Fritsch», in: Slgs.kat. Emanuel Hoffmann-
Stiftung, Basel, S. 201-205

1992   **Tropismes. Colleción Fundació «la Caixa»**, Ausst.kat. Centre Cultural
de la Fundació Caixa de Pensions, Barcelona
Cooke, Lynne, «The Site of Memory», in: Doubletake: Collective
Memory and Current Art, Ausst.kat. Hayward Gallery/Kunsthalle Wien,
S. 23-39
Curiger, Bice, «Epater le bourgeois - revisited», in: Doubletake. Kollek-
tives Gedächtnis & Heutige Kunst, Ausst.kat. Kunsthalle Wien/Parkett,
Zürich, S. 20-22
Deitcher, David, «Art of the Installation Plan: MoMA and the Carne-
gie», in: Artforum, Bd. 30, Nr. 5, S. 78-84
Faust, Gretchen, «Katharina Fritsch at Luhring Augustine Gallery», in:
Arts Magazine, Bd. 66, Nr. 5, S. 84-87
Gillick, Liam, «Doubletake», in: Art Monthly, März 1992
Heynen, Julian, «Mann und Maus», in: 7: Thomas Bernstein, Günther
Förg, Katharina Fritsch, Isa Genzken, Hubert Kiecol, Wilhelm Mundt,
Thomas Schütte, Ausst.kat. Galeria Zacheta, Warschau, S. 22-29
Lillington, David, «Always on my mind. Interview with Greg Hilty», in:
Frieze, April/Mai 1992
Morgan, Stuart, «Thanks for the memories. Review of *Doubletake*», in:
Frieze, April/Mai 1992, S. 6-11
Wulffen, Thomas, «RED BOX, Thomas Wulffen über Katharina Fritschs
Roter Raum mit Kamingeräusch», in: Meta 1, Stuttgart 1992

1993   **Ammann, Jean-Christophe**, «Dauergeschöpfe aus Gier und Energie.
Wächter der Ohnmacht: Katharina Fritsch im Dia Center for the Arts in
New York», in: Frankfurter Allgemeine Zeitung, 23.10.1993
ders., «Katharina Fritsch», in: Jean-Christophe Ammann, Bewegung im
Kopf. Vom Umgang mit der Kunst, Regensburg, S. 226-231
Bobka, Vivian, «Katharina Fritsch - Immobilizing the mythical rat pack»,
in: Flash Art, Nr. 171, Sommer 1993, S. 112
Cooke, Lynne, «Parerga», in: Katharina Fritsch, Ausst.kat. Dia Center for
the Arts, New York, S. 5-13
Eccles, Tom, «Katharina Fritsch at Dia», in: Art in America
Rimanelli, David, «Katharina Fritsch at Dia», in: Artforum, Nov. 1993, S. 105
Schenk-Sorge, Jutta, «Rat-King», in: Kunstforum International, Bd. 123,
S. 380/381
Unnützer, Petra, «Doubletake», in: Kunstforum International, Bd. 122,
S. 451-454

1994   **Das Jahrhundert des Multiple**, Ausst.kat. Deichtorhallen Hamburg,
S. 190-192
Meme si c'est la nuit, Ausst.kat. cacp Musée d'art contemporain,
Bordeaux
**Zimmer in denen die Zeit nicht zählt. Die Sammlung Udo und Anette
Brandhorst**, Ausst.kat. Museum für Gegenwartskunst, Basel, S. 118/119
Ammann, Jean-Christophe, «Anonyme Männergesellschaft», in: Jean-
Christophe Ammann, Modernes Museum. Bilder, Objekte, Installationen
im Museum für Moderne Kunst, Frankfurt, S. 56/57

Cramer, Sue, «Katharina Fritsch», in: Power Works from the MCA
Collection, Museum of New Zealand, Wellington, S. 16/17
Lauter, Rolf, «Katharina Fritsch. Das Individuum und die kollektive
Angst», in: Kunstforum International, Bd. 128, S. 216-218
Liebermann, Valeria, «Katharina Fritsch», in: Junge deutsche Kunst in
den 90er Jahren, Ausst.kat. Sonje Museum of Contemporary Art,
Kyongju, Korea, Stuttgart 1994, S. 34-37
Rhomberg, Kathrin, «Katharina Fritsch», in: Aura, Ausst.kat. Wiener
Secession, S. 22-25
Troncy, Eric, «Katharina Fritsch at Ghislaine Hussenot», in: Flash Art, Bd.
27, Nr. 178, Okt. 1994, S. 102/103
Winzen, Matthias, «Katharina Fritsch – Ein Gespräch», in: Das Kunst-
Bulletin, Nr. 1/2, Jan./Feb.1994, S. 10-21

1995   **Zeichen & Wunder**, Ausst.kat. Kunsthaus Zürich, S. 74, 116/117
Sleeper, Ausst.kat. Museum of Contemporary Art, San Diego
Arca de Noè/Noah's Arc, Ausst.kat. Fundacao de Serralves, Porto
Biennale Venedig. Ein Rundgang, in: Kunstforum International, Bd.
131, S. 79-181
Wie eine Weltmeisterschaft, in: Westfälische Nachrichten, 10.6.1995
Ammann, Jean-Christophe, «Ich stecke gewiss in keiner autistisch-
regressiven Phase purer Selbstbespiegelung. Gespräch mit Heinz-
Norbert Jocks», in: Kunstforum International, Bd. 131, S. 72-78
Criqui, Jean-Pierre, «Best of Show», in: Artforum, Bd. 34, Nr. 1, Sept.
1995, S. 35-36
Damus, Martin, Kunst in der BRD 1945-1990, Hamburg, S.370
Flemming, Viktoria von, «Katharina Fritsch: Mythen reichlich im Ange-
bot», in: art, Nr. 6, S. 16-27
Fritsch, Katharina, Museum, Ausst.kat. Deutscher Pavillon, Biennale
Venedig, Stuttgart
Hohmeyer, Jürgen, «Niedlich, aber fies», in: Der Spiegel, Nr. 23, S.
174-176
Liebermann, Valeria, «Katharina Fritsch», in: Leiblicher Logos,
Ausst.kat. IFA Stuttgart, S. 52-57
Metken, Günter und Paolo Bianchi, «Stillhaltezeit», in: Kunstforum
International, Bd. 131, S. 64-69
Müller, Hans-Joachim, «Die Zeit, die Kunst, der Stachelbaum», in: Die
Zeit, Nr. 25, 16.6.1995
Plagens, Peter, «Whistling in the park», in: Artforum, Bd. 34, Nr. 1,
Sept. 1995, S. 39, 106-108
Poschardt, Ulf, «Kein Pardon», in: Vogue, Nr. 6, S. 190-194
Puvogel, Renate, «Katharina Fritsch – Das Ding als Phänomen», in:
Artis, Zeitschrift für neue Kunst, 47. Jahrgang, Nr. 6, S. 32-37
dies., «Biennale Venedig 1995», in: Artis, Zeitschrift für neue Kunst, 47.
Jahrgang, Nr. 8
Criqui, Jean-Pierre, «Best of show», in: Artforum, Sept. 1995
Singldinger, Josef, «Die Chancen der Kunst in unserer Zeit. Ein Ge-
spräch mit Jean-Christophe Ammann», in: Kunst & Kultur, Sonderdruck
der Kulturpolitischen Zeitschrift der IG Medien für die Biennale in
Venedig
Vetrocq, Marcia E., «The Birthday Biennale coming home to Europe»,
in: Art in America, Bd. 83, Nr. 9, S. 72-81

San Francisco Museum of Modern Art
Director: John R. Lane
Elise S. Haas Chief Curator and Curator of Painting
and Sculpture: Gary Garrels

Exhibition Curator: Gary Garrels
Director of Curatorial Affairs: Lori Fogarty
Exhibitions Manager: Barbara Levine
Publications Manager: Kara Kirk
Associate Registrar: Olga Charyshyn
Installation Manager: Kent Roberts
Curatorial Assistant: Jean MacDougall
Exhibitions Assistant: Marcelene Trujillo
Museum Technicians: Carol Blair, James Goldthorpe,
Doug Kerr, Alina del Pino, Rico Solinas, Greg Wilson,
Kimberly Walton,
Secretary, Department of Painting and Sculpture:
Heather Lind

Öffentliche Kunstsammlung Basel
Direktorin: Dr. Katharina Schmidt
Museum für Gegenwartskunst
Konservatorin: Dr. Theodora Vischer

Ausstellung: Theodora Vischer
Ausstellungssekretariat: Heidi Naef
Transporte, Versicherung: Charlotte Gutzwiller
Restauratorische Betreuung: Peter Berkes, Amelie
Jensen
Aufbau: Dieter Marti, Gustav Frutig und Mitarbeiter

Katalog/Catalogue: Theodora Vischer
Katalogassistenz/Editorial Assistants:
Binci Heeb, Annina Zimmermann
Übersetzung ins Englische/Translation into English:
Michael Robinson
Übersetzung ins Deutsche/Translation into German:
Nansen
Übersetzung/Translation H. von Kleist: s. S. 38/see p. 38
Gestaltung und Satz/Design and Layout:
Vischer & Vettiger, Basel
Lithos und Druck/Lithography and Printing:
Birkhäuser+GBC, Reinach

ISBN 3-7204-0097-2
Vertrieb in Europa/European distribution:
Buchhandlung Walther König, Ehrenstrasse 4,
D-50672 Köln.
Tel. ++49-221-20.59.60, Fax: 221-20.59.640
Vertrieb in den USA/Distribution in the United
States: D.A.P./Distributed Art Publishers, Inc.
155 Sixth Avenue, New York, New York 10013.
ph. ++1-212-627-1999, fax: 212-627-9494

Fotonachweis/Photo Credits:
Courtesy Studio Katharina Fritsch; Christian Baur,
Basel; Volker Döhne, Krefeld; Tom Gundelwein, Saar-
brücken; Andreas Gursky, Düsseldorf; Courtesy Jablon-
ka Galerie, Köln; Courtesy Matthew Marks Gallery,
New York; Ian Reeves, San Francisco; Thomas Ruff,
Düsseldorf; Jörg Sasse, Düsseldorf; Ulrike Schnorpfeil,
Düsseldorf; Richard Stoner, Pittsburgh; Nic Tenwiggen-
horn, Düsseldorf; Rudolf Wakonigg, Münster; Elke
Walford, Hamburg; Werner Zellien, Berlin.
Textabb./Figures: Courtesy of George Teyssot (5);
John Cliett (6); Richard Barnes (7)